When
Government
Regulates Itself

When Government Regulates Itself

EPA, TVA, AND
POLLUTION CONTROL IN THE 1970S

Robert F. Durant

THE UNIVERSITY OF TENNESSEE PRESS

KNOXVILLE

Publication of this book has been aided by a grant from the LAWRENCE L. DURISCH MEMORIAL FUND, *administered by the Department of Political Science, The University of Tennessee, Knoxville.*

Library of Congress Cataloging in Publication Data

Durant, Robert F., 1949–
    When government regulates itself.
    Bibliography: p.
    Includes index.
    1. Pollution—Law and legislation—United States.
2. United States. Environmental Protection Agency.
3. Tennessee Valley Authority. I. Title.
KF3775.D87   1985   353.0082'322   84-22058
ISBN 0-87049-458-9

To Gladys, Jennifer and Mark Durant
and to the memory of
Francis Durant

Preface

In his book *Environment and Enforcement,* Keith Haw-
kins has written that "what tend to be taken for granted as 'pollution'
and 'compliance' are the outcomes of organized, sometimes lengthy,
social processes."[1] This study of the attempts of the Environmental
Protection Agency to apply aspects of the Clean Air Act and the
Federal Water Pollution Control Act to the Tennessee Valley Authority
during the 1970s examines these "social processes" in the seldom-
explored world of intragovernmental regulation. My purpose in writing this book was threefold. First, I wanted to describe what could
happen, and why, when one public agency sought to regulate another.
Second, I hoped to assess the implications of the cases for policy
implementation theory. And finally, I sought to investigate the consequences of intragovernmental regulation for the administrative state.

The data informing the inquiry are the product of two investiga-
tive techniques. To chronicle the course of events, I searched exten-
sively documentation provided by actors involved in each case. Those
providing materials included representatives of EPA, TVA, citizen
groups, and state pollution control agencies. Documents included internal agency memoranda, interagency communications, and citizen
group files and correspondence dealing with the two cases. Additional sources consulted included newspaper, periodical, and legal
journal accounts of the cases involved and of the general field of
environmental policy. Extensive use also was made of relevant congressional hearing documents, *Congressional Quarterly* almanacs and
weekly reports, and General Accounting Office studies. These were
essential for compiling background information on the legislative

history and evolution of the Clean Air Act and the Federal Water Pollution Control Act.

The second data-gathering technique consisted of semistructured interviews with twenty-eight actors involved in the controversies. Those interviewed include: past and present members of TVA's board of directors, legal and technical staffs, and program management; representatives of the Environmental Protection Agency at both the Washington and Region IV (Atlanta) levels; representatives of citizen groups including the Tennessee Environmental Council and the League of Women Voters; and state government officials.[2] Taped interviews, lasting an average of an hour and a half, were conducted in two stages. Preliminary background interviews were conducted from July 1979 to February 1980. Interviews dealing with the specifics of each case took place from June 1980 through May 1981. These interviews were useful for reconstructing events and indicating the nuances of relationships.

Selected portions of this book have been adapted from journal articles that I have either authored or coauthored. I wish to thank Michael R. Fitzgerald and Larry W. Thomas, my coauthors, and the American Society for Public Administration for permission to draw heavily from "When Government Regulates Itself: The EPA/TVA Air Pollution Control Experience," *Public Administration Review* 43 (May/June 1983): 209–19. Special thanks as well to the Southern Public Administration Education Foundation, Inc., and again to the American Society for Public Administration for permission to use aspects of the following two articles: "Learning to Survive as a Regulated Agency: TVA and Power Politics in the 1980s," *Public Administration Quarterly* 8 (Summer 1984): 202–22, and "EPA, TVA, and Pollution Control: Implications for a Theory of Regulatory Policy Implementation," *Public Administration Review* 44 (June/July 1984): 305–15.

Acknowledgments

This study would never have been possible without the aid, encouragement, and cooperation of many individuals. Professor Thomas D. Ungs and his staff at the Bureau of Public Administration, University of Tennessee, Knoxville, provided generous financial and emotional support throughout my association with the BPA. Special thanks are in order to William Lyons, Michael R. Fitzgerald, and Larry W. Thomas. Bill was always there, as hc had been throughout my graduate program, to encourage, aid, and make me believe in myself. Mike joined the faculty just as I prepared to write the dissertation upon which this book is based. His analytical talents, creativity, and major assistance during the interview and data collection phase of the study were invaluable, as was his concern and caring for my professional development. Larry also provided assistance, insight, and support throughout the writing of this book. Most importantly, however, all were friends when friends were needed most.

If this book has any merit, the credit must go to my dissertation director and friend, Anne Hopkins. Without her concern, hard work, and guidance, this project might never have begun or ended. When she had no more time to give, she made time; when I saw only obstacles, she saw only opportunities; and when I saw only the trees, she seemed to always be able to spot the forest. I cannot thank her enough for being so demanding, uncompromising, and patient. And most importantly, I cannot thank her enough for believing in me.

Many individuals involved in the cases were more helpful than one has the right to expect. Especially gracious were Attorney Dean Hill Rivkin, Associate Professor of Law, the University of Tennessee; Attorney Barry Walton, Jim Morris, and Bruce Brye of the Tennessee

Valley Authority; Paul Traina, Charles Kaplan, and Attorney Keith Casto of the Environmental Protection Agency, Region IV, Atlanta; Marvin B. Durning, former Deputy Administrator for Enforcement, the Environmental Protection Agency; and Dr. Ruth Neff, of the Tennessee Environmental Council. In addition, several individuals deserve recognition for the invaluable technical assistance they provided in the preparation of this book: Mavis Bryant and Katherine Holloway of the University of Tennessee Press, and Lynn Deming of New Mexico State University, for their hard work and considerable editorial advice; Jennifer Seely, Diane Kosier, and Sandra Binkley for their excellent typing under tight schedules; David Hobbs, Philip Stonecipher, David Bedford, and Anne Schvaneveldt for innumerable services; and Kitty Cornett Fitzgerald and Linda Warmack for their transcription of numerous, sometimes barely audible, taped interviews. Finally, I should like to thank my mother and my son, Mark. To them I owe everything.

Athens, June 1985   R.F.D.

Contents

Tables

When
Government
Regulates Itself

CHAPTER ONE

Anatomy of a Regulatory Dilemma

In his assessment of the relationship between public bureaucracy and constitutionalism, Norton Long asserts that "the folk-
lore of constitutional theory relegates the bureaucracy to somewhat
the same low but necessary estate as Plato does the appetitive element of the soul."[1] This characterization might also be applied to
our society's view of the role afforded the federal bureaucracies that
implement the positive state policies of the New Deal, Fair Deal, and
Great Society. Citizens routinely call upon, and expect, public agencies to promote, provide, and even guarantee essential goods, services, and opportunities in an efficient, effective, and responsive
manner. Yet, this same citizenry tends to view public bureaucracies
with mounting unease, distrust, and distress. This discontent springs
from, among other things, a popular perception that congressional
policy goals are undermined quite often by the parochial appetites
of public managers charged with their implementation.

Ambivalence toward bureaucracy has stimulated much scholarly
interest in what Lawrence Dodd and Richard Schott term the "sublegislative process"—the process whereby law is distilled into administrative action.[2] One component of this interest has been the study
of regulatory policy as it has been implemented by federal agencies.
Most studies of this topic have focused on the impediments to successful policy implementation posed by our system of administrative
federalism. Such a focus was sufficient when efforts to effect national
policies consisted primarily of federal agencies acting either indirectly
through or directly upon state, local, and private sector actors. But
lately the implementation context of regulatory policy has been expanded significantly with the enactment of laws known collectively

as the new social regulation—affirmative action, occupational health and safety, and environmental protection. Today it is not uncommon to find that the activities of federal agencies can have the effect of placing them within the regulatory responsibilities of other federal agencies charged with implementing the new social regulation. And in extreme cases, Congress has even deliberately charged "adversary bureaucracies" with holding sister federal agencies accountable to the law of the land.[3]

In describing the "bureaucracy problem," James Q. Wilson argued that "first there is the problem of . . . getting the bureaucracy to serve agreed on national goals."[4] But when federal agencies must alter the behavior of other agencies that, in turn, are implementing their own policy responsibilities, the potential arises for a very serious conflict over which national goals prevail, in what form, and in whose interest. Regulatory targets typically are reluctant to modify their goals and behavior at the behest of other agencies lest they risk upsetting the delicately tuned equilibrium of their organization's political economy.

It has long been recognized that disparate public policies inadvertently can place federal agencies at odds. A robust politics of administration literature abounds with examples of such internecine conflict. But in enacting social regulatory policies both enforceable by and applicable to federal bureaucracies, Congress has deliberately divided the executive branch against itself. Two consequences emerge. First, a burgeoning and increasingly important arena of bureaucratic politics develops, one wherein conflicting, even mutually exclusive, policy mandates must be somehow reconciled. Second, a new version of our constitutional precept of checks and balances is created, one wherein the appetites of executive branch actors presumably will be checked within that branch by the "bureaucratic oversight" of adversary federal agencies.

Despite the increasing necessity of implementing national goals within the federal establishment, there is a paucity of systematic research dealing explicitly with the topic. This study proposes to refine our largely impressionistic understanding of the intragovernmental implementation process by examining one of its more notable manifestations: the implementation of pollution control policy as it applies to federal facilities. The analytical focus of the study is the experience of the Environmental Protection Agency (EPA) with the Tennessee Valley Authority (TVA) during EPA's implementation of the Clean Air Act (CAA) and the Federal Water Pollution Control Act (FWPCA). Specifically examined are EPA's efforts to apply its sulfur dioxide (SO_2) and thermal pollution control policies to the power program operations of the TVA during the 1970s. The study describes, compares, and contrasts the divergent responses of TVA to EPA's implementation efforts: relatively swift compliance with the thermal pollution standards of the FWPCA, and protracted noncompliance with the SO_2 pollution standards of the CAA.

The EPA/TVA cases illustrate the interplay of social, economic, and political forces that can occur during any significant attempt at intragovernmental regulation. In their disputes over air and water pollution control, the EPA and TVA pursued goals that were at once consistent with individual agency charters and mutually inconsistent in their ends. The resultant conflicts steadily broadened. Holding low-cost energy production as its paramount responsibility, the TVA tenaciously fought to protect its autonomy as a public corporation from the EPA's regulation. The EPA, in the pursuit of its mandates to implement the CAA and FWPCA, battled just as tenaciously to regulate TVA's operations as these affected the environment. Soon realizing that success could not be assured without outside assistance, officials of both agencies sought new allies'and additional resources from public and private actors at the local, state, and national levels. When it became apparent that neither agency could win the disputes within their original boundaries, each sought to manipulate the conflict in a fashion that would create a more advantageous context. That is, as each agency realized it could not unilaterally dictate the outcome of the disputes, both agencies endeavored to broaden their scopes of conflict to a point of decisive advantage; the contexts thus shifted periodically from legislative to executive to judicial arenas. As E.E. Schattschneider predicted regarding political conflicts, the expanding breadth of the EPA/TVA controversies ultimately defined their respective resolutions.

The remainder of this chapter sets the stage for analysis, First, the developments that have helped alter the substance, organization, and context of regulatory policy implementation in this country are reviewed; then TVA's perceptions of the regulatory experiences are placed in context by reviewing the agency's power program development. The chapter concludes with a presentation of the central research questions framing the study.

THE EVOLUTION OF A REGULATORY DILEMMA

Schattschneider has observed that "some issues are organized into politics, while others are organized out."[5] The past two decades have witnessed a substantial expansion of the kinds of issues "organized into" our national political agenda. Congress has passed legislation concerned with housing, medical care, employment, civil rights, the environment, and public health and safety. The zeal of such efforts is reflected in the growth of the federal bureaucracy. Between 1960 and 1976 alone, thirty-four agencies were created to implement the policy initiatives of the positive state.[6]

Aside from the merits or demerits of these various statutes, as products of a disjointed legislative process ill suited to a priori consideration of policy interactions, they have purposes that are not always harmonious. Where disharmony occurs, actions of the agencies charged with implementing these statutes can conflict as well. Typically, officials avoid direct interagency confrontation. The Department of Agriculture, for example, continues to implement policies to promote and protect the tobacco industry at the same time that the Department of Health and Human Services pursues policies to fight lung cancer. Sometimes, incompatible policies pose sufficiently serious problems that they must be coordinated by interagency committees. Recent presidents, for example, have institutionalized coordinating committees for urban, defense, and regulatory policies. In extreme cases, however, the success of one agency's policy may depend *directly* upon its ability to mandate a major change in the behavior of another. This ability becomes critical as agencies acquire responsibility for implementing the evolving regulatory policies of the positive state.

Charles Frankel has noted a "major shift in our civilization's center of gravity — the emergence of science, technology, and bureaucracy as the great driving enterprises of modern society."[7] These three elements merge strikingly in contemporary regulatory policy. Historically, regulatory efforts focused essentially on economic objectives. Independent commissions were established to implement policies designed to prevent free-market inequities and abuses (antitrust violations and price fixing), to improve the quality and volume of services, and to promote commerce through grants and subsidies. With few exceptions, agencies such as the Interstate Commerce Commission, the Federal Trade Commission, and the Federal Communications Commission were structured to oversee particular industries (e.g., railroads) rather than particular problem areas common to industry in general (e.g., occupational safety). And each was "more or less mandated to protect as well as regulate" the industry under its jurisdiction. The epitome of Downs' issue-attention cycle, these agencies have been portrayed by scholars as either "captured" by industry, operating exclusively in their own self-interest, or operating — as originally intended — to protect industry interests.[8]

In contrast, policies known collectively as the new social regulation began to emerge during the 1970s. These focus primarily on attaining noneconomic objectives through agencies structured to oversee particular problem areas (e.g., pollution control) rather than particular industries.[9] As such, they typically affect nearly all aspects of a regulatory target's operations. Agencies such as the Occupational Safety and Health Administration, the Consumer Product Safety Commission, and the EPA effect health, consumer protection, and environmental policies that transcend industry boundaries and cut to the quick of organizational functions. Moreover, they are charged exclusively with controlling rather than promoting industry activities. Implementing agencies presumably are less vulnerable to agency capture as relationships are said to reflect adversarial rather than cooptative characteristics. Consequently, the "cozy triangle" is replaced by an alliance of the implementor, public interest groups, and the press.[10]

Just as the substance and organization of regulatory policy implementation have evolved, so too has its context. Most conspicuous in promoting this development has been the interaction of the two trends noted above: the emergence of the new social regulation, and the expanded distributive and redistributive service provision role consigned to the federal government since the New Deal. That is, as the federal bureaucracies' positive state functions of *providing services* have spiraled, many have found their own activities falling within the positive state functions of *regulation* belonging to other federal agencies. As Richard B. Stewart has suggested, "the distinct spheres of private and governmental activity have melded."[11] In the process, federal agencies, like their counterparts in the private sector, have increasingly become the targets of regulatory scrutiny.

LEARNING TO SURVIVE AS A REGULATED AGENCY

Francis Rourke has written that "the portents are favorable today for a substantial expansion in public control over bureaucratic organizations that had once seemed immune to it."[12] There exists no less immune a bureaucracy, and no more visible a target of this emerging public scrutiny, than the TVA. An agency statutorily immune from state regulation since its inception and relatively free from congressional oversight since the late 1950s, TVA's power program operations today place the agency on a collision course with those seeking to implement environmental protection policies. The agency is exposed to a degree of congressional, bureaucratic, and public scrutiny seldom experienced by TVA officials since the Morgan/Lilienthal era. In the words of one TVA staff member, the agency has had to "learn how to survive as a regulated agency."[13]

TVA's thinking and activities in its power program have historically reflected its commitment to producing power at the lowest rates possible while meeting the rising demands of its Tennessee Valley service area. This commitment has occasioned program decisions regarding generating fuels and technologies that critically have altered the political economy of the organization. These alterations in turn have produced three analytically distinct administrative eras at TVA: the regulatory yardstick, self-regulation, and regulatory target periods.[14]

Regulatory Yardstick: 1933–1959   TVA was the embodiment of one of President Roosevelt's most cherished goals: a public power utility that would serve as a yardstick against which the operations and rate structures of private utilities would be measured. Low-cost electricity production was to be the mission of the TVA power program, and the power produced was to fuel the economic development of the sorely depressed Tennessee Valley. To this end, the agency was designed as a "corporation clothed with the power of government, but possessed of the flexibility and initiative of a private enterprise."[15] Its organization, policies, and programs were left to the discretion of a three-member board of directors. No provision was made for representation of, or regulation by, officials of its seven-state service area. Federal oversight was provided, however, through the congressional appropriations process.

Responsibility for the power program was initially assigned to board member David Lilienthal. Convinced that TVA could function as a yardstick only if economies of scale were realized, Lilienthal nearly tripled TVA's hydropower generating capacity by the end of the 1930s.[16] So successful was his strategy that TVA was able to produce electricity up to 70 percent below private utility rates and to develop a rural electrification program in areas previously excluded from service by private utilities. Lilienthal also felt that efficiency and "grass roots democracy" dictated a two-tier power distribution system: TVA would wholesale electricity directly to industrial customers in the Valley while indirectly distributing power to residential users through municipal governments and rural cooperative retailers. These distributors, portrayed by Lilienthal as vehicles by which the "people themselves . . . determine their own standards of efficiency of service and level of rates," quickly became staunch, readily mobilizable supporters of agency causes before the Congress.[17]

TVA's success in low-cost power production stimulated both private utility lawsuits and a fivefold increase in demands for its power by the close of World War II.[18] Stimulated by an influx of energy-intensive industrial and government facilities, these demands soon outstripped the agency's hydropower generating capacity. TVA turned for relief to coal-fired plants as a supplementary power source. Congress, propelled by a supportive Democratic majority, disregarded the objections of private utilities and funded construction of the agency's first steam plants as the 1940s ended. Because these plants were nourished by the abundant, inexpensive coal reserves of TVA's native Appalachia, they were expected handily to promote the agency's yardstick mission. But the new decade brought the Eisenhower presidency and the election of a more conservative, less TVA-oriented Congress. When the agency sought funding for construction of additional coal plants, Congress balked and thus precipitated the famous Dixon-Yates controversy.[19] So thwarted, TVA sought increased autonomy from the vicissitudes of electoral politics. Agency officials requested congressional permission to issue revenue bonds to finance future program expansion. The proposal eventually became law in 1959 as the TVA Self-Financing Act. Free of state regulation from birth, TVA now became "technically free" from congressional and presidential scrutiny as well.[20]

Self-Regulation: 1960–1969   The Self-Financing Act inaugurated a period of relative autonomy for the power program seldom experienced before, or since, by TVA. Under the act, neither the president nor Congress had the power to delimit the agency's discretion concerning allocation of bond revenues. Though TVA still had to submit program plans to the Congress, the agency was not legally required to follow congressional recommendations as long as it did not use appropriated funds. And even for projects involving congressional monies, annual appropriation acts for TVA typically were "cast in brief and permissive terms" that allowed substantial agency discretion.[21] So unencumbered, the agency used the 1960s to pursue its vision of energy development and environmental protection.

TVA began the decade by substantially expanding its reliance on coal-generated electricity production and ended it by intimating a commitment to nuclear technologies unprecedented in the utility industry. By the mid-1960s, TVA's contingent of coal plants had expanded to twelve facilities operating in three states: Tennessee, Kentucky, and Alabama. These accounted for nearly 80 percent of all the electricity generated by TVA.[22] About this time, however, obtaining coal for TVA plants became more problematic, expensive, and environmentally controversial. Consequently, as agency officials projected a 1-million-kilowatt-per-year increase in Valley electricity consumption during the 1970s, TVA turned to atomic power. Perceiving the atom to be more cost-effective, environmentally benign, and reliable than coal, TVA announced plans to build two nuclear plants, one in Alabama (Browns Ferry) and the other in Tennessee (Sequoyah).

With regard to environmental protection, the agency had a widely heralded record of concern with water quality, having initiated stream sanitation programs in the Valley during the 1930s and researched the ecological threats posed by heated water discharges (thermal pollution) from its coal plants during the 1950s. Moreover, TVA expertise was tapped regularly by Valley states during the development of legislation to control water pollution. Thus, it was not surprising when in the mid-1960s TVA proposed a basinwide plan for water quality management, one the agency fully expected the states to enact.[23]

TVA's attention to air quality, though more recent and suspect, was nonetheless substantial. During the 1950s the agency pioneered the development and use of electrostatic precipitators for controlling particulate emissions. TVA technicians were also world-recognized experts in studying the effects of wind currents on pollution patterns. During the 1960s commitments to such research continued apace, accompanied by two new agency initiatives: an experimental FGD (scrubber) system was installed at one of its plants, and TVA technicians developed a comprehensive sulfur dioxide pollution control program (SDEL) for systemwide use.

Regulatory Target: 1970 to the Present   The 1970s brought not only TVA's formal announcement of a fundamental shift in generating technologies, but also a rekindling of intense public scrutiny of agency operations. TVA officials envisioned the construction of seventeen nuclear units at seven plants and planned not to order any additional coal plants during the decade. Moreover, they intended to phase out older, more pollution-prone facilities as nuclear units came on line. By 1985, generating capacity was expected to be nearly 35 percent coal fired and 55 percent nuclear powered, as compared with 80 and 0 percent respectively in 1970.[24] But TVA's conversion plan was not without its consequences for the boundary permeability of the agency. To operate nuclear plants, TVA would have to cope with licensing regulations issued pursuant to the Atomic Energy Act. And since its plants would be emitting both SO_2 and thermal pollution in substantial quantities, power program operations also would fall within the regulatory purview of those implementing the CAA and the FWPCA.

Prior to the 1970s, TVA was but nominally inconvenienced by health and safety laws, for the implementation efforts of the Department of Health, Education and Welfare (DHEW) and the Department of the Interior (DOI) were then typically lax.[25] Similarly, until the 1970s the Atomic Energy Commission (AEC) was generally perceived as oriented more toward development than regulation.[26] The new decade, however, brought both a heightened environmental consciousness and a more vigilant, more militant ecology movement. Legislation to redress prior regulatory shortcomings was adopted overwhelmingly by Congress. Not only were the CAA and FWPCA substantially amended to provide legally enforceable timetables, procedures, and decision premises for implementors, but a new agency — EPA — was created and assigned enforcement responsibility for these laws. In addition, the National Environmental Policy Act (NEPA) explicitly required the AEC to consider the ecological impacts of nuclear plants before issuing licenses.[27] The commission itself was later reorganized, and the Nuclear Regulatory Commission (NRC) was charged with pursuing a more vigorous enforcement policy. Scrutinizing all these efforts were increasingly litigious environmental groups, parties granted standing to file environmental lawsuits and permitted to intervene in the nuclear plant licensing process.[28] A formidable regulatory situation thus confronted, and continues to confront, TVA, placing the agency in the unaccustomed role of enforcement target.

CENTRAL QUESTIONS

Those who have investigated intragovernmental regulation genuinely are concerned about its processes and consequences. Most analysts doubt its efficacy, believing that it poses unique problems of implementation and condemning the noncompliance it can produce. John Shenefield suggests that public agencies are distinctly invulnerable to regulation. "Precisely because a particular public authority is acting on behalf of a generalized public interest, it may cease to be subject to laws that frame the rest of the marketplace — laws on disclosure, antitrust, sometimes even health and safety. Service to the public interest at large leads to avoidance of public responsibility."[29]

Similarly, James Q. Wilson and Patricia Rachal ask, "Can Government Regulate Itself?" They conclude that usually it cannot; target agency officials are reluctant to modify their goals and behavior at the behest of regulators. What is more, federal targets are uniquely possessed of the political wherewithal to resist perceived encroachments on their policy-making autonomy. Wilson and Rachal write:

> One agency can control the behavior of another only if the second does not regard the constraint as threatening its autonomy. . . . They will never accept a threat to their autonomy — to their ability to define their own mission and specify their own tasks. . . . Each agency defends or enhances itself [against regulation] by mobilizing allies elsewhere in government — in the legislature, in other agencies, within the executive offices — who share a stake, material or ideological, in the agency's well-being. . . . A government agency can and does deny the sovereign authority of another agency.[30]

Implicit in this argument, and explicit in those of other critics, is the idea that the recalcitrance evoked by intragovernmental regulation is contrary to the public interest. Many question how government can expect the private sector to comply with public policies when members of the federal family refuse to abide by them as well. As articulated by Representative William L. Springer, "One of the frustrating aspects of . . . pollution legislation is the presence of large federal installations either operated directly by the government or under its direction which contaminate the atmosphere on a large scale. How can we expect cooperation or credibility from private sources . . . when the installations controlled by Uncle Sam are some of the worst polluters?"[31]

The central questions of the present study of the EPA/TVA regulatory experiences are culled from the sentiments expressed above. The first set of questions explores the process of intragovernmental regulation as an exercise in regulatory policy implementation. What do the EPA/TVA cases indicate about what can happen, and why, when one federal agency is charged with holding another accountable to the law? How does implementation in this regulatory arena compare with the same in other contexts? Are factors typically said to condition implementation powerful in the intragovernmental arena as well? As representatives of regulatory policy implementation in general, do the EPA/TVA controversies suggest any refinements or amplifications of the conventional wisdom associated with this process? Do they suggest anything about regulatory enforcement that might enrich our theoretical understanding of the process in general?

The second set of questions deals with the broader societal implications of intragovernmental regulation. Of special concern are the consequences of this development for the administrative state, its agents, and the public interest. What do the EPA/TVA experiences suggest about the ability of one federal agency to regulate another? Are federal regulatory bureaucracies really at a distinct disadvantage when trying to hold sister agencies accountable to the law? Under what conditions can intragovernmental regulation be made more effective? What are the consequences of enhanced public scrutiny for regulatory targets? How can federal targets best cope with these consequences? Are federal agency challenges to regulation actually as detrimental to the commonweal as is commonly assumed?

The analysis begins with a description of the organizational structure of implementation provided by the CAA and the FWPCA (chapter 2). The statutory role of EPA and the states, and the enforcement scheme provided by each law, are compared and contrasted. Following this discussion, the study examines EPA's interpretation of the statutes prior to the disputes with TVA and recounts the latter's responses to, and attempts to affect, EPA's actions (chapters 3 and 4). Recounted are the fundamental decisions EPA had to make about congressional intent before it could apply the two laws to the TVA power program. Next, the enforcement phase of EPA's implementation of the two acts is chronicled (chapters 5 and 6). The study concludes by relating the EPA/TVA experiences to the findings of prior research on regulatory policy implementation (chapter 7) and by speculating upon the consequences of intragovernmental regulation for the administrative state (chapter 8).

CHAPTER TWO

Organizing for Pollution Control

THE EVOLVING INTERGOVERNMENTAL DESIGN

Political philosopher James Harrington once wrote that "the law is but words and paper without the hands and swords of men."[1] Certainly, in contemporary America the brandished sword tends regularly to be the authority of the national government. And to the distress of many, the hands wielding the sword are typically the unelected public managers of the administrative state. Yet there is sufficient evidence to suggest that the power of elected officials to condition the policy swath ultimately cut is hardly insignificant.[2] One most telling factor is the statutory language Congress provides when specifying units and methods for effecting policy. Referred to by Charles O. Jones as the organization activities of implementation, this specification is regarded by many as a key factor conditioning the success or failure of policy. It is to the substance of this process as it applies to the CAA and FWPCA that we now turn.

TOWARD POLLUTION CONTROL IN THE 1970S

It is usually wise to counsel, as V.O. Key did, against expecting public opinion to "emerge like a cyclone and push obstacles before it."[3] Yet most agree that public opinion did just that during the stages when problems were being identified and programs formulated in the recent development of environmental policy. In the wake of the sinking of the oil tanker *Torrey Canyon*, the Santa Barbara oil spill, and Nader group studies impugning the integrity of the congressional commitment to pollution control, public concern over environmental degradation grew appreciably during the late 1960s and early 1970s.[4] "Demonstration democracy" was the order of the day, featuring teach-ins, marches, and Malthusian prophecies. And terms such as "ecology," "lifeboat Earth," and the "Greening of America" were the catchwords and phrases of the times. Against this leitmotif, environmental issues came to dominate the national political agenda, with the legislative and executive branches rushing pell-mell to meet the public's demand for government redress. Major elements of this effort emerged in extensive revisions of the CAA and the FWPCA. And these, in turn, significantly affected the implementation of SO_2 and thermal pollution policies as they applied to TVA in the 1970s.

The Clean Air Act   Since the enactment of the CAA in 1955, the federal government's authority to control air pollution from power plants such as TVA's had expanded significantly.[5] Before 1970, amendments to the CAA gradually had increased federal responsibility beyond merely financing state and local air pollution control and research, as provided in the original statute. In 1963 the federal government assumed responsibility for designing abatement procedures for resolving pollution problems in a limited number of circumstances.[6] Then in 1967 Congress mandated the establishment of federal ambient air quality criteria to serve as the basis for state-issued pollution emission standards.[7] These standards were applicable to pollution sources located in federally designated air quality control regions. This evolving nationalization of the formulation and enforcement of pollution control policy continued apace with the enactment in 1970 of major revisions to the CAA.[8] It is generally conceded that the CAA of 1970 made the federal government the "dominant presence in air pollution control."[9]

The 1970 amendments were primarily the product of deep and abiding disaffection with the implementation of the Air Quality Act of 1967. Critics persistently excoriated the act as "ponderous," "disastrous," and "a goddamn mishmash."[10] Most distressing to critics was the seemingly lethargic response of both federal and state agencies to the procedural requirements of the law. For example, the sinew of the 1967 act was specification by DHEW of both air quality control regions and quantitative criteria for hazardous pollutants. At the same time, states were supposed to promulgate criteria-based emission standards and implementation plans. Yet nearly two years after the law was passed, the surgeon general reported to the House Subcommittee on Public Health and Welfare that but twenty of an anticipated three hundred air quality regions were established; that criteria for only sulfur dioxides and particulates had been formalized; and that the states were just beginning to set emission standards.[11] Most telling, perhaps, was that no state implementation plan had received federal approval at that time. Many attributed these administrative delays to what Theodore Lowi terms "policy without law": the act had failed to specify sufficiently clear goals and explicit procedures for implementation.

Nettled by criticism, with the ecology issue at the apex of its issue-attention cycle, and with presidential aspirant Edmund Muskie stung by attacks on his leadership as chairman of the Senate Public Works Subcommittee on Air and Water Pollution, Congress sought to project a "tough posture" and "stern response" in the CAA of 1970.[12] The objectives of this act were consonant with the thrust of prior air quality goals. Sought were the prevention of the deterioration of already clean ambient air, the creation of sufficiently clean air to protect the public health and welfare, and the prevention of "adverse . . . [air quality] . . . effects on any environmental, man-made, or aesthetic process."[13]

The act parted company with its predecessors, however, in its determination to constrain the substantive and procedural discretion of administrators implementing these ambitious goals. Critical to this effort was the precedent-setting stipulation that EPA would have to issue health-based national ambient air quality standards for six air pollutants, and the setting of specific timetables for federal and state agencies to complete their responsibilities for implementation. Under the terms of the act, SO_2 was one of the six pollutants scheduled for control. The procedures and timetables for implementation stipulated by the CAA provided that within thirty days of the enactment of the law, EPA was to release information documenting air pollutants that in the agency's "judgment [had] an adverse effect on public health and welfare."[14] Known as air quality criteria, this documentation was to reflect "the latest scientific knowledge useful in indicating the kind and extent of all identifiable effects on public health or welfare which may be expected from the presence of such pollutants in the ambient air, in varying quantities."[15] These criteria were to be the basis for prescribing air quality standards for each pollutant. The standards were also scheduled for promulgation during the same thirty-day period.

All ambient standards were to be developed solely on the basis of health considerations without concern for the economic or technological feasibility of their implementation. Within ninety days of their publication, during which time opportunity for written comment on their merits was to be provided, the standards were to be published by the EPA administrator in the *Federal Register*. Within nine months of the formal promulgation of these standards, each state was to develop, after "reasonable notice and formal hearings," a plan for their "implementation, maintenance, and enforcement."[16] Referred to as State Implementation Plans, these documents were to be submitted to EPA officials who were to "approve or disapprove such plan or any portion thereof" within four months after the deadline for submissions.[17]

Rules for judging these plans as they applied to each air quality region (or part thereof) within each state were painstakingly detailed. In contrast to the solely health-based ambient air standards, state plans could be based on economic and technological feasibility considerations as well. In addition, each state plan had to include appropriate attainment deadlines for states to meet the ambient standards; emission limits and compliance schedules for polluters to meet primary and secondary standards; procedures necessary to monitor, compile, and analyze data on air quality; provisions for intergovernmental cooperation; procedures for revising the plan to accommodate changes in the ambient air standards; and assurances that sufficient state personnel, funding, and authority would be forthcoming.[18]

To dissuade ineffective implementation of the law by state and local administrators, Congress authorized the EPA to assume responsibility for both preparation and enforcement of State Implementation Plans in certain circumstances. Regarding preparation, should a state fail to submit a plan for approval (as was common under the Air Quality Act) or should the plan, or parts thereof, be inadequate, the administrator could impose either a complete or partial plan for that state.[19] Moreover, without effective state enforcement efforts, section 113 became operative. Under this proviso, when any person was violating emission standards, EPA could directly notify both the violator and the state involved. Should noncompliance extend beyond thirty days of this notification, EPA could—but was not required to—issue a compliance order or seek a civil injunction to stop the violation.[20] Moreover, if the administrator attributed protracted noncompliance to the misfeasance, malfeasance, or nonfeasance of state implementors, EPA was authorized to commence a "period of

federally assumed enforcement" of the entire plan.[21] Optional penalties during this enforcement period subjected convicted violators
to civil penalties, including temporary or permanent injunctions, as
well as criminal penalties for prolonged noncompliance.[22]

As a final bulwark against state *and* federal recalcitrance, the act
formalized the concept of "private attorneys general" acting as environmental custodians overseeing policy implementation. The innovative and ambitious section 304 allowed any person to sue, on
his own behalf, any other person (the United States and any other
government agency included) allegedly violating the CAA or any state
or federal enforcement order. What is more, citizens could sue to compel the EPA to perform any nondiscretionary CAA procedure or duty
previously unperformed. Those contemplating court action had to
notify both EPA and state authorities sixty days prior to filing suit,
thus allowing officials the opportunity to take appropriate enforcement action. The combination of statutorily based, justiciable procedural deadlines and the provision of legal standing for private citizens to enforce these deadlines provided a mechanism for "guarding
the guardians" of air pollution policy.

To summarize, the promotion of air quality sufficient to protect
the public health and welfare from SO_2 pollution was to be realized
through the promulgation of nationally determined ambient air quality standards. These were to be based solely on public health criteria,
excluding consideration of the economic and technological feasibility of the resulting standards. The states were subsequently responsible for developing and enforcing State Implementation Plans to
assure the attainment of the national ambient air quality standards
by statutory deadlines. The EPA retained authority to revise any state
plan, in whole or in part; to directly enforce any provision of a plan;
and to formally assume periods of federal enforcement of the entire
plan if state efforts proved lax. Short of appropriate implementation
of the act by federal or state authorities, private citizens could go
to court to enforce its provisions.

The Federal Water Pollution Control Act   The evolution of federal
participation in water quality control efforts is highly reminiscent
of trends in air quality control. The story is again one "of increasing
federal assumption of authority," a trend nurtured predominantly
by the inability, and sometimes the reluctance, of state officials to
pursue activist pollution control policies.[23] Congress first attempted

to deal comprehensively with water pollution in 1948 with the enactment of the original FWPCA.[24] Concerned primarily with the discharge of effluents into interstate waterways, the act authorized federal research and technical assistance programs, loans to states and localities for constructing waste treatment plants, and the establishment of cooperative state/federal water-basin pollution control programs. The federal role was limited to notifying polluters and state authorities about pollution problems, recommending that states initiate court action against polluters, and holding public hearings to stimulate state enforcement. Thus, as with the CAA of 1955, Congress made clear that water quality control was a prerogative of the states; the federal role was to be advisory at best. The act, however, proved to be a major disappointment. Indeed, general enforcement provisions proved so cumbersome and unworkable that funds for federal activities associated with its implementation were once denied by the House Appropriations Committee on the grounds that the act was "almost unenforceable."[25]

Subsequent amendments to the FWPCA made prior to 1970 sought to redress problems of inadequate federal authority, laggard state efforts, and time-consuming procedures. Amendments enacted in 1956 provided a conference-public hearing-court decree enforcement process.[26] These were followed in 1961 by revisions that extended federal enforcement jurisdiction to interstate waters and eliminated an earlier proviso that state consent was necessary before court abatement proceedings could be initiated by federal authorities.[27] The 1965 amendments followed, creating the Federal Water Pollution Control Administration within the Interior Department to assume implementation responsibility for the act. They required that the states — subject to federal approval — classify by intended use (e.g., swimming, fishing, waste disposal) all water within their boundaries; adopt ambient water quality standards appropriate for these uses by 1967; and then develop implementation plans to achieve these standards. If state standards were not set by the 1967 deadline, federally imposed standards could be promulgated in their stead by convening a standard-setting conference in the recalcitrant state.[28] Although direct enforcement of the standards by the Interior Department was allowed, no civil suit could be initiated without the consent of the governor of the state where standards were being violated.

Despite such legislative refinements, the enforcement performance of pre-1970 federal water quality programs was uninspiring. Indeed, in assessing these efforts, Gordon Arbuckle and Timothy Vanderver concluded that "it was not until 1970 that industrial dischargers were faced with any real threat of prosecution."[29] The most pressing enforcement problem was federal reluctance to assert the authority it had been given. Critics were distressed that despite the 1967 deadline for submission of state water quality standards imposed by the 1965 amendments, many states failed to comply with the deadline — with apparent impunity. During the 1965 to 1969 period, only one federal standard-setting conference had been convened to promulgate federal standards when states failed to do so.[30] In the ecology–conscious, crisis-ridden atmosphere of the late 1960s, demands for changes in water quality policy mounted.

Since revision of the CAA dominated the agenda of Muskie's Subcommittee on Air and Water Pollution at this time, only piecemeal legislative changes could be forged immediately. Most significant for the EPA/TVA controversy was a provision in the Water Quality Improvement Act of 1970. Section 21(b) specified that applicants seeking federal licenses or permits to build or operate facilities that might pollute navigable waterways were to obtain state certification that water quality standards would not be violated by emissions from such a facility.[31] This provision was applicable to a variety of federal permit applications, including AEC (now NRC) permits for constructing and licensing nuclear power plants. Federal facilities such as TVA, however, would not have to get state certification. Instead, the Interior Department (later EPA) was charged with assuring that these agencies complied with all state water quality standards. A history of executive orders mandating federal facility compliance with water quality laws would presumably aid EPA in this chore.[32] In all other respects, however, the implementation framework provided by the FWPCA as amended through 1965 remained intact.

Without the possibility of immediate, comprehensive congressional action, pressure for interim measures mounted. Many looked to the newly created EPA for relief; and William Ruckelshaus, the first EPA administrator, responded quickly. Anxious to buoy public confidence in the federal commitment to environmental quality, Ruckelshaus set about to create a vigorous enforcement image for his neophyte agency. His strategy for establishing this reputation was two-pronged: extensive use of court suits and application of an effluent permit system. So extensive was his use of the former that EPA attorneys referred 371 enforcement actions to the Department of Justice between 1970 and 1972. What is more, these were brought against such luminaries as the cities of Atlanta, Detroit, and Cleveland, as well as against such industrial giants as U.S. Steel, Mobil Oil, and Cities Service.[33] Yet despite the herculean efforts of EPA under Ruckelshaus, the court strategy proved inadequate to the task, making "hardly a dent in the massive number of dischargers that required control."[34]

The effluent permit system established by Ruckelshaus was broad in scope and had as its legal basis section 13 of the Rivers and Harbors Act of 1899, commonly referred to as the Refuse Act.[35] Prompted by two Supreme Court decisions that construed the act as applying to any industrial waste,[36] President Nixon had ordered the establishment of a permit discharge system to be administered jointly by the Army Corps of Engineers and EPA. Shortly after one year of operation, however, the permit program was abandoned, rendered administratively infeasible by a U.S. Circuit Court of Appeals decision in *Kalur v. Resor.*[37] The court ruled that each permit issued — and EPA had received 23,000 permit requests — had to be accompanied by an Environmental Impact Statement to satisfy the requirements of NEPA. With the permit system aborted by the courts, the "suit strategy" rendered innocuous by the dimensions of the water quality problem, and the congressional calendar cleared of air quality legislation, the focus of environmental reform efforts returned to the national legislature. These efforts culminated in the enactment of comprehensive amendments to the FWPCA in 1972.

The FWPCA of 1972 has been termed "the most sweeping environmental measure ever considered by the Congress."[38] The magnitude of the congressional goals established by the act supports this characterization. Section 101 declared that the restoration and maintenance of the "natural chemical, physical, and biological integrity of the Nation's waters" was the intent of Congress. Major waterways were to be fishable and swimmable by 1983 and total elimination of pollutant discharges was to be realized by 1985. Building upon the infrastructure of the 1965 amendments, the new law again made state-set, EPA-approved water quality standards a critical element in its implementation scheme. Section 303 provided that within 180 days after enactment of the 1972 amendments, EPA was required to review for approval all interstate standards previously adopted by the states pursuant to the 1965 amendments. Concurrently, the states were to develop water quality standards for intrastate waters, standards that

EPA would also review. These were to take into account the "use and value for public water supplies, propagation of fish and wildlife, recreational purposes, and agricultural, industrial, and other legitimate uses."

The 1972 act differed from its predecessor — the Water Quality Act of 1965 — on two very significant dimensions. First, it provided for development of nationally uniform, technology based effluent limits that would have to be met in order for dischargers to obtain EPA-issued discharge permits. Second, the 1972 act was more specific in delineating timetables for carrying out administrative responsibilities. Thus, reminiscent of the logic of the CAA of 1970, Congress sought to limit drastically the discretion of agency implementors.

The procedures, decision criteria, and action timetables established by the 1972 amendments were quite comprehensive. Under section 304 of the act, EPA was to issue effluent guidelines by October 1973 for categories of major polluters. The cornerstone of the pollution control strategy, these guidelines were to serve as the basis for EPA's establishment of effluent standards limiting the amount of pollutants each industrial category could discharge. These effluent limits were, in turn, to become the basis for national pollution discharge elimination permits (referred to popularly as NPDES permits) for individual polluters.[39] These permits were to be issued by EPA to all dischargers by December 1974. Pursuant to section 301 of the act, effluent limits were to be developed primarily on the basis of technological feasibility. Dischargers were required to employ the "best practicable control technology currently available" by 1 July 1977, and the "best available technology economically achievable" by July 1983. What constituted the "best" technology for either of these categories, however, was left to the determination of the EPA.

Congress generally intended that the state water quality standards and the EPA effluent limits would be applied as uniformly as possible to individual dischargers within industrial categories. It did, however, provide one exception: the application of these regulations to individual thermal pollution sources. Given that thermal pollution did not have the long-term consequences of more persistent pollutants such as DDT or PCB, and that the desire to take advantage of lax state standards or enforcement reputations was not a critical factor in determining plant sites, case-by-case enforcement was deemed acceptable. Section 316 of the act allowed dischargers such

as TVA an opportunity to challenge any applicable thermal requirement on the grounds that it was more stringent than necessary to
protect the aquatic environment.

The 1972 amendments also provided specific enforcement resources
if polluters failed to obtain discharge permits or violated any standard, limitation, or monitoring requirement. The agency could do
any of four things: issue compliance orders, obtain injunctive relief,
seek civil penalties of up to $10,000 per day, or attempt criminal prose-
cution.[40] Moreover, as it did in the CAA of 1970, Congress sought
to constrain the enforcement discretion of implementors even further by incorporating a citizen suit provision in the act. Section 505
of the FWPCA authorizes "any person having an interest which is, or
may be, adversely affected" to file suit against violators of effluent
standards, or against EPA, for failing to perform nondiscretionary
duties in a timely, expeditious manner. The procedural requirements
of this provision were based upon those of the CAA of 1970.

To summarize, thermal discharge was one of several types of water
pollution that EPA was required to control during the 1970s. As EPA
sought to apply its thermal policies to the TVA during this decade,
it had to work under several sets of organizational parameters provided by the FWPCA. Until enactment of the FWPCA of 1972, EPA's
responsibility was derived from the FWPCA as amended through 1970.
Given the cumbersome, essentially ineffectual enforcement process
provided by this early legislation, EPA turned increasingly during the
1970–1972 period to a thermal pollution implementation framework
that emphasized Refuse Act discharge permits, as well as court suit
enforcement procedures. With the enactment of the 1972 amendments, thermal pollution abatement subsequently would be premised on the notion that control was possible through a system of
state-enacted ambient water quality standards and nationally promulgated effluent limitations for categories of industrial dischargers.

The centerpiece of enforcement under the 1972 amendments was
to be a permit system (NPDES) administered initially by EPA. The permits would translate thermal water quality requirements for categories of industries into effluent limits for individual dischargers.
The operators of these plants could, however, challenge the application of both state standards and effluent limits, claiming that they
were more stringent than necessary to protect the aquatic life of the
bodies of water receiving their heat discharges. As a hedge against
noncompliance, thermal water quality standards promulgated by the

states could be used to halt construction or operation of plants requiring federal licensing. In the case of federal facilities such as TVA, however, no state certification would be required; EPA would be responsible for holding federal government polluters accountable to existing thermal standards. To limit abuse of administrative discretion by those charged with implementing the act, Congress specified legally enforceable procedures, decision premises, and schedules for implementation. What is more, it provided that citizens could file suit against violators of the act, as well as against the EPA, absent timely, effective conduct of nondiscretionary duties and procedures.

SUMMARY

This chapter has reviewed the history, logic, and substance of the implementation designs provided by the CAA and FWPCA for interpreting and applying SO_2 and thermal pollution policies to the TVA. Both designs reflected the federal government's increasing assumption of responsibility for developing and enforcing pollution control policies in this country. As such, they each expressed congressional disaffection with the inability — some said the unwillingness — of the states to cope with environmental problems. Moreover, each incorporated the determination of Congress to constrain the substantive and procedural discretion of all those implementing the ambitious goals of the acts.

With this knowledge as background, it is now appropriate to compare and contrast the units and methods for effecting policy provided by each law as they relate to sulfur dioxide and thermal pollution policy. When the two laws are juxtaposed in this fashion, three primary differences become apparent. First, their decision criteria are strikingly different. In the case of SO_2, the EPA would have to take only health considerations into account when developing the national primary and secondary ambient air quality standards. In contrast, the agency would be able to base thermal standards on factors of both technological and economic feasibility as well.

The second major difference concerns the assignment of administrative responsibilities to levels of government. SO_2 ambient air quality standards would be promulgated by the EPA, but thermal ambient water quality standards initially would be issued by state pollution control boards subject to EPA review. Similarly, although SO_2 and thermal discharges would be subject to enforcement schemes that incorporated the issuing of permits, EPA would directly administer the thermal permit program and the states would be solely responsible for issuing operating permits to SO_2 dischargers.

Finally, the two laws provide different enforcement resources. Although each allows for court suits, civil and criminal penalties, and injunctive relief, one striking difference is apparent. EPA could take advantage of the section 21(b) provision of the 1970 amendments when attempting to apply thermal policies to individual polluters, an enforcement tool unparalleled in the CAA. Pursuant to that provision, anyone applying to a federal agency to obtain a license for constructing or operating a potential source of thermal pollution would have to receive state certification that the operation of the facility would not violate applicable state thermal standards. In the case of federal government facilities such as TVA, standard compliance would have to be ensured by EPA. In contrast, no such provision for adding additional enforcement leverage was available to EPA under the provisions of the CAA.

CHAPTER THREE

Through the Looking Glass Darkly

THE CAA AND
THE TENNESSEE VALLEY AUTHORITY

V.O. Key has written that "to speak with precision of public opinion is a task not unlike coming to grips with the Holy Ghost."[1] No less metaphysical a task often awaits those seeking to comprehend the legislative intent of the U.S. Congress when it passes a law. And no less is expected of public managers implementing the provisions of that law. Confronted by ambiguous, even contradictory, statutory language, administrators somehow must translate legislation into feasible, acceptable program directives. As Murray Edelman has suggested, the rub typically lies wherein statutory imprecision begets "differing interpretations of the same language with different authorities, changing times, altered conditions, and varying interest groups."[2] No more apt characterization exists for describing EPA's efforts to interpret the CAA as it applied to the TVA. What follows are the dynamics and substance of these efforts from the distinctive vantage points of EPA and TVA.

THE VIEW FROM EPA

In contrast to its precision in specifying tasks and timetables for implementation of the CAA, Congress failed to state clearly, or rank in priority, many of its most pressing goals. Most significant for the EPA/TVA SO_2 controversy were ambiguities surrounding the intentions of Congress regarding adequate margins of safety to protect human health, pollution control goals and strategies, and application of emission standards to federal facilities. A chronology of the major events that transpired during EPA's interpretational efforts is provided in table 3.1.

Table 3.1. **Chronology of the SO₂ Dispute: The Inter-
                pretation Experience**

Year	Major Events
1970–1971	—Clean Air Act of 1970 enacted. —TVA begins attempts to persuade states and EPA that intermittent control is superior to constant control.
1972	—EPA proposes regulation disallowing intermittent control; calls for constant control techniques. —TVA continues public relations blitz against constant control and refuses to apply for state operating permits from Kentucky, Tennessee, and Alabama. —Alabama and Kentucky file suit against TVA for noncompliance with procedural requirements.
1973	—TVA submits compliance plans to states asking for intermittent control and exemption from SO₂ emission limits. —TVA gives antiscrubber testimony at EPA scrubber hearings. —EPA proposes regulation permitting intermittent control. —EPA issues invitation to states to relax pollution regulations in wake of OPEC oil embargo.
1974	—EPA/TVA Joint Task Force established; report issued outlining outstanding agency differences. —TVA state permit position upheld by sixth circuit and denied by fifth circuit. —EPA rejects Kentucky proposal allowing intermittent control. —TVA files suit against EPA challenging authority to disallow intermittent control. —EPA notifies TVA of SO₂ violations; issues regulation outlawing intermittent control.

The Question of the Adequate Margin of Safety   Pursuant to the CAA of 1970, EPA was to establish a primary air quality standard for SO₂ that would allow an "adequate margin of safety" to protect the public health. Proposed standards were to be published for public comment on 30 January 1971, and final standards issued on 30 April 1971. But Congress gave little indication of what the term "adequate" meant or how it was to be measured. As Senator Edmund Muskie, floor manager of the bill which eventually became the CAA, stated, "The first responsibility of Congress is not the making of technological or economic judgments. . . ."[3] Such critical details were neglected in the act itself and in the committee reports accompanying the statute. Putting into operation this slippery, albeit fundamental, concept in time to meet the act's deadlines thus was relegated to the sublegislative process for resolution by EPA, the nation's newest environmental agency.

In an ideal world of precise congressional intent and perfect scientific knowledge, setting an adequate standard would have been a rather perfunctory task for the EPA. Knowing the precise point at which SO₂ concentrations would be deleterious to the health of particular segments of the public, the agency could simply set standards below this harm-inducing threshold. As Majone notes, however, "firm knowledge about the amount of damage done by given concentrations under various environmental conditions is simply not available."[4] Whether or not SO₂ was independently responsible for causing and aggravating respiratory health problems was not known. Many scientists believed not. They claimed instead that particulate matter, the synergistic effects of the interaction of SO₂ with airborne substances and meteorological conditions, or toxic materials yet unidentified, were more likely explanations of such problems.

The EPA did not have the data base or the research resources to resolve these issues. Also unavailable was the luxury of waiting for others to resolve them. Pressed by the deadlines of the CAA, the agency subsequently proposed and promulgated primary national ambient air quality standards for SO₂ on schedule in 1971.[5] Since EPA had been in existence less than two months when it first proposed SO₂ standards, the agency based these standards on highly controversial health criteria developed by its predecessors. In so doing, EPA had opted for standards that dealt only with the independent effects of the pollutant; no consideration was given to the synergistic effects of SO_2 in combination with meteorological conditions and other pollutants. Moreover, the agency had set the standards to protect those already afflicted by respiratory disease rather than merely to lessen the likelihood that those unafflicted would fall victim.

The remarks of EPA administrator Ruckelshaus in promulgating these regulations reflected EPA's predicament and presaged its future controversy with TVA. He began by noting that public comments received by EPA when the air quality standards were originally proposed reflected "divergences of opinion among interested and informed persons as to the proper interpretation of available data."[6] He also conceded that the absence of definitive evidence documenting the relationship of SO_2 — in differing concentrations and over disparate time periods — to a variety of health problems allowed, at best, an approximation of what "an adequate margin of safety to protect human health might be."[7] But to those who counseled delay in issuing standards until definitive data could be collected, he responded in two ways. First, he cited the imminent, highly credible threat of citizen suits against EPA should the implementation schedules provided by the CAA be ignored. Second, he asserted that "the need for increased knowledge of the health and adverse effects of air pollution cannot justify failure to take action based on knowledge presently available."[8]

Richard Tobin suggests that "the setting of air quality standards is a political, and not a scientific, responsibility" since it represents a decision as to how much risk a community is willing to accept.[9] Equally political is the defense of such standards once they are issued, particularly when they are based on ambiguous congressional intent and admittedly inconclusive scientific evidence. Once issued, the adequacy of SO_2 standards indeed did become grist for political mills at all levels of the federal system and by all branches of government. Given the kinds of political and economic interests affected by the standards, perhaps no less could be expected. To effectively control SO_2 is to require costly changes in the operations of such economic titans as the coal, steel, and electric power industries. These changes often are perceived as jeopardizing the employment opportunities of such politically potent union memberships as the United Mine Workers and the United Steelworkers of America. Moreover, the standards can exacerbate oil shortage and balance of payment problems should substitutions for coal be made, problems that fall within the purview of other government agencies. But EPA's travails in preserving and applying these standards to polluters in general, and to TVA in particular, are more appropriately the subject of future chapters.

The Question of Sulfur Dioxide Control Strategy   The CAA required that within nine months of the promulgation of national ambient air standards, the states had to obtain EPA's approval for plans implementing them. Since TVA's twelve coal-fired power plants were located in Alabama (two plants), Kentucky (two plants), and Tennessee (eight plants), agency officials were concerned with EPA's treatment of the implementation plans submitted by each of these states. TVA would impugn as overly strict several of the emission limits issued by these states, but its most strident attacks were reserved for EPA's interpretation of acceptable strategies for controlling pollution. With the CAA calling only for "such . . . measures as may be necessary to insure attainment and maintenance" of the air quality standards, there was ample room for challenge.[10]

Basically, there were two closely related aspects to the control strategy question. First, did Congress intend the actual reduction of total SO_2 emissions released into the atmosphere or merely the lowering of SO_2 concentrations in the vicinity of polluting sources such as TVA power plants? Second, did it want the states to consider the economic and technological feasibility of control strategies when developing plans, or could they base them only on health considerations? Depending on which interpretation prevailed, EPA would require either emission reduction or emission dilution. If it chose the former, only constant control systems that reduced the amount of SO_2 leaving the smokestack would suffice.[11] Moreover, emission reduction would require the use of costly low-sulfur coal of questionable availability, along with the installation of expensive and unproven scrubber technology. If EPA chose emission dilution, intermittent control systems and the construction of less costly, technologically proven, tall smokestacks that merely lowered local SO_2 concentrations would suffice.[12]

For all concerned parties, the stakes riding on EPA's interpretation of permissible control strategies were very high. Referring derisively to the intermittent control approach as the "rhythm method" of pollution control, many scientists and environmentalists contended that although relatively inexpensive and easy to implement, it was "flawed by pervasive problems of reliability and enforceability."[13] Furthermore, they excoriated these techniques for "[exacerbating] the problem of derivative pollutants, [subjecting] previously clean areas to new pollution risks, [encouraging] 'acid rain', [limiting] future economic growth, and [reducing] the incentive for development of superior control technologies."[14] For power plant operators such as TVA, however, intermittent control strategies were especially attractive. They would allow plants to meet SO_2 standards in the immediate vicinity of their operation, the only area where pollution could realistically — and hence legally — be attributed to a particular source. What is more, they could meet virtually any standard at considerably less expense.

EPA's evolving, rather tortuous interpretation of appropriate control strategies began in April 1971 with its publication of proposed guidelines for developing State Implementation Plans.[15] After encouraging and evaluating comments on the proposals, EPA prepared and informally circulated a draft of final guidelines during the month of June. These prospective guidelines were a "pleasant surprise" to environmentalists since they said "nothing about cost considerations and neglected many of industries' other social and economic concerns."[16] But the guidelines formally promulgated by EPA in August of 1971 differed considerably from the June draft. Especially dismaying to environmentalists were stipulations that encouraged states to consider the relative social and economic impacts of alternative control strategies before setting control standards. Many felt that this was the Nixon administration's invitation to state officials to allow SO_2 emission dilution rather than reduction because of the cost disparity between intermittent and constant control strategies.

The original Alabama and Tennessee plans were submitted to EPA for approval in January of 1972. The initial Kentucky plan followed in early February of the same year.[17] Under each plan the TVA, as a major source of SO_2 pollution, was required to meet emission standards by mid-1975, but the control strategy options offered by Kentucky and Tennessee did not require the use of constant control systems. Specifically, they provided that "operators could demonstrate that other techniques [rather than constant control systems] would permit the attainment and maintenance of national standards."[18] The question remained, however, whether or not these provisions would be acceptable to EPA.

Approximately two weeks before administrator Ruckelshaus published EPA's review of the proposed State Implementation Plans in the *Federal Register*, EPA notified then-Governor Jimmy Carter of Georgia that intermittent controls such as tall stacks would not be considered an acceptable control technique.[19] Nonetheless, when legally binding state plans were issued in May 1972, Ruckelshaus neither approved nor disapproved their use.[20] Instead, he allowed that if states accepted intermittent control systems as a strategy for controlling polluting sources (such as TVA plants), EPA would treat the action as a revision of the state plan. Consequently, the choice would be subject to EPA review. Forced by CAA deadlines to promulgate plans before sufficient evidence could be marshaled on this and other critical issues, EPA had opted to buy time.

In promulgating the state plans, the agency had also warned the states that they might need to make future revisions, as EPA would make a continuing evaluation of their provisions.[21] The first indication of the need to revise pollution control plans came but two months after the agency's admonition. In July 1972 EPA proposed a regulation disallowing intermittent control systems as a compliance technique.[22] This proposal, however, was never officially promulgated by the agency. Almost a year later, in September 1973, EPA reversed its proposed position on intermittent control. This time it offered for public comment a regulation permitting intermittent control and tall-stack compliance strategies.[23] Again, however, this rule was never actually issued. Confusion seemed to reign at EPA.

In the fall of 1973 what Justice Oliver Wendell Holmes might term "the felt necessities of the times" began to impinge on EPA's interpretation efforts. As the nation braced to confront both an OPEC oil embargo and persistent economic stagflation, it became popular to attack environmental regulations as inflationary and as jeopardizing the nation's energy independence goal. The most vociferous barrage from the private sector against EPA's efforts came from a $3.5 million advertising campaign opposing scrubbers that was spearheaded by the American Electric Power Company.[24] This was accompanied by mounting criticism from within the federal government itself during formal executive branch reviews of environmental regulations coordinated by the Office of Management and Budget (OMB). Under these procedures, any federal agency was given an opportunity to influence, and perhaps even alter, EPA's regulatory policies by formally expressing concern about their impact on national energy shortages or the economy in general. Taking full advantage of these reviews, agencies such as the Federal Power Commission (FPC), the Federal Energy Administration (FEA), the Department of Commerce, and OMB pressed Congress and the president for approval of intermittent control strategies. The Commerce Department even seized these opportunities to develop amendments to the CAA that President Ford eventually submitted to Congress.[25]

EPA responded to all this by inviting the states to review their implementation plans so as to eliminate "overly stringent" provisions that discouraged the use of our abundant coal resources.[26] This invitation was well received by the states where TVA operated its coal-fired plants. Tennessee and Alabama proposed relaxed SO_2 emission limits that intermittent control systems could easily meet,[27] and Kentucky specifically proposed such systems as an acceptable compliance technique.[28] The EPA did not formally respond to the proposed changes of these states until August 1974, almost eight months after the Tennessee and Alabama changes were submitted. The oil embargo by then had been lifted, and the crisis atmosphere supporting the earlier call for relaxations in the state plans was gone. The agency disallowed many of the emission standard proposals proffered by Alabama and Tennessee,[29] and it forbade Kentucky's provision allowing intermittent control systems as a control strategy.[30] These actions were followed in December of the same year by the promulgation of binding EPA regulations mandating constant control systems. This was done amidst uncertainty over the availability of low-sulfur coal and in the face of controversy over the environmental problems caused by the huge quantities of sludge produced during scrubber operation.

After more than two and a half years of vacillation, the agency finally had taken an official, legally binding position on the control strategy issue. It supported emission reduction rather than dilution regardless of the economic and technological feasibility of such constant control techniques as scrubbers and low-sulfur coal.

The Question of Federal Facility Compliance   The final interpretation issue bearing directly on the EPA/TVA dispute dealt with the responsibilities of federal facilities under the CAA. Impatient with prior efforts to control pollution by federal facilities and recognizing that these facilities were among the most notorious SO_2 polluters in the country, Congress used the CAA to vent its displeasure. As Richard Stewart and James Krier suggest, the TVA, as the nation's largest SO_2 polluter, was a primary target of congressional ire.[31] Section 118 provided that all federal facilities discharging air pollutants "shall be subject to, and comply with, all federal, state, interstate, and local requirements respecting the control and abatement of air pollution in the same manner, and to the same extent, that any person is subject to such requirements." Left unclear, however, was whether or not facilities were subject to either the procedural requirements imposed by the states to implement the act or to direct federal regulation.

For most states, the heart of the pollution control program was a procedure whereby stationary sources (e.g., power plants) were required to obtain a permit to operate. These permits were designed to mediate the "gap between pollution sources and national standards," and they allowed state and local authorities to regulate air pollution directly at the source.[32] Aided by monitoring devices, officials presumably would be able to determine exactly when and how ambient air quality standards and emission limitations were being violated, as well as by whom. Environmentalists believed that section 118 authorized the states to regulate federal facility pollution in the same fashion as they did private sources. However, as William Shaw has noted, "The simplicity of the proposal [failed to] ensure its acceptance."[33] Many federal facilities averred that section 118 violated the Supremacy Clause of the U.S. Constitution and the legal principle of sovereign immunity. Though acknowledging that the act allowed state and local authorities to impose substantive air quality standards on their operations, federal facilities argued that it did *not* authorize the imposition of state permit requirements. And as for federal enforcement, many claimed immunity on statutory grounds: only "persons" were subject to enforcement under section 113, and the act had not defined federal agencies as "persons."

The positions espoused by federal facilities were complete anathema to environmental groups, who maintained that for all practical purposes they emasculated the CAA. The EPA shared the environmentalists' view. In seeking to counter the position that federal facilities could not be held to procedural requirements under section 118, the agency argued that such an interpretation essentially granted federal facilities a dispensation from the law. To deny federal, state, and local governments the authority to impose regulations and state procedural requirements on federal installations was, the EPA suggested, to create an "enforcement vacuum which rendered the 'duty' of federal facilities to comply with the CAA 'utterly meaningless.'"[34] Moreover, it occasioned a "dichotomy between federal and private industrial polluters which [could force] the latter to undertake burdensome abatement measures that federal polluters were able to avoid."[35]

THE VIEW FROM TVA

Recall that in the early 1970s, TVA, as the nation's largest electric utility system, was initiating a major transition in its power program. Perceived as the only viable option for meeting the power demands of the Tennessee Valley in the 1980s, a drastic reduction of its dependence on coal for electricity generation was contemplated by TVA, a change that dominated program thinking and action. Agency plans called for the phasing out of several older coal-fired plants during the decade as seventeen new nuclear units at seven plant sites came on line. Anticipated along with the reduction in coal burning was a concomitant reduction of the massive SO_2 emissions normally produced by these coal-fired plants. And this in turn raised agency expectations that the crescendo of environmentalist attacks excoriating TVA as the nation's most prolific — and the federal government's most embarrassing — source of SO_2 pollution would diminish as well. But because TVA intended to reduce, not eliminate, its coal-generating capacity, the agency would still have to cope with the CAA of 1970 as it related to the control of SO_2 pollution. As a consequence, TVA would initiate a campaign determined to obtain what Louis Gawthrop terms a "manipulated agreement" by garnering external support for its perspective on what adequate compliance with that law should be.[36]

The Past as Prologue   TVA began its campaign in late 1970. At that time, the air pollution control boards of Alabama, Kentucky, and Tennessee were holding hearings on the implementation plans that they would have to submit to EPA for approval. TVA naturally was concerned about the types of SO_2 compliance strategies the states would allow. Agency officials hoped to gain approval for their own plan, one that staff members felt would most inexpensively reconcile environmental concerns and their own plans to reduce coal-generating capacity. Known popularly as SDEL (Sulfur Dioxide Emission Limitation system), this plan was based on a strategy of intermittent control. It had three components: increasing the height of plant smokestacks to disperse SO_2 downwind of TVA facilities, thus diluting rather than reducing actual emissions; temporarily shutting down plants when SO_2 concentrations were too heavy; and burning low-sulfur or washed coal when health hazards existed.[37]

Attempts by TVA to influence the development of environmental regulations were neither novel nor regarded as futile by agency officials in these early years. As mentioned in chapter 1, since the mid-1940s Valley states regularly had looked to TVA expertise for guidance in both air and water quality matters. What is more, at the federal level a very cozy relationship had developed between TVA and environmental professionals. In the words of one EPA Region IV official, "there was . . . among the professionals at EPA and TVA a 'sweetheart' relationship. TVA was the acknowledged expert on air pollution in terms of modeling technology, so that in the early days of the CAA . . . TVA was involved to the point where even *staffs interchanged* [emphasis added]. So TVA always had a direct communication to [EPA] headquarters. . . . When they fought this SIP thing, they always went to the Washington folks. . . ."[38]

Symbiotic relationships aside, three additional factors conspired to bolster TVA's confidence that its arguments might yet prevail. First, by assigning implementation responsibilities to the states, Congress had ignored the woeful institutional capacities of most state air pollution programs. The recollections of Harold Hodges, director of the Tennessee Air Pollution Control Division (TAPCD), are revealing; they illustrate the situation in most states in the early 1970s.

> The 1967 Tennessee Air Quality Act gave some pretty broad guidelines as to what our [TAPCD] responsibilities were [but] . . . there were no provisions to fund them [responsibilities]. . . . So they had about four people that they assigned to air pollution control. Increased federal funding started in 1969, so that when I got here in 1970 we had about twenty people and most of those people were relatively inexperienced . . . [just as we had] assumed the task under the CAA of putting together the first state implementation plan. It was more than we had sufficient staff to do, both in quantity and quality.[39]

And alluding to the additional enforcement consequences of this situation, Hodges continued: "[In] any enforcement action that we might get involved in today [1981], I don't feel inadequate . . . [we can] stand the scrutiny of the courts as technical experts . . . whereas back in the early 1970s, we really had some problems claiming we were."[40]

A second factor buoying TVA spirits was the similarly distressing lack of air pollution expertise at both the national and regional levels of EPA. The product of President Nixon's Reorganization Plan No. 3, EPA had inherited the professional staffs of ten distinct environmental bureaucracies (see table 3.2). Inherited as well were their respective competencies, constituencies, and administrative ideologies, each of which was decidedly oriented toward water quality. A comparison of FY 1971 personnel and budget data for the major air (National Air Pollution Control Administration — NAPCA) and water (Federal Water Quality Administration — FWQA) agencies inherited by EPA reveals the preponderance of the agency's "water ethic."

Nearly two and a half times as many water quality professionals were absorbed by EPA, and the old FWQA budget was nearly ten times that of NAPCA. What is more, this ethic was personified in the ranks of the Atlanta Region IV office of EPA — the office within whose geographic area of responsibility TVA operated its power facilities. For example, much of the agency's leadership and staff came from "water backgrounds," were admittedly "more comfortable" with water quality issues, and readily conceded that the regional office "didn't have much of an air enforcement program [at that time]."[41]

The third factor auguring well for TVA's intervention efforts was EPA's initial reluctance to mandate constant control systems. Put most succinctly by an EPA official, "there was nationally, and to some extent regionally [Region IV], a bias toward tall stacks. Remember, this [was] the beginning of the CAA and . . . no one [was] too sure [about constant controls]."[42] With intermittent control techniques the more proven and significantly less expensive control technology, EPA seemed predisposed to err on the conservative side of the SO_2 clean-up debate.

TVA proceeded adroitly to use state hearings to promote the virtues of strategies based on intermittent control. Agency officials argued that only intermittent controls would allow TVA plants to meet national ambient air quality standards by statutory deadlines, that constant controls were economically and technologically infeasible in the immediate future, and that EPA's August 1971 guidelines for State Implementation Plans specifically authorized alternate (as opposed to constant) controls for SO_2 pollution.[43] Although TVA's arguments were persuasive to the Tennessee and Kentucky boards — they proposed plans in 1971 that allowed intermittent control strategies — Alabama refused to allow TVA's approach. It was at this point that EPA Region IV officials began to experience the frustration with TVA that would later result in total communication breakdown between

Table 3.2. **The EPA Inheritance**

Major units	Previous agency	Number of personnel	Fiscal 1971 budget (millions)	Administrator
Federal Water Quality Administration	Interior	2,670	1,000	David D. Dominick
Bureau of Water Hygiene	HEW	160	2.3	James McDermott
National Air Pollution Control Administration	HEW	1,100	110	John T. Middleton
Bureau of Solid Waste Management	HEW	180	15	Richard D. Vaughan
Pesticides Regulation Division	Agriculture (Agriculture Research Service)	425	5.1	G. G. Rohrer
Office of Pesticides Research	HEW (FDA)	275	10.7	
Research on Effects of Pesticides on Wildlife & Fish	Interior	9	0.216	Raymond E. Johnson
Bureau of Radiological Health	HEW	350	9	John C. Villforth
Federal Radiation Council	Interagency	4	0.144	
Division of Radiation Protection Standards	AEC	3	0.075	

SOURCE: Alfred A. Marcus, *Promise and Performance: Choosing and Implementing an Environmental Policy* (Westport, Conn.: Greenwood Press, 1980), 45.

the federal giants. As one Region IV enforcement official recalls, "[The program people] . . . in the trenches were frustrated during the SIP process. . . . It was obvious that the SIP's were changing because of the TVA influence in the states; influence that we [EPA] had no control over."[44]

The issue now was placed squarely before the EPA. As the agency prepared to review provisions in the state plans for approval or disapproval, it came under renewed pressure from TVA in early 1972 to allow intermittent control strategies. This time pressure came in the form of chairman Aubrey J. Wagner's testimony during congressional hearings on the implementation of the CAA of 1970. Chairman Wagner would later summarize the feelings of the TVA board of directors at that time:

> We [TVA] ought not to pollute, but we ought to take into account clean-up costs as well. TVA saw sense in protecting [the environment], but we had other responsibilities — economic development, low-cost energy production for consumers. . . . We had an obligation to resist spending money until we could find out if federal and state [SO_2] standards made sense. We were convinced that scrubber technology had not been proven to work effectively or efficiently at large power plants, and that low-sulfur coal supplies were not adequate to the supply demands that CCS techniques would require. [Moreover], TVA is an independent agency; if it has to take orders from any other federal agency, then it loses its independence.[45]

The Dispute Is Joined   As previously recounted, EPA's interpretation of the question of control strategy took a tortuous, vacillating path. After EPA avoided the question in promulgating approved State Implementation Plans in May 1972 and then proposed regulations disallowing intermittent controls two months later, TVA prepared to plead its case once more before the states and at national hearings sponsored by EPA. Before actually doing so, however, it would show its displeasure with — and some would say its disdain for — having to obtain state permits to operate its plants. TVA, questioning the constitutionality of a federal agency's having to meet procedural requirements of the states, refused to apply for these permits. Taking the stance it would assume throughout the SO_2 dispute, the state of Tennessee — where two-thirds of TVA's plants were operating — took no action to compel TVA compliance. TAPCD officials cited two primary reasons for their inaction: uncertainty over TVA's claims to immunity, and concern over the political and economic consequences of reproaching the agency. As one TAPCD official observed, "The big concern in the early days was 'Did we have the legal authority over federal installations?' We didn't as I saw it . . . the attorneys could never clear me up on that. . . . [What is more] . . . we're unique [from the other Valley states] . . . from a political and economic perspective. TVA is the only public utility Tennessee has, so you couldn't ignore the political and economic ramifications of what impact TVA made on the state."[46] Tennessee's inaction aside, Alabama and Kentucky filed separate suits in the fall of 1972 to require TVA to apply for permits to operate coal plants located within their boundaries.[47]

With its position on state permits pending before federal judges in two circuits, and with EPA proposing to disallow intermittent controls, TVA resumed its public offensive. In late 1972, board chairman Aubrey Wagner strongly attacked constant control systems in a widely publicized speech in New Orleans, citing excessive costs and unproven capabilities.[48] He alleged as well that the sludge produced by scrubbers posed substantial environmental problems. The theme was repeated throughout 1973 by TVA representatives, but with one significant variation: now the emission limitations of the states were attacked as infeasible as well. First enunciated in January when the agency submitted compliance plans to the states asking for exemption from SO_2 emission limitations and approval of its SDEL program, TVA's litany of charges was repeated during testimony at national scrubber hearings sponsored by the EPA in October.[49] These efforts were supplemented by TVA publications and news releases appearing throughout the year extolling the agency's past and prospective pollution control activities.

In the fall of 1973, as a severe onslaught on EPA's interpretation of the CAA mounted in the wake of the Arab oil embargo, and as the agency reversed its position of a year earlier by proposing a regulation allowing intermittent control systems, TVA's hopes soared. Acting EPA administrator John Quarles specifically cited TVA's experiences with pollution controls as a reason for allowing the use of intermittent control "in carefully selected situations." And reminiscent of chairman Wagner's testimony in 1972, Quarles referred to limitations on the technological reliability of scrubbers and the availability of low-sulfur fuels in the foreseeable future. The administrator then proposed a case-by-case approach to future enforcement efforts, calling for a "demonstration by each candidate source . . . that adequate constant emission reduction techniques are not available to attain and maintain the national standards, and that those techniques which are available would be applied to permanently reduce emissions to the maximum extent practicable prior to application of supplementary control systems."[50] Seizing this opportunity, TVA immediately submitted a status report to EPA on SO_2 pollution control at its plants. Not surprisingly, the agency downplayed the effectiveness of constant controls and highlighted the "potential" for using alternate fuels and intermittent control techniques in the Tennessee Valley.

TVA's fortunes took another turn for the better in December 1973 when EPA invited the states to eliminate regulatory provisions from their implementation plans that might exacerbate fuel shortages.[51] Recall that Tennessee and Alabama responded by proposing an increase in allowable SO_2 emission limits in the vicinity of TVA plants, while Kentucky proposed to allow intermittent controls. These revisions in state plans were attributable in large part to the tireless efforts of TVA and its allies to prevent any State Implementation Plan from "locking in" a single type of SO_2 emission control technique until Congress reexamined the question. That spring, the agency, along with the Nashville Electric Service and others, gave testimony rehashing the familiar litany of socioeconomic hardships that implementation of current SO_2 standards would impose. What is more, they introduced two new scenarios: economic dislocation for the eastern coal industry and industrial flight from the Valley. Nathaniel B. Hughes, TVA director of power resource planning, warned: "I can't describe precisely what the effect of our switching to alternate (i.e., low-sulfur) coal might have on the . . . coal industry in the region since high sulfur coal predominates . . . except to say that there would be serious disruptions. . . ."[52] This was followed by a thinly veiled threat leveled by one corporation official: "It's a very dangerous practice to tell a board . . . that we'll shut down or lay off or move out if you carry out a specific regulation, but, gentlemen, I can say in all candor that the economic impact on heavy industry of a thirty percent rate increase by TVA in order to meet constant control requirements would be crippling."[53]

EPA did not rule on the acceptability of these provisions until August 1974. At that time its decision to disallow the proposals led to EPA's first official notification to TVA that it was violating the CAA. But in the interim — with emission limits and compliance strategies still in doubt, news media coverage and speculation mounting, and "bad blood" developing between the agencies — TVA initiated negotiations with EPA.[54] Meeting in April 1974, chairman Wagner and EPA administrator Russell Train agreed to "sort of air differences . . . crystallize positions . . . and find out where there was unity . . . so they [EPA and TVA] could focus on, and resolve, the true issues."[55] To this end, the two leaders established a joint agency task force to produce a document juxtaposing respective agency positions on air pollution control.[56]

Following extensive deliberations, an initial report was issued by the task force in June 1974. Dissatisfied with the report as issued, however, TVA requested that the task force reconvene to consider tall stacks as an alternative control strategy. Interagency talks continued until January 1975, when a final report was issued. Its contents produced few surprises in terms of TVA's position: only SDEL would allow TVA to meet national SO_2 standards by the 1975 deadline; if the CAA did not allow intermittent controls — and TVA argued it clearly did — then the act should be amended; insufficient scientific evidence existed linking SO_2 emissions to health hazards if ambient standards were met; and EPA had indicated its approval of intermittent controls once already. EPA Region IV representatives took issue with TVA's points. Aside from endorsing the economic and technological feasibility of constant controls, the Region IV staff also made several other points: constant controls were mandated by the CAA; SDEL was an unproven approach to pollution control that might jeopardize public health; and Valley power shortages could result when plants were shut down temporarily to combat excessive SO_2 concentrations.

While the task force discussions were taking place, two events transpired that induced a swift hardening of negotiating positions. First, a federal appeals court in the sixth circuit upheld TVA's refusal to apply for state permits to operate its plants. The court decided that TVA did *not* have to apply for such a permit, but had only to conform with the SO_2 standards and limitations contained in Kentucky's implementation plan.[57] However, a fifth circuit court ruled less than a month later that TVA *did* have to apply for a permit in Alabama.[58] Nonetheless, these offsetting opinions gave the agency respite from state enforcement efforts while the decisions were appealed to the Supreme Court.

Second, EPA decided in August 1974 to disallow the intermittent control provision proposed by Kentucky to reduce "overkill" in its plan.[59] With task force negotiations at an impasse, and with TVA convinced that the Kentucky decision was a harbinger of future EPA policy, TVA filed suit challenging EPA's authority to disapprove state provisions permitting intermittent controls.[60] One week after TVA filed suit, EPA officially notified the agency that ten of its twelve plants were in noncompliance with the SO_2 ambient air standards of Alabama, Kentucky, and Tennessee.[61] Then in November and December it promulgated regulations that in effect disallowed TVA's SDEL strategy entirely. TVA, however, made no effort to comply, and agency officials even refused to concede EPA's enforcement power over its operations. They argued that under the definitions section of the CAA (section 302), TVA was not a "person" subject to EPA regulation. For its part, EPA did no more than begin discussing the violations with TVA, even though court suit and plant shutdown options were technically available as noncompliance sanctions. EPA's forbearance is appreciated best by reviewing the comments of those directly involved in the nascent dispute. As two EPA officials explained, "Jack [Raven, EPA Region IV administrator] didn't want to tackle those people [TVA] unless he had to . . . with the enforcement question still so fluid, while we didn't want to test the federal facility court suit question at that time."[62] With regard to the plant shutdown option, TVA board chairman Wagner's recollections are enlightening: "I never believed they'd shut down our plants; the public wouldn't stand for it."[63]

Thus, by the end of 1974, disagreements over SO_2 standards, pollution control strategies, and a federal facility's obligation to comply had resulted in a formal EPA reprimand of TVA's violations of the CAA. Feeling constrained, however, by enduring legal, technical, and sociopolitical factors, EPA moved cautiously to dissuade TVA from continued noncompliance. So gingerly challenged, TVA remained doggedly adamant. In the short term, with no immediate EPA threat of plant shutdowns, the agency's ability to meet electricity demands by Valley consumers was guaranteed. And in the long-term, these coal plants presumably would become less environmentally controversial. After all, TVA was on its way to a nuclear future—or was it?

CHAPTER FOUR

Through the Looking Glass Warily

THE FWPCA AND
THE TENNESSEE VALLEY AUTHORITY

During the EPA/TVA dispute over thermal pollution, interpretation of both the 1965 and 1972 amendments to the FWPCA would significantly affect the operations of TVA's nascent nuclear power program. What is more, federal and state interpretation of these statutes and the CAA would lead Robert Marquis, TVA general counsel, to make the following appraisal in 1973:

> TVA has lost much of the independence it once enjoyed relative to pollution control, and must now do things because they are required by law [not] because they are reasonable or . . . make sense. . . . Faced with this situation TVA is having to learn to live with second best — namely, the administrative process through which these laws are implemented. . . . Unless TVA takes full advantage of these rights [to intervene], it will surrender by default what independence remains to it relative to planning its programs and operating its facilities, perhaps at extraordinary cost to the agency.[1]

In that same year, a well-honed TVA strategy for exercising such "rights" was outlined in an internal agency memorandum: "Not only does rational participation in the administrative process require testifying at hearings, commenting on proposed regulations, and submitting evidence in the record, but it also involves behind the scenes work with federal and state staff people who are actually doing the work so that TVA's position can be presented informally while proposals are still in a formative stage of development."[2] Having examined TVA's early attempts to "participate" in the administrative process afforded by the CAA, we now turn to its efforts with regard to the FWPCA. First, however, it is useful to review the primary interpretational issues involved in the thermal dispute from the perspective of EPA.

John Quarles, former deputy administrator of the EPA, has written that the FWPCA as amended through 1972 "presented a rather bewildering array of requirements" that the agency had to translate into feasible, acceptable program directives.[3] Three products of EPA's taxing experience with interpretation were especially salient for the EPA/TVA thermal pollution controversy. These included the agency's directives concerning acceptable thermal pollution standards, technology-based effluent limitations, and grounds for exempting individual plants from thermal pollution requirements. A chronology of the major events accompanying EPA's interpretational efforts is presented in table 4.1.

The Question of Thermal Water Quality Standards   The 1965 amendments had called on each state to develop and submit for federal approval a set of water quality standards. These would define the maximum permissible levels of various pollutants consistent with the projected uses of a given waterway. A commission established by the Interior Department recommended that standards for thermal pollution be issued pursuant to that mandate. Then in the 1972 amendments to the FWPCA, Congress stipulated that any adopted state water quality standard that was approved or awaiting approval under the terms of the 1965 amendments could be challenged by EPA.[4] In the event of a challenge, EPA was to notify the state and specify changes that had to be adopted within ninety days of notification. If revisions were not forthcoming, EPA could promulgate the necessary changes and hold polluters accountable. The administrative vehicle for doing so was a standard-setting conference convened by EPA where arguments for and against revision could be presented by any interested party.

Most significant for the EPA/TVA controversy, Alabama and Tennessee — two states where TVA would choose to locate most of its nuclear generating capacity — were concerned about excessive heat discharges into the Tennessee River. To allay their fears, they developed thermal pollution standards for portions of that river flowing within their respective boundaries. During the 1970s EPA's review of these standards seriously affected the operations of the TVA nuclear power program and engendered disagreement between the two agencies. At issue was EPA's interpretation of the act's imprecise mandate to determine "maximum permissible levels" of thermal effluent discharge.

Table 4.1. **Chronology of the Thermal Dispute: The Inter-pretation Experience**

Year	Major Events
1965–1967	—TVA proposes basinwide plan for water quality management in the Tennessee Valley; plan calls for 93°F temperature limit and a 10°F maximum temperature rise.
	—TVA testifies before Alabama Water Improvement Commission (AWIC) in favor of its water quality plan.
	—AWIC adopts 90°F, 10°F standards, but then reverses itself to incorporate TVA's standards.
	—TVA proposes to meet standards with diffuser pipe system, temporary plant shutdowns, and management of river flows.
	—TVA claims that meeting more stringent thermal standards would jeopardize electrical power supplies in the Tennessee Valley.
1968–1970	—Department of Interior urges TVA to build nuclear plants to meet stringent thermal standards; advises the installation of cooling towers at Browns Ferry.
	—TVA testifies standards are too strict and designs plants with diffuser systems.
	—TVA announces phase out of older coal plants over the decade with a phase-in of nuclear plants.
	—National Environmental Policy Act enacted.
	—Environmental Protection Agency (EPA) created.
	—EPA administrator Ruckelshaus announces court suit, permit, and conference approach to FWPCA implementation.
1971	—EPA convenes standard-setting conferences for Alabama and Tennessee.

At stake eventually would be an anticipated $640 million worth of construction costs for installing auxiliary cooling tower systems at TVA nuclear plants, towers needed to meet thermal standards that TVA officials thought were unnecessarily stringent.

According to EPA Region IV officials, "[w]aters providing habitat for aquatic life [had historically] received more [research] attention than other water uses because [aquatic life] . . . cannot escape the effects of altered temperature patterns."[5] As a consequence, and in contrast to the SO_2 pollution experience, the cause-effect relationships underlying thermal pollution were well documented by the federal government and widely accepted. Several of the more profound, most irrefutable adverse effects of thermal pollution are summarized in table 4.2. Excess heat discharges undeniably killed fish and other aquatic life through excessive or rapid heat increases (thermal shock) or decreases (cold shock). Equally undisputed were the deleterious consequences of unseasonably high temperatures on aquatic reproductive cycles: spawning failures, "hatchability" problems, and extremely low survival rates among young fish. Uncontested as well was the most egregious source of such problems: the disposal of waste heat from steam electric generating plants, with nuclear units responsible for 40 to 60 percent more heat discharge than comparable fossil-fueled facilities.[6]

Despite the general consensus on what Robert Nakamura and Frank Smallwood term "conceptual complexity" — the matter of how a problem should be defined — uncertainty abounded over the more technical questions associated with heat discharges. For instance, what amounts of heat, at what temperatures, in what concentrations, and in combination with what climatic conditions actually harm different species of fish, at different life stages, and over different exposure levels and rates? Further complicating these questions was the tendency for their answers to vary from site to site. Thus, not unlike the SO_2 standard-setting dilemma, the EPA and its predecessors were charged with determining "permissible" standards, although sufficient technical supporting data did not exist.

The 1965 amendments did not allow time for resolving scientific uncertainties. As stipulated by Congress, the states were to submit water quality standards for federal review by June 1967. The act did provide, however, for criteria guidelines that would be developed by a group of water quality experts to aid the Interior Department (and subsequently the EPA) in reviewing proposed state standards. This group, known as the National Technical Advisory Committee, issued interim recommendations for thermal pollution that were available to federal officials when the first state proposals were submitted. These criteria were based on approximations of what constituted "natural"

Table 4.2. **A Summary of Adverse Effects of Thermal Pollution on Fish and Other Aquatic Life**

- Temperature to a very large degree controls the species of fish that may be present in the aquatic environment, and hence the quality of the fishery.
- High temperatures cause complete displacement of fish and associated biota.
- Temperature changes that are extreme interfere with normal seasonal biological events.
- Higher temperatures promote and favor reproduction and growth of pathogenic bacteria.
- Higher temperatures also stimulate growth of undesirable taste- and odor-causing organisms.
- Temperature also reduces the capacity of receiving waters to assimilate waste and hence affects other water uses.
- Temperature has also been shown to greatly increase the toxicity of other pollutants that may be present in natural waters.
- Higher temperatures reduce the solubility of dissolved oxygen and at the same time stimulate the metabolism, respiration, and oxygen demands of fish and other aquatic life, often with extremely deleterious effects.
- Even with adequate dissolved oxygen and the absence of any toxic substances, there is a maximum temperature that each species of fish or other organism can tolerate; higher temperatures produce death in 24 hours or less. Whenever oxidizable materials are present the rate at which these materials will remove dissolved oxygen is increased by a rise in temperature.

Source: Environmental Protection Agency, Water Quality Office, Region IV, *Water Quality Standards-Setting Conference for the Inter-State Waters of the State of Alabama* (Montgomery: EPA, 5–7 Apr. 1971).

temperatures for particular bodies of water, and they stipulated the maximum temperature extremes and increases that different aquatic life could sustain.[7]

With regard to maximum water temperatures for warm water aquatic life, the committee recommended various temperature levels for different life stages of a variety of fish species. For the reader's convenience, these criteria are listed in table 4.3. Moreover, the report was quite specific about recommended temperature variations.

Table 4.3. **Provisional Maximum Temperatures Recommended for Fish and Associated Biota in the Tennessee River**

93° F: Growth of catfish, gar, white or yellow bass, buffalo, carp-sucker, threadfin shad, and gizzard shad

90° F: Growth of largemouth bass, drum, bluegill, and crappie

84° F: Growth of pike, perch, walleye, smallmouth bass, and sauger

80° F: Spawning and egg development of catfish, buffalo, threadfin shad, and gizzard shad

75° F: Spawning and egg development of largemouth bass, white and yellow bass, and spotted bass

68° F: Growth or migration routes of salmonids and for egg development of perch and smallmouth bass

55° F: Spawning and egg development of salmon and trout (other than lake trout)

48° F: Spawning and egg development of lake trout, walleye, northern pike, sauger, and Atlantic salmon

---

SOURCE: EPA, *Water Quality Standards-Setting Conference for the Interstate Waters of the State of Alabama* (Atlanta: EPA Water Quality Office, 5–7 Apr. 1971).

During any month of the year, heat should not be added to a stream in excess of the amount that will raise the temperature of the water . . . more than 5 degrees F. In lakes, the temperature . . . in those areas where important organisms are most likely to be adversely affected should not be raised more than 3 degrees F. above that which existed before the addition of heat of artificial origin. . . . The discharge of heated wastes . . . must be managed so that no barrier to the movement or migration of fish and other aquatic life is created.[8]

Although many states adopted thermal standards compatible with the advisory commission's guidelines, some did not. Alabama and Tennessee fell into the latter category. After holding extensive public hearings where interested parties, including TVA, testified as to appropriate standards, the Alabama Water Improvement Commission (AWIC) approved in May 1967 a 93° F temperature maximum and a 10° F temperature rise for portions of the Tennessee River where TVA was planning to locate its Brown's Ferry nuclear plant.[9] These were submitted to federal officials in June of that same year. Because they contrasted so sharply with the commission's recommendations of an 86° F maximum and 5° F temperature rise, Alabama's proposed standards were disapproved by federal officials in February

1968. Although protracted negotiations between federal and state officials ensued, as of February 1971 a resolution of their differences was still not in sight. Consequently, EPA administrator Ruckelshaus authorized a standard-setting conference for April 1971 in Montgomery, Alabama. As a result of this conference, EPA officially promulgated an 86° F maximum and a 5° F change limit for sections of the Tennessee River in Alabama.[10]

Much the same pattern was followed in the development of Tennessee's thermal water quality standards. In May 1967 the state water pollution commission proposed a 93° F maximum and a 5.4° F rise standard for portions of the Tennessee River where TVA's Sequoyah nuclear plant would be located.[11] This proposal was rejected by federal officials in favor of an 86.9° F maximum and a 5.4° F rise limitation.[12] Negotiations extended from 1968 until the state voluntarily issued standards consistent with EPA's thermal limits in December 1971.[13] EPA formally approved these revised standards in June 1972. Thus the EPA had pressured the states of Alabama and Tennessee — where all but one of TVA's nuclear plants were expected to be built — to adopt thermal water quality standards more stringent than TVA thought were necessary.

The Question of Technology-Based Effluent Limitation   As noted in chapter 2, the FWPCA of 1972 required all existing sources of pollution to meet two levels of technology-based effluent limitations. By 1977 polluters were to meet limits premised on the "best practicable technology currently available"; by 1983 they were to comply with standards based on "the best available technology economically achievable." The task of translating these vague congressional intentions into feasible, acceptable directives was delegated to the EPA. Section 304 charged the agency with identifying the amounts of effluent reduction technologically possible for classes of industrial polluters. To translate these effluent limitations into regulations for specific discharges, section 402 authorized the EPA to issue pollution discharge permits to individual sources of pollution.

EPA's interpretation of these provisions of the 1972 amendments was very important to the TVA nuclear power program. In order to obtain permits for discharging heated water, TVA's nuclear units would have to be in compliance with the thermal effluent limits developed by EPA, limits that could significantly affect both the capital and operating costs of the agency. Thus, TVA's responses to the directives could significantly affect its ability to meet the needs for power of agency customers in the Tennessee Valley.

EPA's interpretation of the law was complicated severely, however, by the absence of a sufficient data base for promulgating technology-based effluent limits. Congress had charged the EPA with regulating over 200,000 industrial polluters. Such a responsibility required reams of information "about the discharges, manufacturing processes, and technical options of diverse firms operating in different circumstances throughout the country."[14] The agency approached this herculean task by dividing water polluters into 30 categories and 250 subcategories based on such criteria as product, process, size of plant, and age of equipment.[15] EPA staff were then dispatched to industries across the country to develop a satisfactory data base for developing the standards. The results of this effort demonstrated to EPA officials that although Congress assumed that "best" pollution control technologies for industrial types must exist, industry had not identified any. It thus appeared to many staff members that a single technology-based effluent limitation was unrealistic. A summary is provided in table 4.4 of the most popular technological alternatives available as the EPA/TVA thermal dispute began.

Given such a scenario, it is not surprising that the procedural deadlines established by the FWPCA of 1972 were not met. According to the act, EPA was to issue effluent guidelines by October 1973 in order that pollution discharge permits — based upon such guidelines — could be issued to individual pollution sources. However, it was only because of a lawsuit filed by the Natural Resources Defense Council (NRDC) that guidelines for approximately thirty industrial categories were later issued by a reluctant EPA in January 1974.[16] And it was not until March 1974 that effluent guidelines were proposed for thermal pollutants discharged by steam electric generating plants such as TVA's nuclear units.[17] EPA did not issue final regulations for thermal pollution until October 1974, but TVA's early access to their likely substance and enforcement played a major role in resolving the EPA/TVA thermal dispute.

The Question of Thermal Pollution Exemption   The final aspect of EPA's interpretation of the FWPCA that affected the TVA power program involved possible exemptions from thermal standards under sections 313 and 316(a). The former section, akin to section 118 of the

Table 4.4. **Available Technologies for Thermal Pollution
            Abatement**

Technology	Characteristics
Cooling Ponds	Evaporative cooling; given sufficient land, the cheapest and most environmentally benign method; pond effluent can either be returned to plant intake (closed cycle) or discharged to natural receiving body (open cycle).
Spray Systems (Ponds)	Evaporative cooling; require little maintenance; try to increase the exposure of surfaces to atmosphere for cooling; subject to poor operation due to climatic conditions.
Natural Draft Wet Towers	Evaporative cooling; large "chimneys" provide a draft to pull air over a large surface of water; long-term maintenance-free operation; smaller amounts of ground space required; lower mechanical and electrical costs; extreme height (500 feet) causes visibility pollution; fog from evaporation.
Mechanical Draft Wet Towers	Evaporative cooling; much smaller than natural draft towers; better control of outlet temperatures than with natural towers; much shorter (50 feet) than natural draft towers; fog from evaporation.
Natural and Mechanical Draft Dry Towers	Heat exchange between hot water and cooler air; no direct contact with cooling air, thus no fog; much steam piping required for direct system makes it infeasible for large plants.
Diffusers	Pipes distribute and mix waste heat over receiving body of water to attain desired temperatures; heated water may either be concentrated on surface to maximize evaporation, or concentrated in midstream to minimize effects on shoreline biota.

Source: Water Quality Office, EPA Region IV, Atlanta, Ga.

CAA, dealt with the obligation of federal facilities to comply with the law. Section 313 stated that federal agencies

> (1) having jurisdiction over any property or facility, or (2) engaged in any activity resulting, or which may result, in the discharge or runoff of pollutants, shall comply with federal, state, interstate, and local requirements respecting control and abatement of pollution to the same extent that any person is subject to such requirements, including the payment of reasonable service charges.

In addition, a one-year presidential exemption was available to federal pollution sources if the president determined that one was in the paramount interest of the United States.

In contrast to the SO_2 dispute, the issue with regard to section 313 did not involve the obligation of federal facilities to comply with state procedural requirements; under the FWPCA, NPDES permits were issued by EPA itself. At issue, instead, was whether federal facilities had *only* to comply with those requirements that pertained to discharges from pollution sources *as defined in the* FWPCA *itself.* Federal officials tended to claim that this was indeed the case, but most environmentalists saw a broader obligation to comply with *any* and *all* federal, state, interstate, and local edicts. To federal targets, however, meeting "any and all" requirements foreboded a day when, through judicial interpretation of section 313, their multistate operations would become subject to diverse—perhaps even contradictory—state and local land-use regulations and to broadened interpretations of the police power of the states.

The second aspect of the exemption question involved EPA's interpretation of section 316(a) procedural and evidentiary requirements for pollution sources. As illustrated in table 4.5, the factors interacting to influence the environmental impact of heat discharges from a particular plant on a particular section of receiving water are mechanical, geographical, and processual in nature. Realizing that a thermal standard well advised for a whole river section might be ill advised (i.e., economically, technologically, and/or ecologically) for any particular plant, Congress had authorized EPA to assign less stringent thermal standards for individual pollution sources. The FWPCA stipulated only that the burden of proof for exemptions rested on those seeking to be excused. The owner or operator of a plant had to satisfy EPA that the applicable limit or standard was "more stringent than necessary to assure the protection and propagation of a

Table 4.5. **Factors Influencing Environmental Impact of Heat Discharges**

Discharge Characteristics	Power Plant Characteristics
Location	Receiving water type (river, lake estuary, ocean)
Amount	Cooling method (open cycle, "helper" system, closed system)
Temperature	Safe zone
Frequency	Efficiency
	Heat rate
	Unit size
	Capacity factor
	Age

balanced, indigenous population of shellfish, fish, and wildlife in and on the body of water into which the discharge is to be made."[18] Congress made no mention, however, of how a polluter was to convince the administrator that dispensation was warranted. Rather, this was left to the discretion of EPA. As with the question of technology-based effluent limitation, EPA's anticipated interpretation of, and expected enforcement commitment to, thermal exemptions would later help dissuade TVA from continued noncompliance during the twilight hours of the thermal dispute.

THE VIEW FROM TVA

Friends and foes of nuclear power alike took strong note in the fall of 1982 when the TVA board of directors announced it was canceling further construction on four partly completed nuclear power plants in Tennessee. Scotching the plants meant that TVA was writing off $1.85 billion in plant investments made over the previous decade. This decision, when coupled with an earlier TVA plan to place four other nuclear units in a deferred status,[19] meant TVA had effectively abandoned nearly 50 percent of its widely heralded, longstanding commitment to a nuclear future for the Tennessee Valley. Conceived in the mid-1960s and touted as a "technology fix" for making the Valley a twenty-first-century "energy oasis," TVA's nuclear plant contingent had by the late 1970s become a "multi-billion dollar white elephant" as the agency ran pell-mell into the antinuclear and energy conservation movements of that decade.

Paul Schulman has written that "reflexive organizations" increasingly populate our policy-making landscape. These are organizations whose behavior is conditioned by what he terms "reflexive decisions": policy decisions which "in their implementation materially affect the validity of [the] situational assumptions upon which they [are] based."[20] There exists no more apt example of such an organization than the TVA, and no more convincing an explanation of the plight that has befallen its nuclear power program.

TVA planners in the mid-1960s made three assumptions about the situation confronting the agency. Tennessee Valley power needs would continue to grow at an annual rate of 7 percent for the foreseeable future; energy consumption would continue to be the sine qua non for economic growth and improved standards of living; and fossil fuel prices would continue to spiral, such that nuclear power plants would become the most cost-effective sources of electricity. Implementation of the decision to go nuclear to the degree anticipated, however, fundamentally undermined the validity of these assumptions. Cost overruns at nuclear plants contributed mightily to a 500 percent rise in TVA power rates between 1967 and 1982. And this, in turn, lowered consumer demand for power to increases of less than 1 percent annually and threatened to substantially depress economic growth in the region. Most instructive in chronicling this reflexivity are recent assessments of the TVA power program by then-board member S. David Freeman:

> . . . the nuclear plants that TVA was building were the victims of an immature technology. The safety concerns were not fully appreciated beforehand, and extensive changes were required. TVA virtually had to rebuild its nuclear plants while it was constructing them. . . . Until 1979, TVA's reaction to the inflationary aspects of power plant construction was to go full speed ahead, ignoring the fact that the escalating cost of building these plants would reduce future demand and render some of the . . . units under construction unnecessary. . . . TVA [had] not learned that . . . higher priced electricity results in less usage. . . . Electricity at thirteen cents per kwh — which is what the most recently deferred plants would have cost — would not promote economic growth, but would constitute a heavy tax on industry and consumers and would prove a further drag on the economy.[21]

But in the halcyon days of the nuclear power program, long before the agency found itself $14 billion in debt because of nuclear
construction and before officials were claiming that to complete the
program might mean "bankruptcy" or consumer "revolution,"[22] TVA
officials were optimistic about their nuclear future. Chairman Wagner, citing the "exhaustive" internal study that led to the nuclear decision, estimated that about $100 million would be saved on fuel alone
over the next twelve years at the Browns Ferry plant.[23] Similarly, Jere
Ballentine, superintendent at the prospective Sequoyah nuclear plant,
claimed that "two pounds of nuclear fuel can generate as much electricity as one hundred tons of coal."[24] Thus, prior to EPA's creation
in 1970, TVA had already begun construction on two nuclear plants
and awarded contracts for several other facilities. Its primary concerns were not cost overruns or unused generating capacity, but meeting power commitments to its Tennessee Valley consumers at the
lowest rates possible by getting its Browns Ferry and Sequoyah nuclear plants into operation on schedule. To do so, it was critical to
convince the states of Alabama and Tennessee, as well as the Interior
Department, that TVA's version of water quality standards and control techniques should prevail in the Tennessee Valley.

Toward the Dispute   As noted in chapter 1, TVA enjoyed a long-
established, widely heralded record of concern with water quality in
the Tennessee Valley as the agency began its fourth decade of operation. Recognizing the "urgent need" for quantitative data on pollution in the Tennessee River basin, TVA had initiated a stream sanitation program in the mid-1930s. The data generated, along with TVA
consultants, were used by Valley states during the 1940s and 1950s
to develop comprehensive pollution-control legislation for area waters.
Moreover, since 1955 TVA had studied the effects of heated water
discharge from its coal-fired steam plants. Comfortable with a stewardship role that valued water quality as a lever for the "optimum
use and future [economic] development of the Valley's streams and
reservoirs," TVA proposed a comprehensive, basinwide plan for water
quality management in late 1966.[25] One component of this plan dealt
with thermal pollution control, recommending a 93° F temperature
limit with a 10° F maximum rise. Thus, as the states sought to develop thermal pollution standards pursuant to the statutory charge
of the FWPCA of 1965, as President Johnson issued Executive Order
11288 calling for compliance by federal facilities with water quality

laws, and as construction began on the first nuclear units at Browns Ferry, TVA had already developed and was actively promoting its own thermal standards.

From November 1966 to January 1967 AWIC held fourteen public hearings throughout the state on water quality standards. Consonant with the TVA strategy of using the administrative process to attain "some voice in the formulation of standards and requirements with which [TVA would] have to comply," TVA representatives testified at several of these hearings that the agency's comprehensive plan (including the thermal standards proposed) should be accepted by both AWIC and the Tennessee Stream Pollution Control Board.[26] Testifying at water quality criteria hearings in Sheffield, Alabama, in 1966, the TVA director of health and the chief of the Water Quality Branch highlighted the economic development aspects of the comprehensive plan, as well as its progressive nature.

> . . . TVA management has concluded that a comprehensive plan for water quality management developed on a basin-wide concept would fill an important need as people of the region continue to evaluate the Valley's resources and to make plans for economic and social growth. . . . [Such a plan] would be unique in that the management plan would coincide with the natural watershed. Nowhere in this country is such a plan in effect today, [consequently] this is an unequalled challenge and opportunity for TVA and the states to demonstrate a partnership of effort which could assure that the streams of the Valley are permitted to contribute their immense potential to the growth of the area. We are convinced that clean water is of much more value than unclean water to the present and future citizens of . . . the Valley as a whole. The best interests of *all* the people must be served. This means that the special interests of some groups may have to give way in part to the *public* interest.[27]

Formal statements presented at the AWIC hearings on standards applicable to the Browns Ferry plant reflect the breadth of "special interests" concerned with the criteria question. Included were representatives from federal, state, and local governments; civic, conservation, and recreational organizations; and development and industrial interests. When in May the commission initially adopted standards (90° F, 10° F rise) significantly more stringent than TVA had lobbied for, agency officials speculated that it was the "interest" of one Alabama state agency that had largely prevailed. An internal TVA memorandum reads, "the reasons why the Alabama Water Improvement Commission adopted a very restrictive temperature criterion on May 5 are not clear. However, we have learned that the Alabama Department of Conservation vigorously opposed the [TVA preferred] 95° F upper limit [while] the staff of the Commission [AWIC] did not defend with equal vigor even a 93° F upper limit."[28]

In the aftermath of the AWIC decision TVA was contacted by the Alabama Power Company. Agency officials were apprised of the "very serious economic problems" the new limits posed for the utility if left unchallenged: a number of its plants could not be operated in the summer since natural water temperatures regularly exceeded 90° F. The utility strongly urged TVA to oppose these standards at a special meeting it had requested of the commission. M.A. Churchill did so on behalf of TVA, arguing that "experience over the years at our own steam plants supports the conclusion that 93° F as an upper limit is entirely satisfactory for aquatic life."[29] Churchill also assailed the proposed standards as unsupported by available scientific evidence and pointed out that a 93° F limit had recently been recommended to the Ohio River Valley Water Sanitation Commission by an expert aquatic life advisory committee. In the words of one observer, "at the conclusion of the presentations by the power company [Alabama] and TVA, it was apparent that all fourteen members of AWIC — with the only exceptions being those members representing aquatic interests — were quite impressed by the facts presented and were agreeable to doing whatever could be done legally . . . to set aside the criterion adopted on May 5."[30] So "impressed" were AWIC officials that the following day a staff member informed Churchill that the commission had decided to add to the criteria a statement that would, in effect, allow a 93° F, 10° F rise for cooling water discharges.[31] Meanwhile, the Tennessee Stream Pollution Control Board announced that it would adopt a 93° F, 5.4° F standard as its criterion, thus heeding the advice proffered in TVA's Comprehensive Water Quality Plan.

With its position on thermal standards now adopted by both Tennessee and Alabama, TVA moved to design its prospective nuclear plants to meet these standards as inexpensively as possible. Chosen was a control system based on diluting, rather than actually reducing, thermal pollution from its facilities. Classified as a diffuser system, TVA's approach to thermal control consisted of a network of pipes lying at the bottom of any receiving water body. Water would pass through the nuclear reactor as coolant, be discharged as extremely hot water through these pipes, and be dispersed over large areas of the river. The discharge thus would mix with cooler waters to lower its temperature. Moreover, should natural water temperatures at any time be too warm to allow sufficient dilution, TVA would temporarily reduce plant operations.

Recall that under the 1965 Water Quality Act, state standards could not take effect until approved by the Interior Department. To TVA's dismay, Secretary Stewart Udall notified Tennessee and Alabama in 1968 that their proposed thermal standards were too lax.[32] Most significantly for TVA, its diffuser system could not hope to meet the more stringent standards espoused by Interior officials. Discussions between federal and state officials during the spring of 1968 (and, indeed, over the ensuing two years) produced no agreement on an acceptable standard. Consequently, in July the Interior Department officially disallowed the thermal standards of the two states while agency officials continued talks with their representatives. Concurrently, and despite the absence of official thermal standards, the department sought to convince TVA to cooperate voluntarily with Interior's version of appropriate thermal standards when designing Browns Ferry.[33] The water quality standards coordinator in the Southeast Region, Howard Zeller, criticized TVA for planning to operate "under its own temperature criteria" if it chose not to redesign its plants.[34] TVA responded that "you [the Interior Department] may rest assured that water quality in the Wheeler Reservoir [a receiving body of water for Browns Ferry] will be protected . . . [and that] outside a mixing zone of reasonable size, water temperatures shall not exceed an average of 93° F."[35] Zeller remained skeptical, however, convinced that a "distinct thermal barrier . . . with temperatures maintained at a marginal level for fish survival" would result from TVA's diffuser strategy.[36]

Unfortunately for Interior's cause, the data supporting these suspicions were marginal as well. In a memorandum to his files Zeller wrote, "I recognize that detailed study and evaluation are proposed . . . [but] until these effects are demonstrated and the plant is in operation, we will be in no position to make evaluations [since] I know of no comparable operation in comparison that could be made."[37] Under such circumstances, TVA pursued a "wait and see" strategy; it was not about to redesign Browns Ferry and Sequoyah to accommodate "unofficial" standards that would require the installation of very costly ($36–$43 million each) cooling towers. The agency was willing to risk the significantly increased costs of retrofitting these plants should its thermal arguments not prevail (see table 4.6). TVA officials offered instead to supplement diffuser system operations with efforts to increase stream flow and decrease power production during those infrequent times when the 93° F limit was exceeded. To meet "more stringent standards by adding heat dissipation equipment [such as cooling towers]," they contended, "would cause a serious delay in the beginning of plant operations" at the two sites.[38] Moreover, with the "period of critical need" for Browns Ferry power generation being the winter of 1972–1973, such a delay was expected to jeopardize TVA's ability to meet the power demands of the Tennessee Valley.

With TVA pressing ahead on its diffuser system, one Interior Department official summed up his agency's plight in this way: "If we cannot convince TVA . . . then every utility in the country will tell us to go to hell when we tell them they've got to have cooling towers."[39] But TVA, as in the SO$_2$ dispute, was resolute. As chairman Wagner later recalled, "TVA had a responsibility to resist bad standards and we did; [what is more] we felt we were right and that we had a 50/50 chance of convincing federal regulators of it."[40] To this end, the agency began comprehensive recording of water temperature profiles at the Browns Ferry site in the fall of 1968.

Faced with such attitudes, Interior sought to bring additional pressure on TVA by broadening the scope of the water quality debate to include the AEC licensing process of nuclear plants. While hoping to see the AEC formally incorporate Interior's thermal standards as a condition for obtaining construction and operating licenses for TVA plants, agency officials knew this was extremely unlikely. For years, the AEC had asserted tenaciously that environmental concerns were not within its purview given the language of the Atomic Energy Act. Though some, such as Paul Traina, questioned whether President Johnson's Executive Order 11288 on federal compliance might not

Table 4.6. **Cooling Tower Capital and Operating Cost Factors, New vs. Retrofitted Plants (1972 dollars/kilowatt)**

Plant	Capital	Operating Cost
New	$ 3.84	$39.41
Retrofitted	$24.58	$39.43

SOURCE: Water Quality Office, EPA Region IV, Atlanta, Ga.

have expanded the AEC's authority in such matters, both the Justice Department and the federal courts in the *New Hampshire v. AEC* case found otherwise.[41] Still, as TVA prepared its Preliminary Safety Analysis Report for the Sequoyah nuclear plant, a representative of the Secretary of the Interior wrote to the AEC's director of regulations and made the following request: "While [Interior] understands the regulatory authority of the AEC is to be confined to considerations of common defense and security, and radiological health and safety, we recommend and urge that before the permit is issued the dangers of thermal pollution or the potential dangers to fish and wildlife which may result from plant construction and operation be called to the attention of the applicant [TVA]."[42]

From TVA's perspective, any AEC environmental consciousness-raising efforts were likely to be modest. The AEC not only had a widely recognized penchant for promotion rather than regulation of the atomic industry, but also a long and highly valued relationship between its staff and TVA. As Del Sesto writes of the former, "because investments had been so huge, the . . . pressure [on the AEC] to make them pay-off by means of proliferating nuclear generating stations [was] literally awesome."[43] And in regard to the longstanding AEC/TVA relationship, not only was former TVA board chairman David Lilienthal the first head of the AEC, but TVA personnel had also participated in the post-World War II nuclear power studies of the Parker Committee and the Daniel's Pile Project at Oak Ridge National Laboratories. What is more, as TVA began to develop its own nuclear staff in the early 1950s, agency personnel were regularly assigned to various AEC installations, including national laboratories in Washington, for training and experience. Consequently, even when the AEC responded to the WQIA and NEPA in 1970 by announcing it would henceforth give special attention to environmental concerns when issuing licenses, neither TVA nor its cohorts in the private sector had reason to feel especially threatened.

Thus, as EPA came into existence in late 1970, the seeds of its dispute with TVA had already been sown. TVA, Alabama, and Tennessee were all promoting thermal standards unacceptable to the Interior Department. Moreover, Interior's two-and-a-half-year-old campaign to persuade the states to issue stricter thermal standards was still stalemated, while AEC intervention on its behalf was promising in concept, but likely woeful in practice. For its part, TVA was forging ahead and designing its nuclear plants to meet the discredited thermal standards of Alabama and Tennessee despite Interior's warnings. Indeed, earlier in the year TVA announced that although the Sequoyah nuclear plant site "included space for the installation of supplementary cooling facilities if needed," TVA would "make use of its multipurpose reservoirs to control [thermal pollution] by [manipulating] stream flows" in a fashion akin to its Browns Ferry strategy. It was under these circumstances that the first issue to be resolved during the dispute came to the fore: what were the appropriate thermal pollution standards for portions of the Tennessee River where TVA planned to operate its nuclear plants?

The Dispute Is Joined   Recall that under the FWPCA of 1965 EPA could promulgate water quality standards for any state failing to propose such requirements, or for any state proposing limits unacceptable to the agency. To do so, it had only to convene a standard-setting conference and subsequently issue binding regulations for the state. EPA administrator Ruckelshaus saw the standard-setting conference as an effective, highly visible enforcement tool for his neophyte agency. Consequently, after repeated exchanges with the state of Alabama proved fruitless in resolving their disagreement over thermal standards, he notified Governor George Wallace that a standard-setting conference would be held in April 1971 to resolve the problem.[44]

In February 1971, as EPA announced it would convene the Alabama conference and after TVA had let contracts for two more nuclear plants, the Alabama Power Company notified TVA that the state of Alabama did not have "sufficient data to support much of an argument against EPA's proposed thermal standards" and would welcome any assistance TVA could provide.[45] TVA, convinced that EPA would not change its interpretation, nevertheless testified at the conference because, as one official put it, "*someone* needed to protect the public from the 'net-detrimental' effects of thermal standards."[46] The agency contended that EPA's standards were not based on sound technical data and that the public interest required a balance of environmental, energy, and economic concerns absent in its proposals. TVA's rationale for these arguments is best appreciated by referring to an internal agency memorandum issued by M.A. Churchill.

> I suggest we make a statement . . . [that] . . . TVA believes the public interest requires multiple use of our water resources. . . . We need to know

how much protection from any harmful thermal effects aquatic life really need. All the criteria have been proposed by state, interstate, and federal agencies, but soundly based technical data . . . are simply not available. The public interest also requires a healthy power industry which can supply the power needs of the country on a timely, efficient, and economic basis. Thus, in the public interest . . . thermal standards should involve a balancing of these needs.[47]

TVA then recommended that additional research be conducted and that "reasonable" interim standards be issued, standards that could later be adjusted to reflect acquired scientific knowledge. However, the agency also pledged to comply with whatever standard was eventually issued and proposed establishment of a joint TVA/EPA research station at Browns Ferry to collect needed data.

As expected, EPA adhered to its proposal and formally recommended in July 1971 an 86° F, 5° F thermal standard for portions of the Tennessee River where TVA's Brown Ferry nuclear plant was located.[48] Also in July, the state of Tennessee was holding public hearings on its previously disapproved thermal standard. EPA Region IV officials attended these hearings, proposing an 89.6° F, 5.4° F standard for portions of the Tennessee River where TVA's Sequoyah plant was located.[49] State officials, aware of EPA's determined effort in Alabama and seeking to qualify for future pollution control grants, voluntarily accepted EPA's proposal in late October.[50] Most importantly for TVA's future strategy, however, the impression of one agency official attending the Tennessee standard-setting meeting resuscitated agency hopes: "The standards were adopted by the Board with the understanding that they will in all probability be changed at some time in the future when studies indicate more conservative or liberal standards are needed."[51] Thus, as TVA prepared its Browns Ferry and Sequoyah plants for operation, it was presented with thermal standards that its current plant designs could not meet. As in the brewing SO_2 controversy, the agency would have to add expensive pollution control equipment unless EPA relaxed its standards or pursued less than vigorous enforcement.

CHAPTER FIVE

From Defiance to Compliance

APPLYING THE CAA TO
THE TENNESSEE VALLEY AUTHORITY

It has been argued that enforcement of a social prefer-
ence is essential if the preference is to be realized.[1] The EPA/TVA enforcement experience involving SO_2 pollution control was a prolonged,
bitterly contested struggle, one that still rankles many of those who
participated in, or have been affected by, its resolution. Before differences were settled over how the CAA of 1970 could best be applied
to TVA's operations, three fundamental enforcement questions had
to be answered. First, would TVA's challenge of the EPA administrator's refusal to allow intermittent control strategies be sustained by
Congress and the courts? Second, how would these same institutions
react to TVA's entreaties as a federal facility for immunity from state
permit requirements? And finally, with power plant shutdowns eliminated as an option, what credible and legally appropriate enforcement sanctions could EPA apply to expedite TVA compliance?

Aspects of these questions would be debated within EPA itself,
among various executive branch agencies, within the Executive Office
of the President (EOP), before Congress and the federal judiciary,
within the states, and in the arena of public opinion. In the end, the
most expensive environmental clean-up settlement in history would be
reached, but only after a determined, very nearly successful series of
TVA challenges to EPA's enforcement efforts. A chronology of the major events that transpired during enforcement is presented in table 5.1.

NARROWING TVA OPTIONS

In an article coauthored with David Lilienthal appearing in the *Harvard Law Review* in 1941, future TVA general counsel Robert Marquis

Table 5.1. **Chronology of the SO₂ Dispute: The Enforcement Experience**

Year	Major Events
1975–1976	— Supreme Court rules EPA has authority to disallow intermittent controls and that Congress should clarify federal facility/state permit question.
1977	— Congress enacts CAA of 1977 reaffirming EPA's positions on constant controls and federal facility compliance. — EPA issues second notice of violation to TVA without taking enforcement action. — Section 304 citizen suit filed against TVA for noncompliance with CAA. — Marvin Durning becomes new EPA director of enforcement. — President Carter appoints S. David Freeman to TVA board of directors.
1978	— Interagency negotiations resume. — Aubrey Wagner and William Jenkins leave TVA board; President Carter appoints Richard Freeman to TVA board. — TVA board approves negotiated settlement.
1979–1980	— EPA and TVA officially approve $1.02 billion settlement in public signing ceremony. — Settlement challenged as inflationary; errors discovered and settlement costs reduced to $760 million.

wrote, "The usual justification for the regulation of private businesses by administrative agencies is the necessity of ensuring that their operations shall not conflict with the public interest. In the case of a public business, however, such an enterprise itself is no less obligated to serve the public interest in accordance with law than is the regulatory agency: hence the effect of such regulation is almost certain to be simply to duplicate management and dilute responsibility."[2] The EPA/TVA Task Force Report issued in January 1975, nearly three months after EPA's initial notification of noncompliance to TVA, demonstrated vividly how such trust in a common vision of the public interest can be misplaced. Indeed, attorney Dean Hill Rivkin later reflected that "the clash of conceptions" so apparent in this report — with EPA's emphasis on pollution and its carcinogenic effects, and TVA's concern over economic and technological feasibility — "prevented the two agencies from entering into informal mechanisms for resolving problems . . . despite the efforts of the heads of both agencies to resolve the conflict."[3]

The ensuing two years ripened the dispute and witnessed several developments critical to its resolution. First, TVA stepped up its campaign to promote intermittent control systems in anticipation of amendments to the CAA, with the agency hoping to have its versions of the federal facility and control strategy questions safely ensconced in law. Second, federal court decisions related to the dispute brought a TVA promise of compliance and a shift in agency strategy. Third, as EPA's frustration and impatience with TVA rose, an enforcement rift developed among EPA headquarters, EPA Region IV officials, and the Department of Justice. And finally, public concern over TVA nuclear power safety and environmental degradation burgeoned, laying the foundation for subsequent enforcement efforts aimed at the agency by citizen groups. Though EPA's enforcement effort would be hindered by some of these developments, several would severely circumscribe TVA's compliance options as well.

TVA's Promotional Campaign   As the task force report was issued, as the antiregulation mood in Washington intensified, and as President Ford submitted his ill-starred antiscrubber amendments to Congress, TVA escalated its noncompliance campaign. Although they in effect exposed all agency activities to the scrutiny of "friends" and "foes" alike, TVA officials made numerous appearances before congressional committees and state air pollution boards to justify their position on constant control systems.[4] Throughout the spring of 1975 TVA officials made the case for intermittent controls and implored acceptance of less stringent SO_2 standards, as outlined in the Ford amendments. Most noteworthy were appearances before the Kentucky and Tennessee boards, and extensive cross-examination during the first comprehensive TVA oversight hearings since the New Deal. In April chairman Wagner urged the Kentucky Department of Natural Resources and Environmental Protection *not* to abandon its provision allowing intermittent controls. In a letter spiced with provocative "states' rights" rhetoric and emotional appeals to socioeconomic self-interest, Wagner declared:

> We feel your decision to reinstate this alternative control provision should not be affected by the action of the EPA in disapproving it as a part of Kentucky's implementation plan. The legality of EPA's action has been challenged by TVA and others [in federal court]. These cases are of national importance because many other states are interested in adopting similar control regulations. [If left unchallenged] . . . *EPA's view that it can direct how Kentucky will control air pollution . . . and how much Kentucky citizens will pay for it* [will prevail]. . . . *Air pollution control is not the only important aspect of our environment* [emphasis added]. To us, jobs and the social and economic well-being of the people of the region are all important aspects [as well].[5]

The Kentucky appeals were followed by TVA's promotion of its antiscrubber campaign before hearings of the Tennessee Air Pollution Control Board (TAPCB) in June. These were held in response to the charge to the states by the Energy Supply and Environmental Coordination Act (ESECA) to facilitate plant conversions from oil and gas to coal in the interest of energy conservation. At these hearings the TAPCD staff averred that without adequate oil and gas supplies, it was unreasonable to hold polluters to the original State Implementation Plan standards. Thus, TAPCD director Harold Hodges testified that the standards themselves — developed in haste given the press of 1972 statutory deadlines — were in need of change anyway, and the staff recommended a further relaxation of standards. So compelling were these arguments that even EPA Region IV officials and citizen groups supported relaxation efforts. Perhaps anticipating TVA's strategy, however, they drew the line on relaxing control technique requirements as well. Dr. Ruth Neff and Mary Wade of the Tennessee Environmental Council (TEC) were most adamant: "We would strenuously oppose any further relaxation of standards for processing emissions [and] recommend that the Board disapprove all attempts to substitute [the term] 'alternative controls' for 'reduction of emissions.'"[6] Countering environmentalist arguments that the CAA "called for standards that took advantage of technological progress" and that the proposed standard relaxation was adequate, was Dr. Thomas Montgomery of TVA's Air Quality Branch. Montgomery claimed that the relaxation was but an "additional step in the direction of removing 'overkill' from the standards."[7] Further relaxation, he maintained, ought to be made in order to take TVA's tall-stack strategy into account given the "technologically unproven" status of constant controls.

Finally, agency officials took advantage of TVA oversight hearings sponsored by the Senate Committee on Public Works during 1975 to do four things.[8] First, they cited the negative "externalities" of scrubber technologies (1,000 acres of land per year would be needed to dispose of scrubber sludge by-products). Second, they promoted the necessity for alternate intermittent control strategies (the only feasible way for the 1975 SO_2 standards to be met). Third, they excoriated environmental regulations for contributing to spiraling TVA power rates. And fourth, they highlighted the EPA/TVA Task Force Report as evidence of TVA's "willingness to cooperate and comply" with the CAA.

By the same token, however, the agency sustained severe criticisms leveled at all facets of its program. Most telling for the SO_2 dispute was the testimony of attorney Richard E. Ayres of the Natural Resources Defense Council (NRDC), who attacked both TVA *and* EPA for their behavior in the affair. A nationally renowned air pollution expert, Ayres noted his "disappointment" with TVA's failure to assume the lead in deploying scrubber technology, given its status as a federal facility. Moreover, he chastised the task force report as evidence of TVA's success at "coopting" EPA into cooperating with its noncompliance tactics.[9] To the chagrin of both agencies, Ayres delivered a similar message to those holding congressional oversight hearings on EPA's implementation of the CAA.

TVA's themes nonetheless hit a responsive chord in Washington and much of the Tennessee Valley. Thus, when the two met to discuss the task force report in June 1975, chairman Wagner advised EPA administrator Russell Train that the TVA board could not "in good faith" commit Valley consumers "to pay the high costs of scrubbers and low-sulfur coal" before the federal facility and intermittent control issues were resolved by the courts or the Congress.[10] To this, Train retorted, "EPA cannot agree with this approach . . . [since] we believe that the Clean Air Act mandates the use of constant emissions controls."[11]

Court Decisions and Strategic Choices   Movement on the judicial front began in September 1975 when the Sixth Circuit Court of Appeals delivered a powerful blow against TVA's intermittent control strategy. Recall that in a 1974 suit TVA had challenged EPA's authority to disallow provisions of Kentucky's implementation plan that allowed intermittent control techniques. On appeal, the sixth circuit now ruled in favor of EPA.[12] Pursuant to this decision, and as TVA appealed the ruling to the Supreme Court, EPA issued tall-stack guidelines in March 1976 that disqualified most TVA plants from compliance.[13] Reflecting recent fifth, sixth, and ninth circuit decisions, these guidelines made intermittent control and tall stacks available as a control technology only after constant control measures had been taken, and tall stacks were never to be used if the result would be increased SO_2 emissions. TVA's quest for judicial relief on this issue ended abruptly in April of that year when the Supreme Court refused to hear its appeal.[14] However, this decision was followed in June by a Supreme Court ruling that supported TVA's position on compliance by federal facilities, albeit in a less than enthusiastic manner.[15] In finding that the agency had to meet SO_2 emission standards and limits but that it did *not* have to apply to the states for operating permits, the Court noted the ambiguity of section 118 and encouraged congressional clarification of the federal facility issue.

During hearings the previous year before the Alabama Air Pollution Control Commission, the chief of TVA's Air Quality Branch had portrayed the primary question in the SO_2 dispute as follows: "Is spending over a quarter billion dollars more during the next ten years for still more sulfur dioxide control actually necessary in order to get clean air? We believe that the answer to the question is 'no.' We are going to get the same clean air around TVA plants at a small fraction of this cost."[16] The Supreme Court's denial of certiorari in the intermittent control case, however, had effectively answered the same question in the affirmative. TVA's SDEL program was insufficient for compliance with the law. Thus, as Congress pondered major revisions in the CAA, and as further judicial challenges to intermittent control were precluded by the courts, TVA announced in May 1976 that it was "fully committed to complying as rapidly as possible with . . . recent court rulings mandating the use of constant controls."[17] Moreover, the agency pledged to "work closely" with EPA and state officials to develop "necessary control strategies *for each plant*."[18]

Schattschneider has suggested that the way a problem is defined determines the scope of the conflict surrounding it and, ultimately, its resolution. TVA's updated strategy in the fall of 1976 is perhaps best appreciated in these terms. Agency officials hoped to at last "redefine" the SO_2 problem as no longer one of "compliance versus noncompliance," but rather as one of "ideal versus realistic" policy enforcement. And in the process they hoped to mobilize attentive, powerful, and politically astute allies in support of their cause. Their tactic was to continue to negotiate with EPA and state administrators to obtain compliance concessions in the form of "temporary use" of SDEL strategies for particular plants. The rationale for such concessions was twofold: the age of individual facilities and the questionable availability of coal low enough in sulfur. Concurrently, TVA planned to seek statutory relief on the same bases from Congress, to continue pursuit of SO_2 standard relaxation by the states, and, failing in both of these, to seek state variances from existing emission limitations on a plant-by-plant basis. It was thought that, at best, the pressure mounted by impassioned allies might combine with TVA's own efforts to provide congressional or state relief from EPA enforcement. At worst, the delays that these efforts engendered were expected to provide the time TVA needed to phase out older coal plants as the nuclear power contingent came on line.

Several participants in the dispute by then believed that the latter motive was *the* primary strategic concern for TVA. As one EPA Region IV official mused, "Certainly there was principle involved [on TVA's part], but I've been around long enough to know that principle usually translates into economics. . . . They were saying, 'By God, why spend this money when we're not going to have those plants ten years from now because the nuclear plants will be coming into operation. . . .' They were playing sort of a game, trying to put us off long enough so that they wouldn't have to do anything."[19] Thus, as EPA, TVA, and state government officials met during the fall of 1976 to discuss control strategies for TVA plants, EPA Region IV impatience and frustration with TVA grew. Some, such as Paul Traina and attorney Keith Casto, urged EPA superiors to file suit against TVA for noncompliance. At the time, however, these pleas went unheeded and did little more than reveal a significant enforcement rift among federal regulators.

The Enforcement Dilemma   EPA's decision to forsake enforcement sanctions against TVA during the 1975–1976 period drew flak from environmentalists. Some accused the agency of "dragging its feet" when faced with blatant noncompliance by its sister agency.[20] The

comments of Jack Raven, EPA Region IV administrator, are quite revealing of the agency's enforcement perspective: "We were caught in
the middle between the environmentalists and the TVA."[21] Although
EPA maintained that forthcoming amendments to the CAA rendered
enforcement premature, some within the agency indicated that a combination of factors influenced that decision. In addition to noting
the sociopolitical difficulties involved in closing TVA plants, several
interviewees portrayed EPA as somewhat "overwhelmed" by TVA's
widely heralded air pollution staff: "Hell, [TVA] was the international
expert on scrubbers; we weren't always sure we were doing the right
thing . . . their arguments were sometimes mesmerizing and they were
good at presenting them . . . our track record was in water, not air."[22]
Others claimed that some officials empathized with chairman Wagner's economic arguments against retrofitting older coal plants: "Back-
fitting some of those old steam plants . . . requires a lot of money
and the capital investment on some of the upgrading *is* probably more
than the initial investment in the plant."[23] Finally, most interviewees
suggested that EPA's only remaining enforcement sanction—the noncompliance lawsuit advocated by Traina and Casto—was an option
precluded by legal debates both within EPA and between EPA and the
Justice Department.

The Nixon and Ford administrations had maintained a so-called
quiet policy of nonlitigation against members of the federal family.
In TVA's case, however, a Justice Department determination as to the
agency's dependence on presidential direction had to be made before
the policy could be applied to it. At issue was whether TVA was "sufficiently independent" from the chief executive for a "justiciable situation" to exist. If TVA was independent, EPA could file suit. If not,
a presidential directive to the agency would hypothetically suffice to
halt noncompliance, and a "nonjusticiable situation" would exist,
precluding EPA lawsuits. The Justice Department under Nixon and
Ford had opined, and the EPA in Washington had concurred, that
TVA lacked sufficient independence to permit another federal agency
to file suit against it. But with the election of Jimmy Carter in 1976,
hope abounded in some quarters of the EPA Region IV bureaucracy
that the president-elect's touted commitment to environmental protection might change all this. Thus began in 1976 a sometimes heated
internecine debate that continued well into the first year of the Carter presidency, a debate pitting advocates of a TVA court suit against
those dubious of its legality. As a result, three things critical to the

enforcement effort occurred: EPA issued a second notice of noncompliance to TVA *without* applying enforcement sanctions; frustration with the Justice Department mounted among some at EPA; and those disgruntled with EPA enforcement efforts sought extrabureaucratic remedies to resolve the stalemate in the Tennessee Valley.

An Aroused Citizenry   Unimpressed by EPA's enforcement efforts, several citizen groups in Tennessee began to focus national and regional attention on what some characterized as TVA's insensitivity, if not indifference, to environmental protection. In 1975 the Tennessee Environmental Council (TEC), led by Dr. Ruth Neff and Jonathan Gibson, obtained an HEW Office of Environmental Education grant for symposia examining TVA's environmental impact in the Valley. Conceding that these would be "most timely" and "particularly worthwhile from a public education standpoint," TVA agreed to help plan and participate in a series of public forums.[24] The symposia would bring a variety of noted energy, environmental, and legal experts together to discuss various aspects of TVA's operations as they related to the environment.[25] TVA officials saw the symposia as an opportunity to allay Valley fears and to "educate" residents on its perspective that any definition of "environment" should include "the human as well as the natural environment."[26] For their part, TEC planners publicly stated the council's goals as the "stimulation of informed public scrutiny of the complex policy choices facing TVA [and] the encouragement of public participation in TVA decision-making."[27]

TVA was immediately put on the defensive by participants, with presymposia correspondence indicating that many saw the forums as a counteroffensive to TVA's promotional campaign. For example, John Gibbons of the University of Tennessee Environmental Center wrote that his paper would, by implication, "demonstrate the timidity and passivity [I could use stronger words]" of TVA's energy conservation programs when compared with those of other utilities.[28] Gibbons urged that his paper be distributed to what he termed "the TVA Lobby": politicians at the state, local, and federal levels who have "interests" in the TVA. Similarly, S. David Freeman (then of the Ford Foundation) was urged by the TEC project coordinator to challenge TVA's claim that its policies were "responsible in some fashion for whatever economic development occurred in the Valley."[29] Moreover, TEC's Gibson alerted Freeman to data that buttressed the latter's arguments for "alternative growth scenarios" (e.g., clean industry) in the Tennessee Valley. And most importantly for the SO_2 dispute, Region IV officials Paul Traina and Jim Willburn were asked to present EPA's views on scrubber technologies, TVA's compliance status with clean air schedules, the federal facility question relative to TVA, and their assessments of TVA's SDEL rationale.

Though feeling confident that the agency held its own during these proceedings and thanking Dr. Neff for a "fine job on the symposia," TVA officials occasionally expressed their concerns with aspects of the agenda. Reacting to the title of the first symposium, "Is TVA a Law Unto Itself?," TVA information director John Van Mol wrote to Gibson, "I was somewhat amused by the question posed. . . . Memory of the journalism course involving various *propaganda techniques* [emphasis added] escapes me, but you have hit upon a classic in one of the categories — 'begging the question.'"[30] On a somewhat sterner note, after receiving a paper on the legal framework of TVA in which "specific legislative proposals" were offered, Van Mol wrote to Dr. Neff that TVA did not want the symposia to serve as a "platform for debate" of such proposals. Moreover, he emphasized that his understanding was that the symposia were to be educational — i.e., "to make people aware of the issues from both sides."[31]

In the short term, TVA's concern about the use of the symposia as a platform for those antagonistic to its policies was probably well founded. Given the widespread media coverage they attracted, the panels no doubt served as part of an "adverse publicity" regulatory mechanism for the EPA. But as is typical of cycles of attention to issues, public concern predictably shifted elsewhere — in the case of TVA, to its increasing power rates and its alleged insensitivity to safety concerns in the wake of a fire at its Browns Ferry nuclear plant. Thus, the enduring benefits of the symposia for the EPA enforcement effort were most likely (1) the opportunity they afforded for bringing together individuals who would later play critical roles in resolving the SO_2 dispute, and (2) the creation of certain expectations on the part of some environmentalists. With regard to the former, S. David Freeman would become a prime mover in negotiating the clean air settlement as a member, and subsequent chairman, of the TVA board of directors. Paul Traina would lead the negotiating team for EPA Region IV during those same talks. And TEC, led by Ruth Neff, would spearhead a coalition of citizen groups that would file suit against TVA for noncompliance with the CAA. With regard to expectations aroused, TVA board member Neil McBride had talked with

Jonathan Gibson about plans to "follow up on the idea of opening up TVA's decision-making process as it affects the power program."[32] After McBride left the board, however, little follow-up resulted, and this unrealized expectation of citizen participation became a critical element in EPA/TVA negotiations.

REACHING A SETTLEMENT

As 1977 began, interagency talks had produced an exchange of compliance strategies for individual TVA plants but no overall agreement. EPA's proposal, based largely on a study by the consulting firm PEDCO Environmental, Inc., was presented orally to TVA on January 14, four days after TVA had submitted its compliance plan to EPA. Most significantly, TVA's plan called for the *use of low-sulfur coal* and sought to qualify four of its older plants for exemption on the basis of EPA's tall-stack guidelines. The agency argued that these plants should be permitted to meet less stringent emission limits without using scrubbers: EPA had allowed that a source need not apply the "best available technology . . . when it would be economically unreasonable [to do so] or ill-advised for engineering or siting reasons."[33] Nearly two weeks after presenting this proposal and rationale to EPA, TVA submitted the same to the TAPCB. Then in March, the agency petitioned the board for SO_2 emission variances at six of its plants in Tennessee. If variances were granted, TVA planned to take the position that it was "primarily responsible to the state and would act in accordance with state [rather than EPA] compliance directives [and scheduling]."[34]

Despite the comprehensiveness of TVA's efforts, 1977 would prove to be a pivotal year for undoing agency hopes for regulatory relief. Most critical in paving the way for the pollution control settlement of the following year were four developments: the finessing of an "eastern coal strategy" to EPA's enforcement advantage; the filing of a section 304 citizen suit against TVA by a coalition of public interest groups; the enactment of the Clean Air Act Amendments of 1977; and the changing of strategic actors at TVA, EPA, and the Justice Department.

The Eastern Coal Strategy In January, TVA issued a press release detailing the compliance plan submitted to EPA. While reciting its intent to comply with the CAA, the agency noted that "very stringent" emission limits had been set for several older plants, standards that could be met only by using scrubbers or low-sulfur coal. Scrubbers, they argued, would cost more than the original price of the plants themselves, and low-sulfur coal might be "unreasonably expensive," given the bids TVA had received from producers. Then came the linchpin of TVA's strategy to apply political pressure on pollution control officials, affected state legislatures, and the Tennessee and Kentucky congressional delegations. TVA reported that if required for compliance, the "bulk of available low sulfur coal would [have to] come from outside the East Tennessee and West Kentucky areas that now provide most of TVA's coal supply."[35] Put succinctly, TVA would have to import low-sulfur coal from the western states, to the detriment of eastern producer profits and United Mine Worker (UMW) jobs.

As the year progressed, TVA continued to propound this "eastern coal strategy" in a variety of public and private forums. TVA board member William Jenkins used a Knoxville television appearance to point out that although the Kingston plant currently used nearly 38 percent of all coal produced in Tennessee, the agency would have to turn to western low-sulfur coal unless variances from current standards could be obtained for the facility. What is more, as the TAPCB held hearings on variance requests, Jenkins and TVA attorney Lew Wallace conducted a tour of the Kingston plant for members of the Tennessee congressional and state legislative delegations, as well as for representatives of the coal industry. Participants included a Tennessee lieutenant governor who would later work tirelessly to unravel the EPA/TVA settlement eventually negotiated, and a state representative who was the aunt of a future TVA board member similarly prone to question the settlement's merits. What they were told was that present SO_2 standards could "shut this plant down."[36]

That TVA's efforts were effective in raising public concerns cannot be denied. In a poll of the Knox County, Tennessee state senatorial district, for example, 70 percent of those responding favored "lowering the state's air quality control standards to allow TVA to burn higher sulfur coal purchased from Tennessee markets."[37] Nor can the campaign be faulted for ineffectiveness when it came to influencing key figures in Congress and in state government. For example, Senator Howard Baker, normally a staunch supporter of strict enforcement of the CAA, introduced legislation that would have "grandfathered" the four older plants from the more stringent control requirements. And based on TVA's arguments that endorsement of its variance requests by Tennessee officials would be "very helpful" for negotiating EPA approval for extended compliance schedules, state cooperation was quickly forthcoming. During the year the Tennessee legislature enacted a joint resolution urging the TAPCB to grant variances from SO_2 standards to all plants built prior to 1960.[38] Moreover, as TVA entered a marathon ten-hour meeting in Atlanta on 21 March 1977 — to formally respond to EPA's suggested compliance plan — the agency came armed with proposed TAPCB orders supporting four of its variance requests.

Fearing the ecological consequences of large-scale western strip mining, the political fallout of a Democratic administration's putting UMW members out of work, and the headway TVA's campaign seemed to be making with public officials, EPA used the Atlanta meeting to redefine the eastern coal problem, defuse public alarm, and project a tough enforcement image to TVA and the states. At this decidedly adversarial meeting, Region IV officials argued that precisely because economic dislocation issues were real, and because even western supplies of low-sulfur coal were inadequate to the task, scrubbers and coal washing offered the best hope for avoiding economic and environmental hardship in the region. These techniques, incorporating but minimal use of low-sulfur coal, would both be effective and allow TVA to burn the abundant high-sulfur coal of its native Appalachia.

Presented with EPA's compliance plan prior to the meeting, TVA attorney Lew Wallace read a prepared statement that TVA, among other things, disputed the accuracy of the PEDCO data upon which it was based and refused to incorporate any compliance program into a legally enforceable section 113(a) administrative consent order. So far apart were the agencies that agreement on compliance schedules existed for only one of ten TVA plants. Moreover, although EPA agreed that time limits were negotiable, the agency was adamant that TVA acknowledge EPA's regulatory power over its operations by signing consent orders once agreement was reached.

Most important for the ultimate resolution of the controversy, however, was the degree to which the meeting — described by one participant as a "free-for-all" — aroused personal animosities and sowed distrust among the participants. So intense was the animosity that a high-ranking TVA official would allege that "they were so mad at us at EPA that they really [weren't] interested in settling the dispute."[39] And some EPA officials would disparagingly caricature chairman Wagner's attitude as, "The law — don't talk to me about the law — I

am the law."[40] Indeed, participants in negotiations that later would
lead to an interagency settlement suggested that "the animosity toward Red [chairman Wagner] was so great that there was just no way
in the world that he could be involved."[41]

Several EPA Region IV officials left the Atlanta meeting feeling
especially betrayed, frustrated, and determined to file a lawsuit against
TVA.[42] Their feelings are best described by EPA attorney Keith Casto.

> The premise for the whole meeting was that EPA, the states, and TVA were
> going to hammer out administrative orders that would reflect a compli-
> ance program acceptable to all concerned. The meeting disintegrated when
> TVA said they weren't subject to Section 113 orders, and that they may
> or may not comply but it had to be voluntary compliance, not ordered.
> At that point Paul [Traina] said, in effect, "If that's the way you feel about
> it, maybe administrative orders aren't the way we should go. *Maybe liti-
> gation is the way to proceed.*"[43]

Such feelings were further exacerbated by the tone of, and what some
felt were the "overstated costs" reported in, TVA's news release after
the meeting:

> If we could press a button today and have the [air compliance] program
> in operation, it would mean a rate increase of $282 million a year to users
> of TVA power. . . . Actually, it will take until the early 1980s to complete
> construction of the large facilities this program requires, and by that time
> the effects of inflation probably will increase that cost by almost another
> $100 million a year. To put these costs into perspective, total production
> costs for the TVA power system were $242 million in 1970. . . .[44]

In the short term, the threat that court suits might follow produced only a petition for Justice Department advice on the matter
from EPA's new administrator, Douglas Costle. Subsequently, the
likelihood of an EPA-initiated court suit diminished dramatically
with the release of a Justice Department opinion that TVA lacked
"sufficient independence" from the president to be sued in this fashion.[45] Congress, however, had foreseen such circumstances. Consequently, it had used section 304 of the CAA to "provide that citizens
[could] seek, through the courts, to expedite" federal facility compliance with the act.[46] By providing statutory standing to sue for
citizens dissatisfied with the pace or quality of regulatory efforts,
Congress had institutionalized the concept of "private attorneys general" as an enforcement tool. Welcomed, encouraged, and joined even-

tually by EPA itself, a section 304 citizen suit became a critical factor in resolving the TVA enforcement stalemate.[47]

Sparks from the Grass Roots   TVA's news release at the Atlanta meeting concluded with a statement that agency officials would continue to press EPA and the states for "more reasonable" SO_2 pollution control options that would not "adversely affect the environment in any way."[48] What is more, it claimed that such efforts were conducted not for TVA's benefit, but "for the benefit of the consumers of TVA power." However, over the years some of these "consumers" had grown weary of what they charged was TVA's pursuit of one "benefit" above all others: electric power production. Consequently, a relatively small yet vigilant group of environmental, health, and "good government" organizations had faithfully monitored TVA's power program since the first hearings for implementation plans were held in the states. As we have seen, some such as the TEC both participated in and sponsored public forums dealing with TVA's impact on the environment. Concerned as well with TVA's operations were national environmental groups such as the NRDC and the Sierra Club. Throughout the controversy, these organizations released legal and technoscience information that helped provide Valley groups with the wherewithal to challenge TVA policies. In addition, through congressional testimony, these groups attempted to focus macropolitical attention on TVA's recalcitrance.

Three events—TVA's eastern coal strategy, the issuing of TVA's January 1977 compliance plan, and the quandary over an EPA/TVA lawsuit—led environmental groups and some at EPA to believe that no end to the dispute was in sight. As William Chandler, then of the Tennessee Citizens Wilderness Planning Committee (TCWP), later recalled,

> Ruth Neff [of the TEC] . . . felt that a well-represented group was needed to force a lawsuit because EPA was not allowed to file one. . . . The EPA [regional] folks told us that they wanted to sue; that they were trying. They had written all their briefs . . . but the Justice Department wouldn't let them. . . . So through Ruth, her contacts with Dean [Hill Rivkin], and his talks with Dick Ayres in Washington, a coalition of groups was put together.[49]

Attorney Dean Hill Rivkin, reminiscing about the events leading up to his involvement as legal counsel for the citizen coalition and his

efforts to recruit Ayres, provides further insight into the importance
of "networking" for the organizational effort.

> Ruth had expressed her frustration at really not being able to do any-
> thing about the [TVA] situation to some people who were friends of mine
> —that she really would like to get a lawyer to litigate this. I told these
> friends I might be interested in doing it and they communicated that to
> her. I called Dick [Ayres] after agreeing to undertake the case. I had not
> known him personally, but I asked a close mutual friend to call and give
> me an entree. I then laid out what the case was all about to him, why
> I thought it was important, and tried to enlist his personal, as well as
> NRDC's institutional, involvement. He readily saw how important it was.[50]

Enlisting Ayres in the coalition's cause was a major coup for the
would-be plaintiffs. He had served with the NRDC since its incorporation in the early 1970s, was regarded as its leading expert on
clean air issues, and had been involved with most of the debates on
clean air legislation as an environmental advocate. Those who were
knowledgeable lauded his strong relationships with key U.S. sena-
tors and their committee staffs. During resolution of the EPA/TVA
dispute, Ayres would become the personification—along with Senator Edmund Muskie—of Eugene Bardach's implementation "fixer."
Throughout, he adroitly counterbalanced TVA's technical expertise
while embellishing his remarks with allusions to congressional intent. With Ayres now a "player," and with access to NRDC resources
now assured, a coalition of eleven citizen groups plus the states of
Alabama and Kentucky issued in March 1977 a notice of intent to
sue TVA for noncompliance with the CAA.[51]

The importance of this suit, filed by a coalition of resource-poor
citizen groups loosely coordinated by one woman (Ruth Neff) working out of a parking garage in Nashville, cannot be exaggerated. First,
it effectively "broke the inertia . . . of certain elements within the
agencies [EPA and the Justice Department] who thought we ought
to work with TVA as, quote, 'our sister federal agency.'"[52] Second,
it meant that any rift among regulators over initiating a suit against
TVA was now moot, since "there was nothing Justice could say about
us [EPA] joining a suit brought by others."[53] And finally, the morale
of Region IV enforcement officials rose: their pledges to coalition
leaders to press for EPA intervention and to place EPA resources at
their disposal if the citizen groups filed suit had brought action. One
EPA Region IV official summarized the situation best:

[Lew] Wallace [TVA deputy counsel] used to say, "We'll work this out through the normal regulatory processes," and I'd say, "Lew, what the hell does that mean? You've been doing that for ten years!" Before the suit was filed we were certainly in communication with the plaintiffs, providing them a lot of information. When they filed the suit we said, "Oh, Boy!" TVA didn't have the legal argument anymore, nor did we. The citizen suit is the only thing that keeps *us* honest, and by us I mean EPA and others. . . . When you get to certain levels in any organization the system starts controlling you. So you need somebody on the outside who can bring you to your knees and say, "By God, you know you're screwing up, fellas!"[54]

Though perhaps initially on the outside, the citizen coalition quickly became a key insider to the enforcement dispute. Invited as observers to the March 21 Atlanta meeting, coalition representatives would later help negotiate the EPA/TVA "treaty," would be consulted by the Carter administration on the acceptability of a key appointment to the TVA board of directors,[55] and would issue press releases highlighting the benefits of compliance to counteract TVA's emphasis on its costs.[56] As for TVA, in a letter to attorney Rivkin, general manager Lynn Seeber sought to abort the filing of the suit: "We believe the overall public interest would best be served by having the states, the Environmental Protection Agency, and TVA continue to work out . . . problems without judicial intervention of the type you seek."[57] What is more, TVA would look again to the states and the Congress to resolve the court suit issues involved. To TVA's distress, both would be less accommodating than they had been previously.

The Quest for Standard Relief   Conspicuously absent as a plaintiff in the section 304 citizen suit was the state of Tennessee, despite the location of most of the violating plants within its borders and despite the degree to which its citizens stood to lose or gain from the dispute's resolution. By abstaining from the suit, Tennessee officials had ironically excluded themselves from significantly affecting the settlement some would come to resent.

TAPCD officials would later suggest that failure to join the suit was predicated on two factors: the state could not compete with TVA's resources and a challenge would take too much of the staff's time.[58] Certainly, the unique socioeconomic and political situation of Tennessee vis à vis TVA, as outlined earlier, was also a major factor affecting that decision. As one TAPCD official recalled,

When the suit was in its embryonic stages, the TAPCB was asked if they wanted to join. . . . Since they felt there were enough people [including two states] involved in it to render a decision, [they decided] not to join the suit. . . . [Personally], from the standpoint of trying to operate in a politically astute way, I've tried to stay in between the double yellow line down the middle of the highway, realizing that [TAPCD] could get run over by either one of them [EPA or TVA]. I've mentioned the economic position of TVA in Tennessee. Well, on the other side you have EPA overviewing most of what we do, funding possibly 50 percent of our programs. . . . My philosophy is that if either the industry regulated or the environmentalists think you're 100 percent right, then you're probably doing something wrong.[59]

This official's comments likely reflect any state administrator's plight when statutory responsibilities collide with the intragovernmental regulation process. Moreover, his informed speculation as to the TAPCB's reaction to the negotiations that took place among EPA, TVA, and the citizen groups is equally revealing of the subtle, yet important, shift in the board's approach to TVA's pollution control requests that began in 1977: "We were not a party to the negotiations. And although we had been invited and they had tried to keep us abreast of what's going on, they were still making the decisions rather independently of what we thought. So I feel that the philosophy of the Board was, 'Why should we get all worked up about it when we have two federal giants making decisions without really giving a damn what we think about it?'"[60]

Perhaps because of these feelings, and because the SO₂ "statistical grit" possessed was of a higher quality than in the early years, "friendly" TAPCB staff recommendations could no longer be taken for granted by TVA. For example, when the agency had sought TAPCB support for its variance requests prior to the Atlanta meeting, the staff support rendered failed to include the two plants—Kingston and Johnsonville—that TVA had used to "symbolize" EPA's alleged regulatory unreasonableness. Furthermore, after TVA released its initial compliance plan, Harold Hodges notified agency officials that their failure to incorporate any of the staff's recommendations had caused him to consider supporting EPA's position instead.[61] It is also significant that when TVA asked for a postponement of state hearings on its plant variances until terms of the CAA of 1977 were known, TAPCB denied the request. And in perhaps the greatest testimonial to a change in its historic attitude toward TVA, the staff was later upbraided by some for not "working harder" to oppose the EPA/TVA settlement and for not trying to get TVA to "assume a stronger position in the negotiations."[62]

A more serious setback to TVA's hopes for regulatory relief were the long-anticipated Clean Air Amendments of 1977. Congress incorporated several general provisions that substantially buttressed EPA's enforcement arguments and sanctions in the TVA dispute. First, Congress endorsed the use of constant control techniques and specified that SO_2 emissions be reduced, not merely diluted.[63] Second, by declaring a preference for the use of high-sulfur eastern coal in the famous Metzenbaum Amendment, the solons had effectively endorsed and assured the use of scrubber technology. Third, Congress clarified its intent that federal facilities such as TVA be subject to state permit requirements.[64] And finally, addressing EPA's dismay over the lack of credible enforcement sanctions provided by the CAA of 1970, Congress provided market incentives for polluters to comply with the act.[65] These penalties included fines that could be offset by the costs of pollution control equipment, fines based on the economic benefits realized by a polluter while in noncompliance, and reduction of fines when violators cleaned emissions beyond what was required by law.

Congress also took actions directly related to the controversy. Specifically, it first rejected an attempt by Senator Howard Baker to gain less stringent emission limits for tall stacks already in place at older installations (such as TVA's) across the country. According to chairman Muskie, this original Baker Amendment was rejected by the Senate Committee on Environment and Public Works because, "[We] simply did not want to trigger a policy of widespread approval of tall stacks as a method of continuously controlling pollutants."[66] The defeat must also be attributed largely to the timeliness, persistence, and persuasiveness of the citizen coalition's arguments and activities.

Counteracting nearly two dozen TVA antiscrubber appearances before House and Senate committees, coalition attorneys went on the offensive as debate on the Baker Amendment began. Their arguments, based largely on data provided by EPA, emphasized that compliance with current standards would not be as costly as portrayed nor would it severely disrupt eastern coal markets. Moreover, they claimed that TVA plant exemptions would be unfair to those who had already complied, and this might compromise future enforcement efforts. The coalition also deliberately timed the actual filing of the section 304 suit to precede debate of the Baker Amendment. As attorney Rivkin explained, "We wanted to show [Congress] that this was a serious problem, and that . . . what Howard Baker was really trying to do was get a TVA 'relief' bill. Sure it included lots of other plants, but the main focus of the bill, we were alleging, was TVA. We wanted to show the case was in litigation, and that TVA shouldn't be let off the hook at the last minute by any change in the law that would have been contrary to the interests of clean air throughout the East. . . ."[67]

Some at EPA would later claim that Baker had never "worked that hard" for this "private bill" for TVA. Still, Baker was able to persuade even Senator Muskie that TVA "was justified in constructing tall stacks at [its] Kingston plant . . . given EPA's 'confusion' on the question of dispersement enhancement techniques at the time [of construction]."[68] Reworded so that the exemption could apply only to Kingston, the Baker Amendment was incorporated into section 123 of the 1977 amendments. TVA now could claim tall-stack credit at that plant, credit permitting less stringent emission limitations that could easily be met without constant controls. Nonetheless, TVA was now confronted by a Congress and TAPCB less patient with its entreaties, an EPA armed with congressional mandates and more credible enforcement sanctions, and a coalition of litigious citizen groups and state attorneys general. And if these were not enough, an unsympathetic Carter administration began to make its presence felt as well.

The Changing of the Guard   The impact of the Carter administration began, albeit indirectly, in 1977 with the president's State of the Union message.[69] In that speech Carter announced his intention to see the TVA become an energy *and* environmental yardstick for the nation. Then in July of that year, shortly after the citizen suit was filed, a vacancy occurred on the TVA board of directors. After soliciting the advice of environmentalists,[70] Carter appointed TVA critic S. David Freeman to the position on the three-member board. This was followed in August by his appointment of Marvin B. Durning, a Seattle environmental lawyer, as deputy administrator for enforcement at EPA.

The president's activities continued apace throughout 1978 as Carter was presented with, and took advantage of, several opportunities to affect the course of events in the dispute. Early that March, William Jenkins resigned from the TVA board, protesting EPA's inter-ference in TVA's affairs.[71] Later in the month chairman Wagner an-nounced his retirement.[72] Carter responded by elevating S. David Freeman to the chairmanship and, after consultation with the citi-zen suit plaintiffs, by appointing Richard Freeman to fill the remain-ing vacancy. What is more, on several occasions the president indi-rectly applied pressure for resolution of the dispute. In his State of the Union message, he declared that federal facilities must take steps to come into compliance with environmental laws. Then in October he issued an executive order committing his administration to the "goals of achieving and maintaining a clean environment,"and to mak-ing the federal government "the leader in that effort."[73] As one EPA staff attorney suggested, the president's attitude provided "new mes-sages to TVA about its responsibility as a public agency to do more than produce low cost energy."[74]

Environmentalists had been among the first to rally to Jimmy Carter's campaign for the presidency, and he earnestly rewarded that allegiance once in office. As one EPA official put it, "The NRDC and the Sierra Club were almost decimated; he took almost all of their lawyers and put them in high government positions . . . all through EPA and the Justice Department."[75] Certainly, the most telling ac-tions taken by Carter with regard to the EPA/TVA dispute involved his studied use of the power of presidential appointment to place those with staunch environmental credentials in positions of strate-gic significance. Most critical were his appointments of S. David Free-man and Marvin Durning. Freeman, reflecting Carter's views, felt that TVA had to be a leader in showing the private sector how to rec-oncile energy and environmental concerns.[76] The best way to do this according to Freeman was not to encourage consumption of electric-ity by maintaining artificially low rates as TVA had historically done to encourage economic development. Rather, Freeman felt that en-ergy conservation made possible by internalizing the true costs of electricity production—especially the environmental costs—was the long-term solution for reconciling such values.

The EPA appointee, Marvin Durning, was said to have "brought life" to that agency's enforcement effort, coming to Washington with a "hit list" of polluters that made TVA his number-one enforcement target.[77] Moreover, in contrast to his predecessors and to the delight of regional EPA officials, he indicated his willingness to prosecute fed-eral facilities that remained in noncompliance with clean air laws.[78]

Emphasizing the depth of his commitment to this litigation philosophy, Durning successfully proposed to administrator Costle that EPA
"run like hell to catch up with the citizen groups" by joining their
lawsuit and by offering the agency's technical support to their challenge.[79] In his own words, Durning "was *very* happy to advise [inter-
vention], a decision that put EPA and another federal agency [TVA]
on opposite sides of the courtroom."[80]

The two Carter appointees also shared a similar philosophy about
TVA's role as a public agency. Each felt that TVA was, as a member
of the federal family, "more than just another power company"; it
was a social agency with a social purpose and the holder of a public
trust.[81] Consequently, TVA ought not wait until ordered by a court
to conform to the law of the land; rather, it had a moral, as well
as a legal, duty to comply with both the spirit and letter of pollution
control statutes. And if such attitudes were not enough to cause each
man to wish an end to the interagency dispute, Freeman's courtesy
call on Senator Muskie during his confirmation hearings certainly
helped. Muskie lectured Freeman: "I'll vote for you on one condition; that you get those sons o' bitches by the nape of the neck and
you shake the hell out of them because they're thumbing their nose
at *my* law."[82] Beyond that, Muskie, as chair of the Senate Budget
Committee, made it clear to Freeman that noncompliance would result in rejection of TVA's request for an increase in the bonded indebtedness ceiling it needed to complete its nuclear power program.
"He [Muskie] said he was going to throw the book at TVA; that they
needn't come to see him about anything. . . . There was zero chance
that [without complying] TVA could have gotten any increase in the
ceiling. And the agency would have been left sitting with these half-
completed nuclear plants up the creek without a paddle, raising rates
or going broke."[83]

Upon joining the TVA board Freeman learned just how difficult
Muskie's charge would be to carry out. Rampant animosity and
distrust between the two agencies had caused a total breakdown in
negotiations. But Freeman had many friends within the Carter administration, not the least of whom was EPA administrator Costle.
Indeed, both men had served on the Carter transition team. TVA general manager Lynn Seeber sought to use this friendship to reestablish
talks with EPA. Freeman, paraphrasing Seeber, recalled how the latter beseeched him to contact Costle to get discussions going again:

"Dave, we need to get this air quality litigation settled; we need to get it out of the way . . . [but] we can't find anybody to surrender to!"[84]

Freeman attributed the urgency expressed by Seeber to staff concerns that the power system itself was in danger.

> The power people felt that they just couldn't operate the power system much longer without knowing what to do. It reached the point that had we not been able to get our coal plants shaped up, we'd have been in a hell of a mess with all the delays on the nuclear side. . . . I can't read their minds [the TVA board], but it is a fact that they let the coal-fired plants "go to hell in a handbasket" generally, and the power system nearly broke down. So you have a right to speculate that they'd just written off the coal-fired plants [waiting for the nuclear plants to come into operation].[85]

There exists some question as to whether Freeman initiated negotiations with EPA on his own, as chairman Wagner maintained, or whether he was authorized by fellow TVA board members to do so. Wagner insists he learned of both the negotiations and the settlement itself "from the [news]papers," and that Freeman "didn't keep us [the board] informed."[86] In contrast, Freeman maintains that "the decision to start the negotiations was agreed to by the Board . . . [and] the negotiating parameters . . . were laid out by Lynn Seeber and discussed with [Aubrey] Red Wagner and Bill Jenkins before the discussions began."[87] Whether authorized or not, intensely difficult negotiations among EPA, TVA, the citizen coalition, and the states of Alabama and Kentucky were held between August 1977 and March 1978.

In reflecting upon the numerous and often protracted negotiating sessions, the EPA staff attorney who handled liaison between EPA headquarters and Region IV, Charles Hungerford, characterized their tone as "clearly adversarial." Reflecting the views of most participants, Hungerford claimed these were "true negotiating situations" in which EPA viewed TVA "not as a government entity but as a pollution source."[88] Indeed, S. David Freeman likened the first meetings to "a contest of who could snarl the loudest . . . especially between the EPA Region IV people and the TVA staff." And Marvin Durning recalled that "it was quite sometime before EPA felt that the TVA staff was producing sufficient, accurate information to permit

progress to be made." As a consequence, Durning would ask Freeman to "personally" vouch for the factual statements that the TVA
staff was making in these early days.

Aside from sparring over the factual bases of risk assessment and
control technologies at individual plants, the bargainers focused most
attention on noncompliance fines for TVA and the establishment of
a citizen committee to oversee implementation of the terms of the
settlement.[89] Both, in effect, became significant bargaining chips used
by the negotiators. EPA and the citizen coalition employed the economic benefit of noncompliance penalties afforded in the CAA of
1977 — assessed at hundreds of millions of dollars for TVA — to wrest
an agreement for the installation of "innovative" pollution control
equipment at one of TVA's plants. And TVA used the citizen coalition's passion for participation in agency policy-making — a notion
"dear to their hearts" since director McBride's comments at the TEC
symposia — to gain concessions involving extended compliance timetables. Thus, with Durning and Freeman acting "almost as judges"
whenever snags developed,[90] a consent decree settling the section 304
lawsuit was at last completed in early 1978 by TVA and the plaintiffs.
In the words of one participant, "neither side was entirely happy
with any particular piece of it, [but] we finally got enough momen-
tum going on the settlement and enough feeling of each side getting
something out of it" to conclude an agreement.[91]

THE SETTLEMENT AND ITS AFTERMATH

In the consent decree submitted to the full TVA board of directors
for approval, the parties agreed that "an amicable resolution of this
case would serve the public interest." They then proceeded to specify
exactly how TVA would bring the ten coal-fired plants involved into
interim and final compliance with the national ambient air quality
standards as well as the SO_2 and particulate emission regulations of
Alabama, Kentucky, and Tennessee. Literally, TVA, as defendant in
the litigation, admitted that the ten plants had been operating in violation of the CAA since mid-1975 and it agreed to "comply with the
final and interim emission limitations specified in this consent decree through the use of continuous emission controls."[92] On a plant-
by-plant basis, TVA agreed to implement a mix of constant emission
techniques, including the limited burning of low-sulfur coal, use of
electrostatic precipitators, use of flue gas desulfurization (scrubbers),

coal washing, and mixing of coal. Exactly which type, or types, of constant controls to be used at a given plant was specified, as were provisions for continuous monitoring and reporting of SO_2 and particulate emissions. These monitoring provisions allowed the plaintiffs access to the data necessary for assuring compliance with the interim and final emission limits specified in the agreement. The parties further agreed that, except in emergency situations, the requirements of the consent decree would be met by use of coal produced in the eastern United States.[93] In order to "ensure continued citizen participation in the implementation" of the consent decree, "an implementation committee" consisting of representatives for each of the plaintiffs and TVA was created. Its task was to meet regularly, or whenever requested by the plaintiffs, to "review progress towards the achievement" of the requirements of the settlement.[94] TVA acknowledged that the economic benefit of its noncompliance for the entire TVA power system for the period involved was $260 million, thereby recognizing that it could be assessed at least this much for noncompliance. The plaintiffs agreed to waive this penalty and, in return, TVA agreed to install scrubbers at its Cumberland plant that would clean its SO_2 and particulate emissions beyond what the law required. TVA further agreed to pay stiff penalties if it missed any of the interim or final compliance deadlines.

This very detailed, technical, and complex set of consent agreements committed the TVA to operate constant emission controls for its plants at an estimated annual cost of $377 million. Moreover, TVA's capital investment costs for control equipment alone were $1.02 billion.[95] These costs would be passed on to TVA's electric consumers in the form of increased utility rates. The parties to the agreement hastened to point out that much of this investment would be offset by the health and aesthetic benefits of cleaner air, and each noted that substantial TVA fines had been avoided by compliance in the manner negotiated.[96] Still, there is no question that the financial burden assumed by TVA in the agreement was a heavy one.

At least two of the three TVA board members had to approve the settlement before it could be formalized. To David Freeman's dismay, both Aubrey Wagner and William Jenkins left the TVA board refusing to sign the agreement he had labored so hard to negotiate. Like Freeman, Wagner saw TVA as the holder of a public trust and as more than just another power company. But he saw the agency's obligation to the public interest in a much different light than did

Freeman. Wagner maintained that TVA, as a federal agency, had an
obligation to challenge "unwise" regulatory policies that "didn't make
sense."[97] Precisely because TVA's compliance would be used to bring
pressure on others to comply, and because in his view constant controls would stymie economic growth if applied indiscriminately, Wagner concluded that agency resistance was actually in the national
interest.[98]

For board member Jenkins, "other agency interference" in TVA's
decision-making processes combined with many of Wagner's reservations to make him uneasy about the interagency pact.[99] Indeed,
because he believed as a matter of principle that intragovernmental
regulation threatened TVA's decision-making flexibility, Jenkins resigned from the board nearly two weeks before Wagner's retirement.
Summarizing his predicament, Jenkins confided that although he felt
the settlement was "largely a waste of money," it was a "more cost-
effective" strategy than litigation. Still, because he felt that "the whole
thing was wrong," the only way to have a "clear conscience" was to
resign.[100]

Wagner's appeals to the "greater good" were accompanied by specific concerns about two other aspects of the decree. First, he felt
it unwise to commit TVA to meeting emission standards that had yet
to be set, a commitment he felt would certainly be overturned by the
courts if litigation ensued. Second, he was disturbed deeply by the
breadth and imprecision of the oversight charge given to the citizen
implementation committee. Perceived by several TVA staffers as an
attempt to "institutionalize the continuing participation of the plaintiffs in agency policy-making" and conceived by attorney Rivkin as
mandating "high-level policy work," the committee provision provoked a fascinating exchange among the principals. With Jenkins'
resignation and the chairman's impending retirement, Freeman had
to convince Wagner to sign the agreement or else wait until a suc-
cessor could be chosen to complete the quorum needed before major board commitments (like the settlement) could be made. What
is more, Freeman wanted the "political legitimacy" for the decree
that only Aubrey Wagner's signature could provide to some in the
Valley. Freeman offered to convince the citizen coalition to drop its
insistence on the implementation committee if Wagner would agree
to sign the decree before he left the TVA board.

Freeman today maintains that Wagner "either said or nodded or
left us all with the impression" that he would sign the consent de-

cree. Chairman Wagner, however, categorically and stridently denies this claim. In any event, Freeman spent the weekend prior to the chairman's retirement successfully persuading the coalition to drop the committee provision in exchange for Wagner's approval of the settlement. Freeman later recalled the subsequent events that environmentalists now refer to as the "Mother's Day Massacre":

> I got it all worked out with Red [Wagner], but he never did sign it. He called me from Washington to tell me he wouldn't. I'll never forget it. I said, "Red, you can't do that; you gave me your word!" He said, "Well, I just can't sign it." And I said, "You know, Red, I've dealt with people in the Nixon Administration that never . . . gave me their word . . . and then just broke it like this. . . ." That was the last conversation we had.[101]

It was at this point, with the consent decree now beached on the shoals of a quorum-deficient TVA board, that President Carter appointed Richard M. Freeman to the pivotal post of director. On 14 December 1978 the two Freemans signed the consent decree on behalf of TVA.

In accord with Justice Department policy, the consent decree was submitted for judicial approval to the federal Middle District Court of Tennessee (Nashville) and the federal Northern District Court of Alabama in early January 1979. At that point, the parties to the litigation anticipated no further problems with the case.[102] But, in response to a protest over the EPA/TVA settlement submitted by an aluminum company executive, the director of the president's Council on Wage and Price Stability (COWPS), Barry Bosworth, wrote a letter criticizing the agreement. Bosworth argued that it imposed "an unnecessary cost burden on the residential and industrial users of electric power in the Tennessee Valley." Bosworth also mentioned in his letter that COWPS had previously asked the TVA board to review the settlement because "essentially the same environmental result could be achieved at a lower cost."[103] Bosworth's views on the pending consent agreement subsequently were made public and stirred considerable controversy. U.S. Senator James Sasser of Tennessee sent a copy of Bosworth's letter to the federal judge in the Middle Tennessee District, who was reviewing the agreement. Judge Tom Wiseman, on 30 January 1979, then ordered the parties to the consent agreement to provide him with a statement of the economic impact of the settlement.[104]

The Bosworth letter became, at least initially, a rallying point for critics of the proposed agreement. But the Carter administration soon repudiated the views expressed in the correspondence,[105] and the chairman of the TVA board alleged that "Mr. Bosworth does not have the foggiest idea of what he is talking about."[106] Bosworth himself—under White House pressure—soon expressed regret that his letter was "interpreted as the administration's point of view when in fact it was not."[107] Regardless, the Bosworth letter and its attendant publicity compelled the TVA board to defend the consent agreement at three separate congressional hearings during the winter of 1979.[108]

Encouraged by Tennessee Lieutenant Governor John Wilder and charging that the settlement represented inflationary overcompliance with the CAA, twenty-two electric cooperative power distributors in Tennessee petitioned to intervene in the case.[109] Other TVA distributors later joined the intervention attempt and, despite the Justice Department's contention that the petitioners had passed up their opportunity to shape the EPA/TVA settlement,[110] Judge Wiseman subsequently allowed their intervention.[111] He did so noting that the distributors' views had not been represented adequately during the negotiation of the settlement.[112]

Even though the agreement was now being challenged by intervenors, and although the district courts in Alabama and Tennessee had yet to approve the consent decree, TVA began implementing the compliance program at this time. The TVA board contracted for the needed pollution control equipment and purchased virtually all of the replacement coal needed.[113] Then on 6 June 1979 EPA administrator Douglas Costle and TVA board chairman S. David Freeman at last signed the negotiated settlement on behalf of their respective federal agencies. Both Costle's visit to Tennessee and the signing of the consent decree were taken as a symbolic "burying of the hatchet" between EPA and TVA, one that signaled an end to their longstanding dispute over SO_2 pollution control in the Tennessee Valley.[114] Four months after this symbolic ending of the clean air dispute, a federal district judge in Alabama approved the consent decree, thereby ending the litigation in *Alabama v. TVA* and authorizing the implementation of the settlement.[115]

The settling of the Alabama case and the symbolic burying of the hatchet notwithstanding, the consent decree was still pending before Judge Wiseman. Senator James Sasser became increasingly critical of the proposed settlement, and in January 1980 he sent a letter to the TVA board chairman challenging its implementation absent court approval. Senator Sasser cited a recent General Accounting Office (GAO) report, undertaken at his request, that was critical of TVA's procurement of pollution control equipment before the lawsuit was final.[116] In response, S. David Freeman defended the EPA/TVA settlement as appropriate and declared that the TVA board would continue to implement the decree no matter how the district court ruled.[117] Several TVA power distributors and their representatives were quick to protest Freeman's retort. For example, Frank Perkins, executive director of a Tennessee electric cooperative association, remarked, "It's [Freeman's response] a slap at us. It's a slap at the Senator for even questioning the activities of the TVA board, and it's a slap at Judge Wiseman. In effect, he's saying to hell with how you rule, Judge, we're going ahead and do what we damn well please."[118]

As the controversy over the implementation of the EPA/TVA settlement continued, and as President Carter telephoned Lieutenant Governor Wilder to ask his support for the settlement, the TVA board chairman strongly defended the agreement he had helped negotiate. In March 1979, at a TVA board meeting, Freeman, after noting that the president was "fully in accord" with the settlement, pointed out that

I came here with a mandate from both the President and Congress to obey the law. It's that simple. I have said before that to fight the clean air law would be an expensive and futile piece of symbolism. To continue the fight would be coming near to criminal action. TVA is not above the law. That's all there is to it. There are some things that are borderline decisions. The scales may be weighed heavily on both sides. Personally, this is not one of those decisions. I sleep well with it. It is, in my estimation, a prudent and proper course of action.[119]

The simplicity of obeying the law, however, was soon belied by the inherent complexity of the issues involved in any attempt at technoscientific regulation. In August a miscalculation was discovered in the pollution modeling for the Cumberland plant. Corrected calculations revealed that the scrubbers agreed to in the consent decree were not really needed. This discovery reduced the original $1.02 billion capital cost of the settlement to $806 million. Then, in the summer of 1980, a second miscalculation was discovered that further reduced the need for scrubbers, this time at the Johnsonville plant. Another $80 million in compliance cost was eliminated. Satisfied that their claims of overcompliance and excessive costs had been vindicated, the intervenors abstained from further challenges. With errors corrected, and TVA capital investment costs reduced to approximately $760 million, the consent decree was finally approved by Judge Wiseman on 23 December 1980. The EPA/TVA air pollution dispute was at last history.

CHAPTER SIX

From Complacence to Compliance

APPLYING THE FWPCA TO
THE TENNESSEE VALLEY AUTHORITY

Austin Sarat and Joel Grossman have written that the level of procedural formality and the degree of publicness of a dispute resolving institution typically interact to cause participants to "redefine their interests, goals, and strategies."[1] Having examined the dynamics of this process as they applied to the conflict over SO_2 enforcement, we turn now to the same in the controversy over thermal pollution. EPA's dispute with TVA in this instance was a less acerbic, more dispassionately resolved episode than the SO_2 affair. Not unlike the latter, however, TVA sought relief from EPA's efforts to apply regulations that TVA's staff deemed overly stringent and an infringement on the agency's decision-making prerogatives. TVA officials would present their arguments during interagency negotiations, as they sought to obtain nuclear plant licenses from the Atomic Energy Commission (AEC), and in the arena of public opinion. Yet TVA never did pursue relief in so contentious a manner nor with a strategy so comprehensive and relentless as it did during the SO_2 affair.

Before interagency differences could be settled over how best to apply thermal pollution policies to TVA's operations, four questions concerning enforcement had to be resolved. First, how staunchly would EPA adhere to and enforce the recently imposed Alabama and Tennessee thermal standards? Second, how committed to the letter and spirit of NEPA and the Water Quality Act of 1970 would the AEC be? Third, could individual TVA nuclear plants qualify immediately for exemptions from thermal pollution standards pursuant to section 316(a) of the FWPCA? And finally, would TVA's preferred strategy for controlling thermal pollution — the use of diffusers and combined cycle operation modes — qualify the agency for National

Pollution Discharge Elimination System (NPDES) permits? A chronology of the major events that occurred during EPA's enforcement efforts is provided in table 6.1.

EVOLVING COMPLIANCE

Recall that as of mid-1971 the states of Alabama and Tennessee, with decisive EPA intervention and vocal TVA dissent, had enunciated stringent water quality standards applicable to TVA's Browns Ferry and Sequoyah nuclear plants. Unless relaxed or unenthusiastically enforced, these standards would preclude the use of the plants' diffuser systems and would require the retrofitting of these facilities to accommodate cooling towers. With Browns Ferry originally scheduled to begin operations in late 1972, and with an estimated 2.8 billion gallons of water needed daily to cool its reactor core, TVA was, according to one official, "caught with our pants down. . . . We had acted in good faith and naturally figured everything would work out."[2]

Several of those interviewed maintained that prior TVA actions dealing with thermal pollution had been reasonable and environmentally responsible. Not only had all nuclear plants been designed to meet existing state standards, but TVA had also initiated a multimillion-dollar testing facility at Browns Ferry to study thermal effects and alternative uses for waste heat discharges. The agency had further demonstrated its reasonableness, they contended, by planning to install cooling towers voluntarily at its prospective Watts Barr nuclear plant, where they made ecological, engineering, and economic sense. In the words of board chairman Wagner, "We had to approach it [cooling tower installation] realistically. . . . There are costs that we had to take into account. . . . We were not going to spend one dollar more than we had to in order to sufficiently protect the environment. . . . When you're forced into the kinds of things TVA was, you have to take a look at the law."[3] Thus, in responding initially to the more stringent thermal standards enunciated, TVA only agreed to study the feasibility of installing cooling towers.[4] Moreover, its research consisted primarily of assessing the legitimacy of EPA's preferred standards.

By the end of 1972 TVA's efforts led to or were affected by three primary actions of its "regulatory community." First, EPA sent strong signals to TVA concerning its unflagging commitment to thermal standard enforcement. Second, federal courts disallowed the AEC's con-

Table 6.1. **Chronology of the Thermal Dispute: The Enforcement Experience**

Year	Major Events
1971	— EPA establishes strict thermal standards for Browns Ferry at standard-setting conference; TVA is unable to meet these standards with diffuser systems. — Calvert Cliffs Coordinating Committee v. AEC. — TVA applies to AEC for Browns Ferry nuclear plant operating license and construction permits at Sequoyah. — EPA submits comments to TVA on Browns Ferry Environmental Impact Statement calling for installation of cooling towers operated in closed-cycle mode.
1972	— TVA agrees to install cooling towers at Browns Ferry but proposes to operate plant with diffusers only during 18–24-month period before construction of towers is completed. — Alabama attorney general threatens to file suit and intervene in AEC licensing process to stop TVA's interim operation plan. — FWPCA of 1972 enacted; permits individual plant exemptions from thermal standards; requires NPDES permits for plant operation. — EPA/AEC Memorandum of Understanding issued dealing with complementary responsibility problem. — Petition for AEC intervention filed by Vanderbilt professor opposing installation of cooling towers as a violation of NEPA.
1973–1974	— TVA agrees to meet EPA standards as a condition for obtaining AEC operating license at Browns Ferry; Alabama drops intervention petition; TVA cites threat of electricity shortages if Browns Ferry does not operate on schedule. — TVA learns EPA will interpret thermal exemption clause in ways precluding immediate exemption for Browns Ferry and Sequoyah. — TVA informed diffusers not acceptable control technology for NPDES permits. — TVA announces plants will be equipped with cooling towers at an eventual cost of $640 million; agency says further licensing delays would jeopardize power supplies in Tennessee Valley.

tention that its environmental responsibilities lay solely with the radiological aspects of plant operation. And finally, in order to prevent Browns Ferry from opening on schedule, environmentalists and the state of Alabama reacted to a TVA compliance counterproposal by threatening lawsuits and intervention in the AEC licensing process.

The Assault on Thermal Standards   Although EPA aggressively confronted thermal pollution problems in the early 1970s, agency enforcement efforts were severely complicated by chronic uneasiness over thermal standards and criteria. As Tarlock, Tippy, and Francis observed at the time,

> . . . there is sharp debate over the [temperature criteria] and standards to be applied. The Environmental Protection Agency has avoided the establishment of a firm thermal standards policy. Instead, they have preferred to negotiate agreements with utilities . . . that cooling towers will be constructed. . . . The drafting and enforcement of thermal standards present several serious problems. . . . Because of the variations in both surface and flow characteristics of bodies of water, thermal criteria must be individually established for each site and must be coordinated for long reaches of a stream or estuary. . . . Furthermore . . . standards are especially vulnerable to judicial attack on the grounds that they are unreasonable. Courts have required a showing that probable injury to a beneficial use will result . . . and absent such a showing, have found that the discharge does not constitute pollution because the injury is speculative. . . . Finally . . . regulation is complicated because states do not have adequate technical information to assess a proposed discharge. . . .[5]

With thermal enforcement challenged so successfully, with revisions to both the thermal criteria of the National Advisory Committee and the FWPCA itself anticipated in 1972, and with state standards still vulnerable to relaxation pending promulgation in the *Federal Register,* TVA's hopes for administrative, legislative, or judicial relief were technically alive.

During the remainder of 1971 TVA sought to marshal and publicize evidence supporting its earlier claims that EPA's thermal standards for the Tennessee River were too stringent and lacked scientific justification. In October TVA's manager of health and environmental science, Dr. O.M. Derryberry, requested a staff evaluation of the data presented at the Alabama standard-setting conference by the director of EPA's National Water Quality Laboratory, as well as an assessment of the relationship of the data to TVA's heat dispersion plans for Browns Ferry. The staff issued a lengthy memorandum challenging much of the director's testimony concerning lethal temperature maximums, the impact of temporary plant shutdowns on fish morbidity, and the necessity for standards to be met over the entire receiving body of water. The memo concluded with a comment by M.A. Churchill, chief of TVA's Water Quality Branch, who lauded the expertise of the director but complained, "My most serious criticism . . . is that none of the [thermal standard] values [he] proposes are data which he personally has developed. So far as I can determine, all the quoted values on both the lethal and recommended temperatures are taken from the [EPA] 'literature.'"[6]

Simultaneously, similar issues were raised regarding the Sequoyah nuclear plant when TVA charged, and EPA acknowledged, that applicable thermal standards were based heavily on studies of the Ohio rather than the Tennessee River. Although EPA contended that the two rivers were strikingly "similar" with regard to fish specie temperature requirements and that historical temperature records for the Tennessee River had been factored into its calculations, TVA maintained that EPA's action violated the latter's own procedural policy for criteria development. A GAO study subsequently concurred with TVA.

> EPA's policy statement of thermal criteria states, "The individual water body must be analyzed to define the individual species or community to be protected." EPA set the standards based on the best survival temperature of two Tennessee River fish: the walleye and the sauger. However, it did not make a specific study of the Tennessee River basin. . . . [Moreover] . . . EPA officials stated that the original state thermal standards for the Tennessee River would have been damaging to the river as well as to its aquatic life. However, they did not know the extent of damage the river would sustain, or the percentage of fish that would be killed. They stated only that under the law they are obligated to protect the river and its aquatic life from any damage, no matter how little.[7]

Any hopes TVA harbored for quick EPA relaxation of the standards, however, were quickly squelched during interagency talks in December. Because Alabama technically could propose relaxed standards within six months of EPA's Notice of Proposed Rulemaking in the *Federal Register*, Region IV administrator Jack Raven sent a firmly worded yet conciliatory letter to TVA declaring, "It [is] important for you to know that [EPA] will not accept any maximums [temperatures]

other than those [proposed] and that we . . . believe adoption is imminent."[8] Deflated at this time as well were any hopes TVA had for
immediate exemption from standards at its Browns Ferry or Sequoyah plants. The agency argued that it had already "acted in good
faith" to bring both plants into compliance with state standards by
designing them with diffuser systems.[9] Just as the plants were scheduled to begin providing needed electricity to TVA customers, EPA had
"revised" the standards so that TVA now had to retrofit them with
cooling towers. TVA felt enforcement concessions were not only justified but also in the public interest. Retrofitting would be very expensive, and environmental studies had already caused construction
delays and schedule setbacks that threatened power supplies in the
Tennessee Valley. Unpersuaded, Region IV EPA officials forwarded
copies of the Alabama and Tennessee revised standards to TVA; they
also sent critiques of TVA's Browns Ferry and Sequoyah Environmental Impact Statements to EPA headquarters in Washington. This
occurred as events were transpiring elsewhere that would bring additional regulatory pressure on TVA from an unexpected source: the
AEC.

Judicial Impatience with the AEC   As Ruckelshaus began his campaign to establish the credibility of EPA's enforcement commitment
in early 1971, TVA was already well immersed in the lengthy, two-step
process for licensing nuclear plants that was provided by the Atomic
Energy Act. The AEC had previously issued construction permits for
the Browns Ferry plant, and public hearings had begun on TVA's applications for Sequoyah. Moreover, since the agency intended to begin generating electricity at Browns Ferry in mid-1973, TVA was also
preparing for AEC hearings on its application for operating permits
at that facility.

The AEC's announcement in December 1970 that henceforth it
would incorporate environmental impact as a condition for licensing nuclear plants was neither voluntarily undertaken nor well received. Although section 102 of NEPA stipulated that all federal agencies had to evaluate and assess "the full environmental impact" of
their activities, and that these Environmental Impact Statements had
to be made publicly available for comment and critique, the AEC responded characteristically that nonradiological issues were not its concern. When the commission refused a request by an environmental
coalition to require preparation of an Environmental Impact State-

ment for a nuclear facility at Calvert Cliffs, Maryland, however, it became the object of a court suit challenging its regulatory stance. At that point the AEC issued what Judge Skelly Wright later characterized as "the Commission's crabbed interpretation of NEPA": environmental factors needed to be considered only if raised by AEC staff or outside intervenors; nonradiological issues could not be joined if the hearing notice appeared prior to 4 March 1971, thus exempting all plants under construction before that date; independent Environmental Impact Statements by the AEC were prohibited if prior environmental certification had been provided by other federal, state, or regional agencies; and, until operating licenses were issued, the AEC would not consider environmental factors that required retrofitting on facilities already issued construction permits.

In the landmark *Calvert Cliffs Coordinating Committee v. AEC* decision, Judge Wright termed the commission's position "a mockery" of NEPA. He asserted that not only was it the duty of the AEC to consider environmental values fully before issuing licenses, but also that the commission had to give attention to all nonradiological effects of plant operation. Moreover, the court ruled that the AEC was responsible for conducting its own independent impact statement since certification by individual agencies was insufficient to ensure the overall "balancing" of environmental values required by NEPA. Finally, the decision rendered all nuclear plants vulnerable to environmentally related modifications or retrofitting, regardless of when construction permits were issued. In Judge Wright's words, NEPA was enacted to "tell federal agencies that environmental protection is as much a part of their responsibility as is protection and promotion of the industries they regulate."[10] And as the "decade of the environment" dawned across the land, the opinion of this jurist sent a similar message to all concerned in the EPA/TVA thermal dispute.

The *Calvert Cliffs* decision had significant implications for the AEC regulatory process, for the TVA power program, and for the EPA effort to control thermal pollution. For the AEC, the decision meant that it would now be liable for environmental lawsuits challenging its licensing decisions. For TVA, it meant not only that Browns Ferry was no longer exempt from AEC-imposed plant modifications because of its pre-1970 construction permits, but also that its plans for controlling heated water discharges would now have to be approved by EPA, the states, and the AEC. And for EPA, it meant that a credible enforcement tool for coaxing TVA compliance was potentially at hand:

it was now possible that without TVA compliance with thermal standards, the agency's highly touted nuclear plants would be denied operating licenses. Still in doubt, however, was if and when the AEC would accept EPA's stringent standards as a condition for issuing licenses for TVA nuclear plants. But TVA could ill afford the luxury of awaiting resolution of this or any other enforcement question. The agency felt that if Browns Ferry — already once delayed — failed to begin operation on schedule, there was a substantial risk of severe power shortages for the entire Southeast.[11]

Grudging Compliance at Browns Ferry   In December 1971 EPA headquarters forwarded comments to TVA on the latter's draft impact statements for Browns Ferry and Sequoyah. These revealed that differences of opinion existed within EPA. The commentary on Sequoyah incorporated most of the language submitted by Region IV, but the evaluation of the Browns Ferry Environmental Impact Statement was "significantly watered-down" from that provided by regional staff members.[12] Charles Kaplan of the Region IV Water Quality Division summarized these differences in a memorandum to the chief of the Federal Facilities Branch: (1) the water quality standards and cost-benefit sections had been "'weakened significantly' especially in relation to [TVA's] proposed method of interim control by [river] flow and/or reduced power levels"; (2) the alternative heat dissipation and socioeconomic sections were "basically deleted"; and (3) requests had been deleted for discussion of the possiblity of thermal effects caused by damage to diffusers by river traffic and by discharge interaction between plants. Still, though some regional officials attributed EPA headquarter's more moderate stance to TVA's appeals to Washington,[13] and though some at TVA later acknowledged that "we had obtained some concessions from EPA in the development of water standards,"[14] all acknowledged that EPA demonstrated none of the enforcement diffidence displayed during the SO_2 controversy. For example, Art Linton of the Federal Facilities Branch later recalled,

> We played with the standards a little bit, but they were still higher than what Alabama set originally. . . . But they [TVA] still had to know whether or not we'd stand behind what we said. After getting the guidance needed, we told them we would stand by the standards even through litigation. . . . I went to a meeting with TVA and told them, "Goddamnit, there's going to be a cooling tower on that plant [Browns Ferry]."[15]

With the *Calvert Cliffs* decision raising the spectre that Browns Ferry might not qualify for an operating license, and as its parrying with EPA and the states portended only long-term, marginal prospects of success, TVA announced in February 1972 that it would install cooling towers at the plant.[16] In the announcement, however, TVA officials voiced strong reservations about both the thermal standards and the EPA's logic. Terming the action a "$43 million 'extra insurance' policy against environmental damage and an electric power shortage," a TVA spokesman proclaimed,

> The available scientific knowledge about [thermal pollution] is still not adequate to determine precisely what temperature limits are necessary to ensure protection of aquatic life. TVA and the Environmental Protection Agency are undertaking a research program . . . which will contribute to a more exact determination, but it will be a considerable time before results . . . will be available. Meanwhile, the limitations on heat discharges necessary to meet applicable water quality standards could result in serious curtailment of generation at the plant after all three units are in operation. That in turn could endanger the reliability of electric power service in the region because this plant is a major part of the new generating capacity that will be necessary to meet future power demands. Proceeding now with cooling towers will provide extra insurance against adverse effects on aquatic life and guard against this potential hazard to power service.[17]

The announcement then characterized the thermal standards as "environmentally unnecessary" and prophesied that TVA's expenditures for the towers would provide "no appreciable improvement to the environment": the water temperature of the Tennessee River naturally exceeded 86° F in the summer anyway. What is more, the multimillion-dollar cooling towers were patently cost-ineffective because the restrictive standards would be violated only 28 percent of the plant's operating time.

Though TVA patiently recited these and its "good faith" claims in a variety of public and private forums over the ensuing months, the agency gained neither sympathy from environmentalists nor regulatory respite from state pollution control boards. For example, when raised before the Tennessee Water Quality Board, these arguments were countered by sportsmen who spoke of the ecological and economic impact of fish kills at the Sequoyah plant and who implored TVA not to exceed an 87° F maximum. Similarly, and in effect countering chairman Wagner's congressional testimony and his correspondence to Senator James Allen (D-Ala.) and Representative Jamie Whitten (D-Miss.), Charles D. Kelly of the Alabama Game and Fish Division alleged that "false information" regarding the natural temperatures of the Tennessee River was being used. Further, Kelly refused to abide the agency's complaint that the belated shift in state standards imposed unreasonable hardship. Recalling his and the Interior Department's efforts to persuade TVA in the late 1960s to alter its plant designs, Kelly said the agency opted instead "to have [Alabama] approve a temperature standard that would have been most destructive to the fishery of Wheeler Reservoir."[18] And when TVA claimed Alabama's standards required inordinate capital investments for marginal water quality improvements — a practice increasingly disparaged as "withdrawing needed resources from other environmental efforts" — AWIC took no remedial action.[19] Still, it was TVA's actions in the wake of the Browns Ferry announcement that aroused the most sustained, and potentially debilitating, ire of environmentalists. At that point, TVA proposed and sought to persuade EPA to allow interim operation of Browns Ferry with only diffusers until construction of cooling towers was completed.

Counterproposal   As noted, TVA's decision to install cooling towers at Browns Ferry came extremely late in the construction phase of the plant. Specifically, two of the plant's three units were scheduled to begin operation in March and December of 1973, respectively, while the third was to come on line in July of the following year. Construction of the first cooling tower, however, could not be completed until July 1974, and the last could not begin operation until January 1975.[20] Thus, during interagency talks described by all participants as "highly professional,"[21] and in a letter from Region IV administrator Raven to Dr. Gartrell of TVA, EPA requested that TVA refrain from exceeding the 86° F, 5° F standards during the "interim period" of plant operation.[22] TVA countered, however, that critical peak load demands, expected in the summer of 1973, could not be met if Browns Ferry were held to those standards: the plant would have to be shut down temporarily to ensure compliance. Agency officials also suggested that if this happened simultaneously with equipment failures at other TVA plants or with shortages of coal supplies in the Valley, the TVA power grid could become totally crippled. TVA proposed to meet a less stringent 93° F, 10° F standard using diffusers during the eighteen to twenty-four months of interim operation, maintaining that it "did not consider the interruption of service to power consumers to be an acceptable alternative."[23]

In offering its proposal TVA raised not only the threat of power blackouts but also the infeasibility of, and environmental havoc wrought by, alternative strategies.

> Meeting the proposed thermal standards of a 5° F rise and 86° F maximum would involve the regulation of upstream reservoirs to provide additional stream-flow at Browns Ferry, the reduction of generation by the Browns Ferry units, or a combination of the two. Although it is feasible to use limited regulation by the TVA reservoir system to meet the 10° F rise and 93° F maximum criteria, the greater regulation which would be required to meet the more stringent criteria would result in drawdowns of upstream reservoirs so large that TVA does not consider this approach to be practicable. . . . TVA considers that the adverse impacts to the environment from increased generation by fossil-fueled [coal] plants as a result of reducing generation at Browns Ferry would exceed the questionable environmental benefit to aquatic life, particularly in view of the small percentage of time the [more stringent] standard would be exceeded during the interim period due to plant generation.[24]

TVA next used its final Environmental Impact Statement for Browns Ferry to broach an equally controversial proposal. Published in September 1972, about one month before Congress enacted comprehensive amendments to the FWPCA, the statement detailed TVA's intent to operate the plant permanently in a combination cooling mode. That is, the agency proposed to operate Browns Ferry either in once-through (diffuser), helper, or closed-cycle cooling modes, depending upon variations in river flow and temperature at the plant. As depicted in table 6.2, these operating modes are progressively less harmful to the ecology as the intake of water into the plant is reduced and ultimately eliminated. EPA officials immediately notified TVA that unacceptable environmental damage would occur during the once-through and helper modes of operation due to the impingement and entrainment of aquatic life. Moreover, given the unevenness of reservoir flows from TVA hydropower dams during peak power periods, these officials strongly doubted that Browns Ferry could comply with thermal standards if operated in this fashion.

Both environmentalists and the state of Alabama quickly took issue with TVA's proposals. A member of the attorney general's staff, William Garner, termed TVA's plan a "menace to the ecology of the

Table 6.2. **Processes and Environmental Impacts of Alternative Cooling Methods**

Cooling Method	Process	Impact
Once-Through (Open Mode)	Heated water is returned directly to receiving body of water.	Most water intake; mortality to aquatic life near intake structure and drawn through the plant (impingement and entrainment).
Helper	All or part of heated water is partially cooled all or part of the time by a tower, pond, or ditch before returning to receiving body of water.	Less water intake and consequently less aquatic mortality.
Closed-Cycle	All water is cooled by tower or pond and continuously recycled; only water imported to system is to replenish amounts lost through evaporation.	No water intake; no environmental hazard.

[Tennessee] river" and threatened to join environmentalists in taking legal action to block the plant's opening.[25] Similarly, Assistant Attorney General Hank Caddel claimed that the plant might eventually use "a third of the river's flow and raise its temperature twelve degrees."[26] Acknowledging that the state was contemplating a lawsuit, he insisted that TVA should be treated no differently than any other pollution source. Attorney General William Baxley then announced his intention to intervene in forthcoming AEC hearings on operating licenses for Browns Ferry unless TVA agreed to comply with EPA's more stringent thermal standards. Now under legal and administrative siege by those disgruntled with its policies, and anticipating more time-consuming interventions during the AEC's reevaluation of its construction permits in light of *Calvert Cliffs*, TVA looked to the Congress in late 1972 for statutory relief. Although initially buoying agency spirits, the FWPCA of 1972 would instead result in TVA's decision to design and build all its nuclear plants with cooling towers at an anticipated capital cost of $640 million.

TOWARD SYSTEMWIDE COMPLIANCE

The FWPCA of 1972 brought both hope and apprehension to TVA officials. The former was perhaps best articulated by chairman Wagner in a letter to Senator Allen of Alabama. Noting that "it has not been demonstrated to our [TVA's] satisfaction that thermal discharges of the sort proposed . . . for any of our plants adversely affect the aquatic environment," Wagner wrote:

> That the degree and manner to which thermal discharges need to be regulated is still open to question is evident from the . . . FWPCA of 1972. Congress required the EPA to conduct continuing comprehensive studies of the effects and methods of thermal discharges [sec. 104] . . . [and] EPA was further directed to publish criteria for water quality which will provide a scientific basis for state water quality standards. *If the scientific basis for standards had been free from doubt, none of this would have been necessary* [emphasis added]. In addition, under Section 316(a) of the Act, it is not possible to establish a standard for thermal discharges on a case-by-case basis that will be either more or less stringent than actually required to fully protect [aquatic life] . . . as it exists in the particular reservoir into which a discharge is made. As studies and demonstrations are made in order to establish standards under Section 316(a), we are sure that . . . TVA's position [on standards] will be substantiated.[27]

TVA's apprehension stemmed from the statute's ambitious goals to eliminate all pollutant discharges into the nation's waterways by 1985. Operationalized in terms of the installation of the best practicable control technology by 1977 and best available technology economically achievable by 1983, this goal animated TVA's fears that it would be required to operate cooling towers in closed-cycle modes at all its nuclear plants in order to obtain NPDES permits from EPA. Three events directly related to these and other aspects of the FWPCA helped bring the cooling tower dispute to an end by late 1974. First, an EPA/AEC Memorandum of Understanding resulted in the incorporation of EPA's thermal standards as conditions for TVA's obtaining nuclear plant operating licenses. Second, TVA learned that procedures for exemption from section 316(a) would most likely preclude successful appeals before Browns Ferry and Sequoyah would have to begin operation. And last, EPA persistently communicated to TVA the strong likelihood that best available technology requirements for obtaining NPDES permits would indeed specify closed-cycle cooling systems.

Resolving a Problem of Complementary Responsibility   As previously recounted, the *Calvert Cliffs* ruling made it abundantly clear that the AEC had to consider the environmental impact of thermal discharges when issuing licenses to petitioners. With the enactment of the FWPCA of 1972, however, Congress made it clear as well that EPA also had authority over thermal discharges whenever a license or permit from the AEC was necessary for plant operation (section 402). Cognizant of these "complementary responsibilities," Congress stipulated in section 511(c)(B) that nothing in NEPA should be construed to authorize any federal licensing agency to "impose, as a condition precedent to the issuance of any license or permit, any effluent limitation other than [those already] established pursuant to this Act [FWPCA]." Thus, in January 1973 EPA proposed NPDES permitting procedures specifying that any licensing application from a federal facility had to be submitted for state comment on its compliance with existing thermal standards. What is more, the AEC, the EPA, and the Council on Environmental Quality issued a Memorandum of Understanding implementing section 511. Most significant for the EPA/ TVA dispute, the AEC agreed not to "impose different [effluent] limitations or requirements . . . as a condition to any license or permit" than those already established. Noting, however, that some licenses would necessarily be issued prior to EPA's promulgation of technology-based limitations in 1974, the memorandum also provided that the AEC would give "due regard" to EPA's views on all Environmental Impact Statements accompanying license applications. In return, EPA agreed to consider "not only water quality" in establishing those standards, but also monetary costs, other environmental impacts, and energy production needs.

The EPA/AEC pact would raise the spirits of TVA's friends and foes alike. To Alabama Attorney General Baxley, his staff, and environmentalists, the agreement meant two things. First, Alabama's insistence on TVA's compliance with more stringent thermal standards now would have to be considered formally in the AEC licensing hearings on Browns Ferry. Second, if the AEC's "due regard" for the impact comments of EPA included acceptance of its 86° F, 5° F standards, meeting these standards could become a binding condition for issuing a license for Browns Ferry. After negotiations among the principals, these hopes became reality in mid-1973. No doubt fearing that to do otherwise would invite lawsuits by environmentalists,[28] the AEC announced that it would defer to EPA's version of appropriate thermal standards at Browns Ferry. TVA, wary that severe licensing delays would ensue from Baxley's continued intervention and threatened lawsuit, agreed to comply "with all applicable thermal standards of the state of Alabama and the United States."[29] What is more, TVA agreed to stipulate this commitment formally in its Browns Ferry license. In return, Baxley withdrew Alabama's petition for intervention.

In contrast, Vanderbilt University professor Frank Parker felt that TVA's concession to install cooling towers was unwarranted given the memorandum's emphasis on cost and non-water quality considerations. Parker, an environmental and water resource engineer, petitioned to intervene in the AEC hearings on Browns Ferry, maintaining that TVA's decision violated NEPA since it failed to assess adequately the cost-benefit ratio of cooling tower expenditures to total environmental impacts.[30] Specifically, he alleged that "no monetary benefits from reducing the thermal load on the reservoir could be demonstrated" and that the Environmental Impact Statement neglected the "environmental and aesthetic diseconomies of the cooling towers." For example, the towers would require reduced boat traffic, would cause increased fog, and would raise noise levels in the area. In January 1973, however, TVA officials informed Parker that although they agreed with the substance of his arguments, they felt that the AEC licensing process was the wrong forum for challenging thermal standards. It was time-consuming and thus threatening to TVA's nuclear power production needs. They therefore encouraged Parker to consider instead section 316 of the FWPCA, which afforded a more legally appropriate and promising opportunity for regulatory challenge. TVA attorney David G. Powell then urged Parker to withdraw his intervention petition.[31]

Precluding Section 316(a) Exemptions Following enactment of the FWPCA of 1972, and as agency officials sought operating permits for the Sequoyah nuclear plant, TVA assessed the likelihood of Sequoyah's qualifying for a section 316(a) exemption. The results of this analysis were discouraging to TVA officials. The agency lacked "sufficient information" at that time to seek an exemption at Sequoyah no matter what criteria EPA would require as evidence for dispensation.[32] Reviewers noted that TVA had two options: either install cooling towers at the plant or ask the president of the United States for a national security exemption.[33] Others raised the possibility that TVA could claim exemption as a federal facility. With presidential exemption viewed unlikely and federal facility exemption perceived implausible, TVA staffers still advised postponement of cooling tower installation: "Before pursuing . . . [other] alternatives [e.g., cooling tower installation], we believe TVA should undertake a comprehensive research study at Sequoyah to determine the effects of thermal discharges. This study could be used to form the basis for Section 316 exemption. We believe valuable data could be gained from operation of [the plant] with once-through cooling [diffusers] in conjunction with an extensive monitoring program. . . ."[34]

As representatives of TVA's Office of Power and Divisions of Law and Environmental Planning met to discuss the merits of this proposal, the agency received information concerning the procedures EPA most likely would adopt for obtaining section 316(a) thermal exemptions. TVA learned throughout 1973 from the Utility Water Act Group (UWAG) and from its own informal contacts with EPA officials that the agency favored and intended to promulgate guidelines that allowed three ways to qualify for exemption.[35] First, operators could show that the existing discharge from a plant had not caused "prior appreciable harm" to aquatic life and, consequently, had not disturbed the "balanced indigenous community" of fish and wildlife in or on the receiving body of water. In making this demonstration, the interactive and additive effects of prior thermal discharges were to be considered. EPA also provided that even with prior appreciable harm, it would consider an alternative standard if it could be shown that the substitute would protect waterlife. Admissible evidence supporting these claims might include data from the applicant's prior operation of the plant as well as proof of the facility's compliance or noncompliance with previous state water quality standards.

A second method for justifying an alternative standard required proof that "representative, important" fish species in each receiving body of water would be protected and allowed to propagate. To qualify for this designation, a species would have to be classified as essential, in terms of biological needs, for maintaining a balanced, indigenous aquatic community. Evidence supporting an operator's claim would have to demonstrate that the plant's thermal discharges would comply with all water quality criteria developed by EPA pursuant to section 304 of the act dealing with "growth, reproduction, and survival" of designated species.

The final exemption method specified was one designed for plants that had no previous record of operation. Again the goal was to protect and ensure the propagation of a balanced, indigenous community of aquatic life. This alternative provided, however, that without actual plant operating data, an operator could submit biological and engineering models of anticipated effects to bolster exemption arguments. Supporting documentation might include extrapolations from the operations of comparable polluting sources based on new or historical biological data and physical monitoring as well as the results of engineering and diffusion modeling.

Because TVA's nuclear program was so new, the first option of demonstrating the absence of prior harm at Sequoyah or Browns Ferry was eliminated immediately. Also removed was the option of extrapolating from the experiences of comparable plants, since none existed. When disagreement arose over the specification of a representative species for the Tennessee River, the only option remaining was thermal diffusion modeling.[36] However, a joint EPA/TVA analysis convinced agency officials that sufficient data were unavailable; in effect, the necessary extrapolations could not be made in time to get either plant operating on schedule.

EPA/TVA communications during this period also revealed additional time pressures bearing on TVA's decision-making. As outlined in an EPA memorandum circulated among TVA staff, the risks of section 316 exemption delays were especially grave: "If a source fails to prove absence of [aquatic] harm to qualify for automatic 316(a) relief . . . then between March 1974 and March 1975 the source applies for . . . relief and conducts biological studies. However . . . this late schedule could result in noncompliance with the Act's 1977 requirements."[37] The enormity of such a failure was paramount in the minds of TVA planners: noncompliance meant that the birth of a twenty-first-century "energy oasis" in the Tennessee Valley could be stillborn for want of NPDES permits as the twentieth century moved inexorably to a close. The agency's technical staff thus advocated, and TVA officials readily authorized, accelerated and comprehensive biological studies at all plants in order "to give maximum lead time for meeting requirements of the [FWPCA] in areas where studies show that a plant will be in noncompliance."[38] Although TVA would pursue such efforts intensively, EPA's thermal exemption posture was about to merge with its persistent predilection for closed-cycle cooling systems to resolve the cooling tower issue.

NPDES Woes and Systemwide Compliance   As TVA was receiving cues about forthcoming thermal exemption guidelines, EPA and state officials were sending similar signals as to their likely enforcement posture with regard to NPDES permits. These signals began in January 1973 when EPA forwarded staff comments on the final Browns Ferry Environmental Impact Statement to TVA officials. As mentioned previously, EPA applauded TVA's decision to install cooling towers but expressed deep concern that operation in a combined-cycle mode would preclude compliance with applicable thermal standards and inflict severe ecological damage. In that same document, EPA fired a second enforcement shot across TVA's bow by linking closed-cycle operation of the towers to TVA's ability to qualify for NPDES permits. EPA officials noted that although definitions of best practicable technology and best available technology "have not been promulgated [as yet], requirements . . . can be anticipated."[39] The agency then outlined how even standard exemptions under section 316(a) probably would not ensure plant operations as TVA's dependence on nuclear power spiraled over the next decade.

> It is to be noted that variances for thermal discharges can be authorized by the Administrator under certain conditions in conformance with Section 316(a). However, Section 316(b) requires "that the location, design, construction, and capacity of cooling water intake structures reflect the best technology available for minimizing adverse environmental impacts. . . ." TVA would be well advised to . . . evaluate alternatives available to eliminate recirculation of the heated plume to the plant intake. Use of a totally closed-cycle cooling tower system as previously recommended should rectify this problem.[40]

Additional warnings were issued by EPA throughout the year, most prominently (1) in an affidavit presented by Region IV administrator Raven to the AEC, (2) in a letter to TVA attorney David Powell, and (3) during interagency meetings. Raven's affidavit, for example, stipulated explicitly that EPA intended to designate off-stream, closed-cycle cooling as the best practicable technology requirement for obtaining NPDES permits under section 402 of the act.

State intentions in this regard, though somewhat clouded in mid-1973, also were unsettling to TVA. For example, after attending a meeting in Tennessee to "explore the possibilities of TVA working informally with the state . . . to develop mutually acceptable, plant specific water discharge standards," one TVA official speculated that the state would "probably require the best practicable treatment to meet thermal standards."[41] He then identified the problems for the power program posed by the three most likely outcomes of the state's determination:

> ... the standards developed by Tennessee ... may result in the following: (1) Tennessee programming plans being disapproved or delayed [by EPA] because the standards developed may not meet guidelines yet to be released; (2) Tennessee coming up with more stringent standards than may ultimately be contained in EPA guidelines — TVA would be committed to meeting these more stringent standards according to the FWPCA; and (3) the standards developed by Tennessee becoming criteria used by EPA for considering approval of TVA's NPDES permits.[42]

Despite EPA's tireless recitation of its NPDES philosophy, TVA nonetheless submitted its Browns Ferry permit application in April 1973 without provision for continuous closed-cycle operation of its cooling towers. Instead, TVA officials reasserted their intention to use diffusers and river flow regulation as a primary cooling mode. Four months later general manager Lynn Seeber, critical of EPA's failure to act expeditiously on the agency's NPDES applications, wrote to the EPA acting administrator John Quarles. Seeber advised him that TVA took strong exception to EPA's insistence on closed-cycle cooling.[43] He then again proposed using a system of combined modes at Browns Ferry and labeled the adoption of EPA's recommendation "entirely inappropriate" and "premature." Alleging that the recommendation was based solely on EPA's "anticipation as to the eventual outcome of the rule-making proceedings currently underway" to establish NPDES requirements, Seeber charged that Quarles' interpretation of the FWPCA was faulty. EPA, he suggested, could not impose closed-cycle systems on regulatory targets solely on section 316(b) considerations.[44]

The mode of operation aside, by late 1973 TVA's nuclear power situation relative to thermal pollution standards was clear. Needing AEC construction and operating licenses for all its plants, TVA officials knew they would be required to meet EPA's more stringent standards. And needing NPDES permits from EPA to operate its facilities in compliance with the FWPCA, TVA staffers were certain that off-stream cooling (most likely towers) would be designated as the best practicable technology for obtaining these licenses. Thus, despite indications from the AEC that means other than cooling towers (such as limitations on power levels) might satisfy their licensing conditions,[45] and despite the possibility that the National Technical Advisory Committee might issue less stringent thermal criteria in forthcoming revisions, TVA took immediate steps to assure compliance with EPA's standards at all its plants. Unlike the SO_2 dispute, there were neither court challenges to EPA pollution limits or authority nor appeals to Congress for legislative relief. Instead, TVA announced in September that it would install cooling towers at its Sequoyah nuclear plant (at a capital cost of $42 million) in order to meet Tennessee's 86.9° F, 5.4° F thermal standards. The agency's rationale: doing so prevented delays in TVA's nuclear plant licensing schedule that could jeopardize power supplies throughout the Southeast. Then, in the aftermath of EPA's promulgation of effluent guidelines in October 1974, TVA announced it would design and operate all its present and projected nuclear plants with cooling towers.

So equipped, TVA's nuclear contingent would be able to meet any thermal standard EPA was likely to issue in the future regardless of stringency. Consequently, the spectre of shortfalls in power production occasioned by EPA or AEC licensing delays was eliminated immediately. As for EPA, TVA's announcement represented a major victory for the agency in intragovernmental enforcement. TVA would continue to oppose EPA's use of section 316(b) as the sole basis for requiring closed-cycle operating modes at the towers—a policy EPA initially was unsure enough about to invite legal opinions from other federal agencies. And TVA staffers would continue to pursue exemptions under section 316(a) when they appeared promising. Still, a major compliance commitment by the nation's most illustrious nuclear power advocate had been secured in relatively short order and with comparatively moderate resistance.

CHAPTER SEVEN

The Cases Revisited

AN ANALYTICAL PERSPECTIVE

Political scientist James E. Anderson has written insightfully that all public policies contain an element of social control, one "designed to cause people to do things, refrain from doing things, or continue doing things that they otherwise would not do."[1] To refine our appreciation of social control in the arena of intragovernmental regulation, the preceding chapters have chronicled two noteworthy examples of the process. The study now returns to the research questions posed in chapter 1, specifically, those concerning the comparison of intragovernmental regulation to implementation in other contexts, and the implications of the cases for developing a predictive theory of regulatory policy implementation in general.

INTRAGOVERNMENTAL REGULATION AS POLICY IMPLEMENTATION

Nearly a decade has passed since Erwin Hargrove termed implementation the "missing link" in policy analysis.[2] A multidisciplinary rush to study the topic subsequently has ensued, with heightened interest of late in understanding implementation in the regulatory arena.[3] Examined most often have been national policies where implementation success required changes or modifications in the behavior of reluctant regulatory targets. In both national and cross-national contexts, implementation has been portrayed most often as a transactional bargaining process wherein policy goals are negotiated with, rather than dictated to, regulatory targets.[4] Researchers characterize it as a rational pursuit of participant self-interest, with compliance most readily expected when the benefits outweigh the costs of noncompliance.[5] This determination, in turn, is conditioned by a host of inter- and intraorganizational factors.[6] For example, it usually is suggested that when policies directly conflict with the policy views, personal dispositions, or organizational predilections of regulatory targets, implementation difficulties abound. Similarly, implementation is portrayed as more difficult as the number of actors involved increases,[7] as the sociopolitical environment becomes less supportive,[8] as the validity of the policy's causal theory looms more problematic,[9] and as the adequacy and credibility of enforcement resources appear most dubious.[10]

The EPA/TVA cases demonstrate clearly that the dominant metaphors of the regulatory policy implementation literature are characteristic of the intragovernmental arena as well. Once more, implementation appears to be a bargaining process where the compliance of reluctant regulatory targets is negotiated, rather than dictated; where the behavior of those targeted is predicated on a rational pursuit of self-interest narrowly defined; and where a circular bargaining process can develop, with participants striving to affect enforcement in whatever forum — public or private — and at whatever stage of the policy process they deem useful. The cases also reinforce the specific findings of previous implementation research: factors found to condition regulatory policy implementation in other contexts appear powerful as well in the intragovernmental arena. What follows is a discussion of those analytically distinct factors that were most influential in resolving the EPA/TVA controversies.

Policy-Mission Proximity   One of the most powerful factors in influencing TVA's divergent behavior in the two cases was the difference in the degree to which SO_2 and thermal policies affected TVA's power program mission. As noted, TVA projected that nearly 55 percent of its generating capacity would be nuclear powered by 1985, whereas its dependence on coal-fired steam plants would be cut approximately in half by that date. To effect this change in nuclear generating capacity, TVA had stopped ordering coal-fired plants, begun phasing out older ones then in operation, and started accepting bids for five nuclear plants. Given the long, and ever-increasing, lead times needed to license and get nuclear plants into operation, TVA officials felt that they could not afford any delays in operating their nuclear contingent if they were to meet the power needs of the Tennessee Valley. Thermal standards threatened this timetable when the AEC decided to make TVA's compliance with EPA's thermal standards a condition for obtaining construction and operating licenses at its plants. TVA faced an apparent no-win situation. If the agency agreed to meet these standards, the operation of its nuclear plants might be delayed for eighteen to twenty-four months while cooling towers were constructed. But to challenge their stringency, or to risk the intervention of friends or foes in the nuclear licensing process, could cause even longer delays that would seriously jeopardize its ability to complete its mission to produce electric power. Although doubting the wisdom of EPA's thermal policies — and although AEC, congressional, and even legal appeals were available to the agency — TVA abstained from further challenges to avoid the mission-threatening delays they would engender.

In contrast, the agency's coal-fired plants were already on line and were gradually being deemphasized as a source of TVA power production. Delay in this case was an asset. The longer TVA could resist installing constant control systems, the fewer coal plants it would have in operation. Consequently, less SO_2 pollution would be emitted from its facilities and its operations would become less of a regulatory target. Moreover, delay provided additional opportunity for EPA, the Congress, or a new administration to relax SO_2 policy. Because TVA "got away from fossil fuels and into nukes,"[11] it could pursue challenges in a variety of public and private forums without jeopardizing its ability to meet the power demands of the TVA service area.

Complexity of Joint Action   A second factor influencing TVA's strategy in the two cases was the difference in the number, types, and perspectives of implementation veto points. Researchers typically refer to these characteristics as the complexity of joint action. Unlike its efforts in the thermal dispute, EPA's attempts to apply SO_2 policy to TVA were severely complicated by OMB's regulatory review procedures. Recall that all EPA regulations, in effect, had to be reviewed by other federal agencies for their impact on energy supplies and the economy. Consequently, antagonists such as the Commerce Department and FPC — as institutionalized "veto points" — were able to raise repeated challenges to SO_2 pollution control efforts. What is more, these challenges were sometimes quite productive; witness President Ford's submission to Congress of Commerce Department amendments to the CAA. Results such as this not only frustrated EPA's interpretation of the law but also buoyed TVA's hopes that either legislative or administrative relief might be forthcoming. And this no doubt fueled the agency's recalcitrance.

Similarly, the need for TVA to obtain licenses for its nuclear plants from the AEC was unparalleled in the SO_2 controversy. This made a significant difference in the two cases, speeding TVA's compliance with thermal standards. While potentially an obstacle to EPA's efforts since the commission could have issued licenses based on less stringent standards, the AEC chose instead to incorporate EPA's recommendations as conditions for licenses at Browns Ferry and Sequoyah. Moreover, the potential for delay occasioned by the lengthy licensing process was critical to TVA's decision not to pursue further challenges and to install cooling towers at all its nuclear plants.

Validity of Causal Theory   A third factor influencing TVA's behavior was the validity of the causal theories underlying SO_2 and thermal pollution control. Causal validity refers, in these cases, to the certainty of the relationship between limiting pollutant emissions and actually protecting human health and aquatic life. Differences on this dimension accounted in part for differences in the nature and tone of the SO_2 and thermal application challenges. These, in turn, affected the duration of the two controversies, prolonging the former while curtailing the latter.

As EPA sought to apply its SO_2 policy, TVA persistently raised fundamental questions about the cause-effect relationship involved. For example, agency officials maintained vehemently that insufficient evidence existed linking long-term SO_2 coal-plant emissions to respiratory deaths and acid rain problems. And chairman Wagner asserted tenaciously that SO_2 actually "sweetened the soil," increased crop yields, and thus indirectly improved the nutritional health of Valley residents.[12] TVA also joined those chastising scrubber technology as essentially unworkable at large power plants. Given the technical limitations and conceptual complexity of the problems at hand, definitive evidence refuting these charges simply was not available to EPA in the early 1970s.

In contrast, TVA never challenged the link between thermal pollution and harm to aquatic life because the relationship between the two was documented so well; since 1962, the federal government had compiled an inventory of acknowledged thermal pollution fish kills.

Agency officials also conceded that TVA nuclear plants could pose a severe thermal problem, acknowledging that plants of this type typically produced 40 to 60 percent more heat than conventional facilities. And because cooling towers were accepted by the engineering profession as an effective thermal control device, TVA never disputed the ability of these towers to protect the aquatic life around its plants. Agency officials raised only the more technical issues concerning temperature criteria and standards rather than the threshold question of whether emissions really harmed aquatic life. As opposed to the SO_2 dispute, this difference in causal validity led to more professional, less confrontational discussion between the two agencies. This, in turn, resulted in a more compromising attitude on the part of thermal discussants, and thus forged a quicker resolution to the cooling tower issue.

Policy Communication   Differences in the manner in which EPA communicated its policies to TVA during its interpretation and application efforts were also critical in influencing the latter's behavior. During the SO_2 affair, EPA struggled over a two-and-a-half-year period to come to grips with the question of strategy: constant versus intermittent control. After notifying then-Governor Jimmy Carter that intermittent control would not be considered an acceptable control strategy, the agency neither approved nor disapproved such strategies when it reviewed the original State Implementation Plans. Following this, EPA initially proposed a regulation disallowing intermittent control, and then proposed one allowing it. In the end, the agency rejected such strategies, but only after a prolonged period of flip-flopping on the issue.

EPA's vacillation concerning control technology was a major factor delaying TVA compliance with the CAA. Several TVA officials cited it as justification for noncompliance. And representatives of environmental groups, EPA, and the states suggested that this inconsistency encouraged TVA recalcitrance in two ways: first, by offering hope that EPA might still be persuaded to accept SDEL, and second, by providing political ammunition to those seeking antiscrubber amendments to the CAA.[13]

EPA's vacillation in the SO_2 case was unparalleled during the thermal interpretation and application effort. EPA, and before it, the Interior Department, consistently encouraged TVA to design its

Browns Ferry and Sequoyah plants to meet the most stringent thermal standards possible. In so doing, they effectively required TVA to install auxiliary cooling systems such as towers at these plants. Moreover, despite the absence of a sufficient data base for promulgating its technology-based effluent limitations, EPA maintained and communicated to TVA a consistent posture, requiring closed-cycle cooling towers as the best practicable control technology for obtaining discharge permits. EPA's steadfast positions on issues such as these offered scant hope that its interpretations could, with patience, be reversed. Nor did they invite the disparagement of those hostile to their substantive decisions concerning thermal pollution.

Enforcement Credibility   Juxtaposing the two application processes also suggests that the likelihood of EPA enforcement affected TVA's behavior. EPA's credibility was sorely compromised prior to the enactment of the CAA of 1977 by the limited range of enforcement sanctions provided by the 1970 act—sanctions that did not require the application of fines to violators. Moreover, interviewees conceded that the draconian measure of temporarily or permanently closing down TVA plants—the only other sanction available to EPA when dealing with the federal facility—was never seriously considered.[14] EPA could not request, federal courts were not about to order, and TVA would never view as likely, an action so disruptive to the economic and social fabric of the Southeast. Also inhibiting implementation was the well-known reluctance of EPA and the Justice Department to file lawsuits against sister agencies. This enforcement predicament, however, was eased somewhat after 1977 by two developments. First, Congress amended the CAA to require injunctive relief and/or civil penalties in cases of noncompliance, and it added market incentives to EPA's enforcement arsenal. Second, President Carter's EPA and Justice Department appointees indicated a willingness to change the nonlitigation policy of the two agencies. Only at this point did TVA view enforcement likely and look for "someone to surrender to."

    In contrast, EPA's enforcement credibility peaked during the thermal controversy. Under Ruckelshaus, the agency quickly had established a tough thermal pollution enforcement reputation, one founded on the standard-setting conference and fortified by an aggressive court-suit strategy. The agency's ability and propensity to seek court-ordered imposition of fines was always taken seriously. What is more, after the FWPCA of 1972 was enacted, TVA officials viewed the NPDES permit system—the heart of EPA's enforcement scheme—as a highly effective compliance mechanism. When the discharge permit system was combined with the likelihood of fines and the AEC's decision to support EPA's thermal standards, TVA's noncompliance option became highly unattractive. To challenge either the technology-based standards supporting the permit system or to pursue relief from the AEC's decision would have threatened TVA's mission to produce power. And to absorb fines that TVA rate payers would have to subsidize was politically infeasible.

Intergovernmental Task Assignment　A sixth factor affecting TVA's behavior was the assignment of implementation tasks to various levels of government. The organizational infrastructure (i.e., the specification of units and methods for implementing policy) provided by the CAA assigned initial enforcement responsibility to the states. Alabama, Kentucky, and Tennessee opted for a permit system as the cornerstone of their enforcement effort. However, TVA as a federal facility refused to apply for state permits, citing the Supremacy Clause of the U.S. Constitution as its basis for refusal. Court suits were immediately filed against TVA by Alabama and Kentucky. While conflicting court opinions were reconciled by the Supreme Court in TVA's favor, Congress stipulated in the 1977 amendments that federal facilities had to apply for state permits. Whether motivated by principle or by a desire to further impede implementation of the CAA, TVA's challenge of the state permit system seriously prolonged resolution of the SO$_2$ dispute. Not only was delay inherent when, as expected, TVA's recalcitrance was challenged in court by Kentucky and Alabama, but the challenge itself fueled the frustration and hardened the bargaining positions of EPA and environmental groups. It thus made resolution of the dispute more difficult and time consuming.

Because administration of the NPDES permit system was assigned to EPA rather than the states by the FWPCA of 1972, TVA had no sustainable basis for a similar challenge during the thermal dispute. When questioned about TVA's abbreviated and unsuccessful attempt to claim exemption as a federal facility during that episode, one of the persons interviewed responded: "The [FWPCA] was much clearer on the duties of federal facilities than the Clean Air Act was," and "we raised the issue briefly, but . . . I don't think they [the TVA legal staff] really thought they had a case."[15] The absence of such a challenge helped lessen interagency antagonisms, afforded a less confrontational atmosphere for negotiation, and facilitated compromise and expeditious resolution of the issues.

Sociopolitical Environment   Analysis also reveals the importance of differences in the sociopolitical environment surrounding the two enforcement experiences. As EPA interpreted and applied its SO_2 policies, acute oil shortages and economic stagflation plagued its efforts. Environmental regulations were attacked relentlessly as inflationary and as detrimental to the goal of energy independence enunciated by the Nixon and Ford administrations. Pressure mounted to relax these standards, and the federal government was divided over the proper balance of environmental, economic, and energy values. The FPC, the Commerce Department, and the FEA pressured EPA to require only intermittent controls such as TVA's SDEL program. EPA responded by encouraging the states to eliminate "overly stringent" regulations from their implementation plans. Tennessee and Alabama, in turn, proposed to relax SO_2 emission limits around TVA plants, and Kentucky sought to allow intermittent controls. Although both proposals subsequently were rejected, EPA's disapproval was uncertain until the last minute. These events all played an important role in conditioning TVA's behavior in the SO_2 dispute. First, they offered hope to TVA that challenges to EPA's efforts might prevail with patience and persistence. Second, they provided TVA officials with an abundant supply of highly sympathetic, strategically placed, and stridently vocal allies. What is more, these were sympathizers who actively promoted intermittent control systems within the Executive Office of the President, during administrative proceedings, and before Congress.

In contrast, as EPA implemented its thermal policy, national interest in the heat discharge problem was increasing. Throughout the late 1960s and early 1970s, environmentalists successfully had raised concern over thermal pollution in a number of nuclear plant siting and operating cases, including the *Calvert Cliffs* decision. Successful legal challenges also had raised the consciousness of the national legislature over thermal pollution. In 1970 Congress enacted FWPCA amendments that ended the confusion over who had jurisdiction over heat discharge from nuclear plants, and in the FWPCA of 1972 Congress made sweeping changes in the organizational infrastructure for controlling thermal pollution. Thus, interest in air pollution waned and attacks on its regulation mounted during the SO_2 dispute, but interest in thermal pollution intensified until late in the thermal controversy and the advent of the Arab oil embargo. A much more favorable implementation environment for thermal pollution resulted, one that discouraged, rather than encouraged, TVA recalcitrance.

Dispositions of the Actors Finally, differences in the attitudes of the actors involved in the cases help account for TVA's behavior. First, variations in EPA's confidence about thermal and SO_2 policies were critical. Second, TVA's actions were affected greatly by differences in chairman Wagner's attitudes toward air and water pollution in general, and SO_2 and thermal pollution control technologies in particular. EPA's lack of confidence in dealing with TVA on the SO_2 issue stemmed from TVA's reputation as an "international expert" on air pollution and scrubber technology,[16] and from the relative inexperience of the EPA air quality staff. As one regional EPA official remarked, "We weren't sure we were doing the right thing; they came in with their modeling flow charts and their data on scrubber technology problems, and we just couldn't match it at that time."[17] Another official identified the effect of TVA's surfeit of expertise on EPA's enforcement strategy: "We could only hang in there and say 'you're violating the law.'"[18] When this attitude is coupled with administrator Ruckelshaus' statements that "definitive data" supporting SO_2 national ambient air standards were unavailable, much of EPA's early difficulty in regulating TVA is understandable. So too, in part, is TVA's laggard response.

In contrast, EPA exuded confidence and consistency in applying thermal policy to TVA. This can be attributed to the water quality branch's long track record in the water quality arena and to the validity of the causal theory underlying the thermal problem.[19] Moreover, several interviewees suggested that EPA's "professionalism" in this regulatory arena translated into a more "reasonable" attitude toward implementation on EPA's part when compared with its posture in the SO_2 dispute.[20] This reasonableness, in turn, provoked the TVA general manager, Lynn Seeber, to recommend that a more conciliatory TVA attitude was warranted in the thermal dispute.[21]

Equally important in shaping TVA's behavior were differences in the attitudes of board chairman Wagner toward air and water pollution, as well as toward SO_2 and thermal control technologies. Indeed, some speculated that these differences made the chairman's opposition to towers less truculent and uncompromising than his opposition to scrubbers, thus abbreviating the thermal dispute.[22] TVA had been concerned for decades with water quality. Beginning with its stream sanitation program in the mid-1930s, continuing with its development of water pollution control legislation during the 1940s, and culminating in its studies on the effects of heat discharges at TVA coal-fired plants in the 1950s and 1960s, the agency's commitment was unassailable. Chairman Wagner, because of his long association with the agency, was quite comfortable with a stewardship role that saw water quality as the lever for the "optimum use and future economic development of the Valley's streams and reservoirs." Thermal pollution, according to one interviewee, threatened this vision: "Dead fish floating on the water simply weren't conducive to [these goals]."[23]

In contrast, the problems that environmentalists and some health professionals associated with SO_2 pollution were less visible, less immediate, and less attributable to TVA operations. What is more, chairman Wagner was "more skeptical" about those effects and the control technologies associated with them. He maintained that TVA's heralded air pollution modeling and its experience with experimental scrubbers gave little support to the contentions of environmentalists.

IMPLICATIONS FOR A THEORY OF
REGULATORY POLICY IMPLEMENTATION

Despite the breadth of the literature across substantive policy areas and the heuristic value of the conceptual frameworks and propositions derived therefrom, a predictive theory of regulatory policy implementation has proven elusive.[24] One reason for this might be that the conventional wisdom is based inordinately on strikingly similar research designs that unduly limit our attention to certain aspects of implementation to the exclusion of others. Few have studied the actual process of regulatory enforcement at all, and those studying the topic typically have performed aggregate, rather than in-depth, analyses of particular experiences.[25] Moreover, until recently researchers have focused on either implementation success or failure, eschewing systematic comparisons of dissimilar cases.[26] And perhaps most significantly, the process has been studied almost exclusively from the perspective of regulators rather than from the distinctive vantage point of enforcement targets.[27]

This study has applied a decidedly different analytical approach that compensates for the design shortcomings noted above. This approach has proven useful for understanding the particulars of the cases themselves and for appreciating the dynamics of intragovernmental regulation. Moreover, it also has revealed that implementation difficulties are anticipated best if the interaction patterns of two factors are known: (1) the degree to which the application of a policy directly affects activities central to a regulatory target's mission, and (2) the extent to which the delay inherent in challenging policy implementation is perceived by the target as compromising or even foiling mission success. For convenience, we can refer to the interaction of these factors as the "noncompliance delay effect."

Thinking of delay as a determinant of implementation difficulty, rather than as a measure of the degree of difficulty experienced, is rather uncommon in the literature.[28] Atypical as well is the treatment of bargaining delay as a cost rather than a benefit to regulatory targets. Prior research, however, generally does support the notion that regulatory targets anticipate the impact of policy application on agency missions and calculate the costs and benefits associated with compliance or noncompliance strategies. What the EPA/TVA cases illustrate is that one primary, and hitherto less appreciated, intervening variable in that calculus is the degree to which the delay inherent in noncompliance strategies threatens the abilities of targets to realize program missions. Indeed, given its apparent centrality in the resolution of these controversies, this variable could constitute a "missing link" for advancing a truly predictive theory of regulatory policy implementation if found to be prominent in future studies. To demonstrate how pervasive and powerful the noncompliance delay effect can be, an analysis of its impact on the conventional wisdom should be made. The analysis focuses on three prominent concepts of the literature: extent of behavioral change required, complexity of joint action, and sociopolitical environment.

Behavioral Change   Policy analysts have identified several organizational factors — and the extent to which a policy requires changes thereof — as powerful conditioners of regulatory policy implementation. Collectively, these factors fall within the rubric of what organization theorists term the "institutional mission" or "goal" of an agency.[29] This concept refers to an organization's dominant official philosophy or administrative ideology and is directly associated with its maintenance and survival needs. It is identifiable in an agency's technical programs, procedures, and decision premises, and it represents the view held by the organization's dominant group about agency capabilities and ends. The implementation literature suggests that the greater the anticipated extent of behavioral change required by a policy with regard to bureaucratic routines, agency expenditures, or policy-making autonomy, the greater the likelihood of long-term delay.[30] Put differently, the more a target agency's mission is inconsistent with, alien to, or hostile toward a policy, the greater the amount of behavioral change required and, consequently, the more likely implementation will be difficult.

The EPA/TVA cases, however, illustrate how knowing the degree of behavioral change required by a policy is insufficient for predicting target agency compliance or noncompliance. In both the SO_2 and thermal controversies, successful implementation involved substantial changes in TVA's preferred pollution control routines and expenditures and severe impacts on the agency's decision-making autonomy. Nonetheless, TVA's responses in the two cases differed drastically. It appears instead that implementation difficulties can be anticipated more accurately if the interaction patterns of those factors making up the "noncompliance delay effect" are known.

In the thermal pollution case, EPA sought to apply a policy that, if not expeditiously complied with, would have directly threatened TVA's power program mission. Clearly, the central mission of this program was to meet whatever demands for power generation TVA consumers placed upon it. In phasing out its older coal plants, by failing to order more of the same during the 1970s, and by intending to generate over half of its electricity with nuclear plants by 1985, TVA made its mission a hostage to the vagaries of bringing nuclear plants into operation according to agency timetables. Agency officials thus perceived thermal regulations as directly imperiling TVA's mission if TVA did not comply with them expeditiously. Failure to comply promptly, or to have the standards amended in time to construct pollution control facilities acceptable to federal regulators, was expected to result in power shortfalls throughout the Southeast. Fearing the delay that regulatory challenges would bring, TVA complied with EPA's standards in relatively short order.

In contrast, SO_2 regulations were not perceived initially as threatening TVA's mission. Agency officials anticipated that coal plants would play a significantly less critical role in power production as the decade proceeded. SO_2 standards thus affected a power source viewed only as the bridge to an increasingly nuclear-powered future, one wherein SO_2 regulations would become progressively less relevant to SO_2 operations as the oldest, most polluting coal plants were phased out and nuclear plants came on line. This expectation — combined with EPA's well-known aversion to closing TVA plants and the possibility for relaxed EPA enforcement with changing national priorities and agency leadership — made noncompliance an eminently rational and affordable strategy that posed no threat to TVA's power production mission until the late 1970s.

Complexity of Joint Action   A second factor said to condition implementation is the complexity of joint action involved.[31] This concept typically refers to the number of actors, in addition to the principals, whose explicit or implicit agreement must be secured before a policy can be successfully implemented. Some have referred to these actors as "veto points." Delay is reputedly the price of obtaining such agreement and is portrayed as a function of the number of decision points, the number of participants at each point, and the direction and intensity of their preferences.[32] The conventional wisdom thus suggests that the more decision points and participants there are, and the greater the number of interdependent decisions required, the longer implementation delay.[33]

Analyzed from the perspective of regulatory targets, the EPA/TVA cases provide an expanded view of the power of veto points. When analyzing the implementation process in the regulatory arena, one must look at more than the number of actors and the direction and intensity of their attitudes. Equally important is the potential impact of the delay posed by the intervention of their number and kind on the mission of regulatory targets. This may have a significantly greater effect on compliance, an effect that allows the complexity of joint action to facilitate, rather than frustrate, regulatory policy implementation.

Those studying implementation have tended to view the complexity of joint action from the perspective of those effecting policy and, consequently, have tended to view extended bargaining delay as beneficial to regulatory targets. Delay, as well as the less stringent controls adhered to during noncompliance, is expected to result in lower target costs.[34] This focus on implementors has led, however, to a failure to appreciate the problems veto point delay can pose for regulatory targets. As noted, TVA's ability to sustain delay and still realize its mission varied dramatically between the disputes. In the SO_2 affair, TVA welcomed the existence of, and deftly used, external veto points. It did so because the delays that the veto points could occasion in no way threatened TVA's ability to produce sufficient quantities of electricity. In contrast, during the thermal episode TVA officials feared the impact that veto points might have on timely electricity production. The involvement of the AEC, the courts, and private interest groups — though possibly supportive — meant delay that could seriously jeopardize TVA's power production goals. The EPA/TVA cases thus demonstrate how the complexity of joint action and the noncompliance delay effect can interact to structure regulatory policy implementation. The more a regulatory target views the delays inherent in the complexity of joint action as detrimental to its mission, the less likely prolonged implementation difficulty will occur.

Sociopolitical Environment   A third prominent theme of the literature involves the sociopolitical environment of implementation. Legislation is the product of conditions and coalitions at a single point in time, but implementation must occur over time. Consequently, it is acutely vulnerable to shifting public concerns, policy attitudes, and political agenda that can render implementation unpopular and extremely difficult.[35] These shifts benefit recalcitrant targets by activating equally disaffected, politically powerful actors whose efforts may compromise enforcement zeal, produce policy alterations, or result in outright statutory repeal. Some researchers even suggest that targets actively mobilize those who share a stake — material or ideological — in frustrating implementation through executive, legislative, or judicial appeals.[36] It frequently is posited that the more inconsistent a policy's goal is with the priorities of the current political agenda, the more likely that allies willing to challenge implementation will be abundant for mobilization. Consequently, it is less likely that such a policy can be effected without long-term delay.

Though useful as an explanation for prior compliance behavior, this conventional wisdom has unimpressive predictive power. As the EPA/TVA cases illustrate, knowing that an inhospitable political climate exists and recognizing that allies spawned by that climate are available and readily mobilizable tells little about the compliance strategies of a prospective target. In both the SO_2 and thermal cases such conditions existed, yet TVA's behavior in each was drastically different. During the thermal controversy, the agency complied in relatively short order despite the emerging antiregulation, proenergy production agenda of the country. Indeed, TVA spiritedly discouraged the intervention of those sympathetic to its noncompliance cause during the AEC licensing process.

In contrast, the agency pursued a determined, relentless strategy of noncompliance during the SO_2 dispute while it patiently awaited the denouement of implementation challenges mounted by the Department of Commerce, the FPC, and the FEA as the political agenda shifted from environmental to energy concerns. What is more, TVA's tireless public relations campaign to promote intermittent control strategies and SDEL was specifically designed to activate such allies and thereby expand the scope of implementation conflict. TVA's disparate behavior in the two cases again is best accounted for by the noncompliance delay effect. Unlike the SO_2 controversy, TVA feared that mobilizing allies might delay the issuance of critically needed operating licenses for its nuclear plants and thus compromise TVA's ability to meet the power needs of Valley consumers.

An amplification of the implementation themes associated with the sociopolitical environment thus seems warranted. The more inconsistent a policy is with the priorities of the current political agenda, and the less mission threatening regulatory targets perceive noncompliance delay to be, the greater the degree of implementation difficulty. Targets are more likely to view the intervention of sympathetic allies as beneficial when the delay their participation occasions is perceived as nonthreatening to agency responsibilities or goals.

CONCLUSIONS

Three primary conclusions can be drawn from analysis of the EPA/TVA pollution control experiences. First, regulation in the intragovernmental arena is driven by many of the same factors found to affect implementation in other regulatory contexts. Second, more analytic attention should be given to the role of time in the compliance decision calculi of regulatory targets, with special concentration on the "noncompliance delay effect" as a major intervening variable in the regulatory enforcement process. Third, additional research — viewing implementation from the perspective of regulatory targets and using a variety of research designs — appears useful and necessary for the development of policy implementation theory in the regulatory arena.

What is most interesting about the EPA/TVA cases from a theoretical perspective is the emergence of the noncompliance delay effect as a pervasive, even overriding, influence on implementation in both experiences. Indeed, it appears as though many of the most widely recognized determinants of implementation success or failure can be affected themselves by the degree to which targets perceive the delays inherent in their noncompliance behavior as mission threatening. Hence, sensitivity to the noncompliance delay effect can provide a better appreciation for the relationships among policy, target agency mission, and implementation difficulty.

Traditionally, implementation has been portrayed as growing more problematic as policies more drastically disturb the political economies of regulatory targets, involve substantial numbers of potential veto points, and are applied in hostile sociopolitical environments. The noncompliance delay effect clarifies the conditions under which the all-too-familiar exceptions to these expectations arise. Implementation actually appears less difficult not only when target missions are less threatened, complexity of joint action is less pronounced, and political agendas are more supportive, but also when the opposites of these are true yet challenge must be eschewed because of the mission-threatening effects of delay.

Certainly extreme caution is warranted before generalizing from the findings of one comparative case study to the universe of regulatory policy implementation experiences. It is hoped, therefore, that the validity of the noncompliance delay effect, as well as the modified propositions derived therefrom, will be tested in different implementation contexts and with a variety of research designs emphasizing the perspective of regulatory targets. Given the intragovernmental focus of this study, research designs investigating regulatory policy enforcement in the intergovernmental and private sector arenas seem appropriate. Equally promising are designs that compare and contrast the responses of the same regulatory target to enforcement efforts across regulating agencies or policy types. Finally, the implementation efforts of a single agency from the perspectives of different regulatory targets might prove useful as well. It appears that decidedly uniform designs thus far have characterized implementation research in the regulatory arena, and that these probably are responsible for our tendency to overlook the dynamics reported in this study. Thus, though fostering a seemingly ambitious agenda, the scope and content of the research designs suggested seem necessary for the emergence of a truly predictive theory of regulation.

CHAPTER EIGHT

The Regulatory Dilemma Revisited

IMPLICATIONS AND PROSPECTS
FOR THE ADMINISTRATIVE STATE

JUDGE WISEMAN: I understand, but Mr. Ayres, you purport to represent the public?

MR. AYRES: Certainly that is true.

JUDGE WISEMAN: And the EPA purports to represent the public?

MR. AYRES: Yes, sir.

JUDGE WISEMAN: And the Department of Justice represents the public, and TVA is a public agency. The Tennessee Cooperative Association represents the public users of power in the Tennessee Valley. All of you tell me where the real adversity is. It is citizen against citizen here, and they are the same people. That is why I am saying this is not a normal type of adversarial relationship.

MR. AYRES: You are certainly correct that each of the parties purports to represent the public. I don't think that is particularly important. The point is that each of them had a different perception of what the public interest is.

JUDGE WISEMAN: Yes, sir. And I suppose it is my responsibility to try to resolve those.[1]

The second set of research questions posed at the beginning of this study concerned the implications of intragovernmental regulation for the administrative state, its agents, and the public interest. This concluding chapter probes the EPA/TVA cases to see what they reveal about such issues. There is a paucity of research on regulation in the intragovernmental arena, and the following discussion is offered in the hope that it might stimulate interest in, and systematic analyses of, the topics addressed.

IMPLICATIONS FOR REGULATORS

The EPA/TVA cases clearly support the conventional wisdom that regulators should not expect sister agencies to be more compliant or less formidable enforcement targets than their counterparts in the private sector. What is more, they advise those supportive of, as well as those effecting, the new social regulation in the intragovernmental arena to apply adequate resources to the task. The counsel of an internal TVA memorandum issued in the early 1970s indicates both the resistance to be expected and the budgetary and personnel "arsenal" regulators will need if they are to counter such efforts effectively:

> Skillful manipulation of this [administrative] process to achieve what TVA regards as a reasonable implementation of the law requires that necessary personnel and other resources be made available on a priority basis to prepare technical and economic studies, develop evidence, plan alternative compliance strategies, prepare and present testimony at hearings, and prepare permit applications and suggested permit terms and conditions which satisfy the requirements of both the law and TVA.[2]

In short, regulatory agencies must be funded adequately and manned with professional expertise capable of marshaling evidence and patiently articulating agency claims of "regulatory reasonableness" in a variety of legislative, executive, and judicial forums throughout our federal system.

Building and maintaining capacity, however, are necessary but hardly sufficient conditions for regulatory success in the intragovernmental context. Because federal targets may try to invoke the authority and immunity of the state in their cause, regulatory success can depend upon the ability to adroitly manage the support of elected, appointed, and judicial sovereigns. For example, during the SO$_2$ dispute TVA, well aware that "the best point at which to manage conflict is before it starts,"[3] asserted its privileged status as an agency traditionally exempted from intragovernmental regulation. Failing in that, agency officials sought to manage the conflict by involving parties — local and state officials — that had traditionally supported the agency. Throughout the 1970s, the arena of conflict continued to shift at an accelerating speed among interagency negotiations, state regulatory boards, state and federal courts, state and federal legislatures, and within offices in the White House itself — to the growing attention and scrutiny of the press. By 1978, the contagiousness of the conflict made an interagency dispute over regulation a political conflict of the first magnitude, such that the decisive, if subtle, intervention of the national chief executive was necessary to aid enforcement.[4]

Clearly, enforcement can be aided immensely by a president positively disposed toward regulatory goals, one who will attempt to facilitate intragovernmental efforts directly and/or indirectly. A clearcut example of this is the direct intervention of President Carter via telephone to Lieutenant Governor John Wilder of Tennessee, requesting him to desist from continued challenges of the air pollution consent decree. Similarly helpful were Carter's assurances (issued through the Justice Department) that, contrary to the statements of the COWPS, his administration fully supported the negotiated EPA/TVA agreement. President Carter demonstrated, as well, the power of indirect presidential interventions. Using his appointment power, State of the Union messages, executive orders, and public statements regarding TVA, Carter created an enforcement context more conducive to successful regulation. For example, most officials who were interviewed acknowledged how important Carter's appointments of strategic actors at EPA, TVA, and the Justice Department were in resolving the SO_2 dispute in EPA's favor. They also conceded his deftness in creating a "climate of compliance expectations" around TVA. Most noteworthy in this regard were his executive orders exhorting all federal facilities to conform immediately with environmental protection laws and his speeches proclaiming TVA's revamped energy and environmental yardstick role. What is more, Carter did all this without jeopardizing the scarce political "capital" typically at risk when presidents become involved in controversial policy issues.

This is not to suggest that regulatory agencies should overestimate the propensity for presidential intervention and thereby underestimate the difficulty of intragovernmental regulation. No guarantee exists that they will receive the support — direct or indirect — of any given president. Clearly, the relationship between the *time* that the SO_2 dispute reached its climax and the nature of its resolution illustrates this. Had the critical points in the dispute occurred somewhat later, during the Reagan administration (with Howard Baker as the majority leader of a Republican-controlled Senate), the balance of forces might well have shifted in favor of TVA's position of noncompliance. Regulators thus must be prepared at all times to spar aggressively with regulatory targets for presidential favor and succor. Equally uncertain is whether a president sympathetic to a regulatory cause will even have an opportunity to make friendly appointments in non-complying agencies, be able to pay sustained attention to enforcement problems, or be disposed to risking precious political capital on federal family squabbles. Consequently, when enmeshed in intragovernmental conflicts, regulators must be prepared to counter aggressively — without presidential support — efforts by sister agencies to mobilize legislative and judicial support for their antiregulation cause.

Certainly all is not lost for regulators when appeals to Congress or the courts are made. Indeed, as the EPA/TVA cases indicate, congressional and judicial actors often must, and do, expedite intragovernmental regulation through statutory clarifications. For example, when ambiguities concerning federal facility compliance threatened to stall the application of SO_2 regulations to TVA coal plants, Congress used the CAA of 1977 to specify its intentions in ways favorable to EPA's interpretation of the law. Moreover, it took action at the prodding of the Supreme Court. Equally illustrative of the supportive role these institutions can play were: (1) Congress' rejection of Senator Baker's attempt to "grandfather" TVA plants; (2) the fifth circuit's decision to disallow TVA's challenge of the EPA administrator's discretionary authority with regard to control technology; (3) Senator Muskie's role as implementation "fixer" during confirmation and budget hearings; and (4) the statutory precision provided by the FWPCA in regard to federal facility compliance. But the SO_2 and thermal cases also illustrate that support from these institutions should be seen by regulators as no less precarious nor episodic than that of the president. Witness, for example, the off-setting federal facility compliance rulings delivered by the fifth and sixth circuits during the SO_2 controversy. Moreover, regulators are ill advised to take solace even when supportive actions are taken; these often afford necessary but hardly sufficient conditions for compliance, given the ever-present hope of statutory amendment or successful judicial appeal.

With support for their efforts so capricious, challenges to their interpretations of ambiguous statutes so likely, and the constitutionality of suing sister agencies so clouded, do other enforcement resources exist for intragovernmental regulators to draw upon? The EPA/TVA cases strongly suggest that a most potent weapon in this arena is an aroused, determined, and litigious public. Though hardly guaranteeing compliance in either the SO_2 or thermal disputes, actual or potential public involvement in both cases was critical to their resolution. The section 304 citizen suit in the former and the likelihood of citizen intervention and court suits related to the AEC licensing process in the latter seriously delimited TVA's compliance options. Once citizens took advantage of the legal standing afforded them by the CAA, the agency no longer could rely on the "quiet policy" of not suing sister agencies espoused by EPA and the Justice Department, nor on the constitutional questions concerning such actions, to stymie civil suits. Similarly, the heretofore nonthreatening regulatory posture of the AEC took on new meaning for TVA after *Calvert Cliffs* and NEPA combined to increase both the legal liability of the commission and the probability that citizen actions would challenge licensing decisions.

Unfortunately for regulators, effective, sustained public support is never guaranteed. Consequently, they must be prepared to court public opinion with the same intensity they display when marshaling executive, legislative, or judicial support for their cause. Three useful strategies for doing so can be culled from the EPA/TVA cases: (1) use adverse publicity to alert regulatory constituencies to violations, (2) actively encourage citizen actions consonant with regulatory goals, and (3) diligently provide technical expertise to those activated. Using the media to alert citizens to health and safety hazards has long been recognized as a legitimate regulatory tool; the use of adverse publicity is a well-known, effective star in the constellation of enforcement resources available to regulators when dealing with intransigent targets. EPA Region IV officials repeatedly used the media to headline TVA's intransigence by funneling news items about TVA's pollution problems to newsmen and making appearances at the TEC Regional Symposium heralding TVA's environmental woes. EPA also provided the citizen groups with emotional and technical support.[5] Not only did both Washington and Region IV officials contact them to welcome their legal intervention and to encourage their pursuits, they also placed EPA's consulting firm, PEDCO, at the litigants' disposal. Citizen group leaders readily acknowledged that their success might not have been possible without EPA's timely and unflagging assistance.

Paul Weaver has argued that an alliance of regulators, public interest groups, and the media will come to dominate the politics of the new social regulation. This "rubber triangle" of proregulation interests is expected to thwart any tendency toward agency capture by the antiregulation forces of the "iron triangle." The EPA/TVA cases, as well as the unenthusiastic regulatory efforts of the Reagan administration, cause one to be less sanguine about the inevitability of such a prospect. Still, it is clear that the strategy of public and media arousal and support employed by EPA is available and effective. Indeed, as the cases illustrate, such a strategy can be determinative in the intragovernmental arena — especially when the delays posed by such actions can jeopardize the perceived mission of a regulatory target. And when supplemented by staunch congressional, executive, and judicial support, the strategy can make intragovernmental regulation much more manageable than commonly portrayed.

IMPLICATIONS FOR REGULATED AGENCIES

Matthew Holden defines the constituency of an agency as "any group, body, or interest to which [an administrator] looks for guidance, or which seeks to establish itself as so important that he 'had better' take account of its preferences even if . . . averse to [them]."[6] As TVA celebrated its fiftieth anniversary, key decisions involving its power program combined with dramatic changes in its regulatory environment to expand the agency's constituency, cause an attitudinal reorientation in its traditional grass-roots clientele, and profoundly erode its policy-making autonomy. The strategy of "rational participation" in the administrative process advocated and pursued by the TVA legal staff in the early 1970s seems today woefully inadequate to the regulatory challenges of the 1980s and beyond. TVA officials now must cope additionally and simultaneously with an aroused multiple clientele, a less deferential and more vocal grass-roots constituency, and a formidable effort to publicly scrutinize its administration.

TVA's regulatory predicament illustrates what Francis Rourke has termed "repoliticized administration": the national trend toward delimiting bureaucratic autonomy through heightened public control of the administrative state. As such, it seems useful to chronicle the impact of, and TVA's responses to, the enhanced boundary permeability that intragovernmental regulation has wrought for the agency. Doing this allows guarded speculation as to the implications of, and prescriptions for coping with, intragovernmental regulation and the repoliticized administration it can spawn for regulatory targets in general.

TVA, Multiple Clients, and Grass-Roots Democracy   The composition of TVA's attentive public, and consequently its power program politics, has indeed been substantially altered by intragovernmental regulation. No longer dominated by those espousing a production ethic — with power production at the lowest possible cost as their animating spirit — TVA's constituency today also includes those interests concerned with environmental protection. The latter view the TVA yardstick function in a new light: the agency should become a national beacon demonstrating how environmental and energy production values can best be reconciled. And their preferred course of action is the internalization of the "true" social costs of energy production (e.g., environmental and replacement costs) in TVA electricity rates. Such a policy is, of course, foreign to TVA's traditional constituencies, who presume that higher rates dampen regional economic growth. Thus, the agency's task for the foreseeable future is to accommodate the sometimes incompatible policy preferences of its newfound and heterogeneous clientele.

As the SO_2 and thermal pollution cases clearly demonstrate, TVA can no longer confidently "announce," and routinely expect adoption of, power program or pollution control policies. The agency now has to weigh the preferences of state and federal regulators, Valley residents, power distributors, and national public interest groups. What is more, the opinions of these actors can carry the weight of law when exercised pursuant to the CAA, FWPCA, AEA, and NEPA. Considering the prolonged, costly, and even mission-threatening legal remedies available to the disgruntled, TVA today ignores these preferences at its own peril. Indeed, as the thermal dispute illustrates, the agency even has to fear the use of these remedies by those sympathetic to its causes! Gone, too, is the era of benign congressional oversight of TVA operations. As the agency's electricity rates soared, as substantial cost overruns developed at its nuclear plants, and as its power demand projections became suspect, congressional scrutiny intensified. TVA's budget requests were scrupulously reviewed in the 1970s, and Congress initiated the first comprehensive TVA oversight hearings since the late 1930s.[7] Given the probability of future rate increases and sustained attention to energy and environmental concerns, congressional interest in agency affairs will likely continue.

Most unlikely to continue is the level of agency support historically tendered to TVA by its grass-roots, production-oriented constituency. Although Martha Derthick could write in the early 1970s that TVA was able to keep "enough control over its local partners to make sure that programmatic goals [were] thoroughly protected" and their discretion limited, the SO_2 controversy revealed a decidedly less deferential distributor clientele.[8] Excoriated for their complicity in spiraling utility rates,[9] feeling excluded from TVA policy deliberations, and viewing the consent decree implementation committee as the precursor of an "institutionalized" policy role for utility critics, distributors revolted in the late 1970s.[10]

Repoliticized Administration: For Better or Worse?   Some welcome repoliticization, but others are more anxious, fearing its consequences for professional efficiency and organizational effectiveness.[11] During the 1970s TVA's response to this development reflected each of these positions at different times. This is best seen by examining the strikingly different views on regulation and public participation held by the two men who served as board chairman during the decade: Aubrey J. Wagner and S. David Freeman.

The attitudes toward regulation held by Wagner and Freeman stemmed largely from their perspectives on how TVA best serves the public interest.[12] Both believed TVA was "more than just another power company": as a quasi-public corporation, it was the holder of a public trust and the legatee of the yardstick philosophy. For Freeman this meant that TVA was "not above the law," that it was in the agency's "interest and [that] of the people . . . to carry out the congressional mandate [of environment laws]." Freeman, for example, saw TVA's acceptance of the air pollution consent decree as "the agency performing its yardstick role as it should." Not only was TVA demonstrating how to reconcile energy and environmental protection values, it was also removing the agency's noncompliance as a justification for private utility violations. In contrast, Wagner saw TVA's obligation to the public interest as compelling the agency to challenge the enforcement of "unwise" environmental regulations. Precisely because TVA is a federal entity and because its compliance is used to bring pressure on private utilities, the agency had, in Wagner's view, a responsibility to fight the implementation of "ill-advised, very costly" regulations. What is more, Wagner felt the enforcement of these laws represented "other agency interference" in the TVA policy-making process. For Wagner, EPA's insistence on massive capital investments to meet SO_2 standards interfered in the agency's plans to phase out its older coal plants.

Similarly, the approaches of the chairmen to citizen participation in TVA policy making were largely the product of two very different conceptualizations of service delivery. Wagner's was more akin to the professional-technocratic model of the process: service delivery "as decidedly unidirectional, an active bureaucracy providing services to a consuming, but largely inert, citizenry."[13] Associated with TVA since the 1930s, Wagner had participated in, was comfortable with, and highly valued the agency's very successful stewardship approach to resource development. Importantly, this was an approach that most often afforded little opportunity for participation by nonpolitical and nonprofessional Valley residents: "I feel citizens ought to have an input, [and they do], through elected officials and the [power] distributors." His philosophy thus was reminiscent of the early administrative reform movement — valued above all else in policy making was professional expertise. Accepting a consent decree that provided for a citizen implementation committee challenged everything Wagner had learned about administration in over forty years as a highly valued and nationally respected TVA public manager.

Freeman, in contrast, espoused a more participatory philosophy of service delivery. Before his replacement as chairman he instituted telephone hot-lines and research surveys to spur citizen feedback. In addition, he held board meetings throughout the TVA service area and ultimately agreed to establish the citizen implementation committee so unpalatable to Wagner. In the process, Freeman seemed to be taking the first tentative steps toward a coproduction model of service delivery.

Toward a Coproduction Ethic for Regulatory Targets?   The coproduction model of service delivery envisions coequal participation of a bureaucracy and its constituency as essential for effective provision of public services.[14] In contrast to the professional-technocratic model, coproduction demands the interaction of service provider and citizen recipient in defining the content, scope, and ends of agency policy. This interaction process has three critical elements: citizen requests for agency service, citizen provision of assistance and cooperation to the service provider, and mutual adjustment between citizen and agency. Operationalized administratively, these elements require "passive" vehicles for citizen participation (surveys, public hearings, advisory boards) and more "active" mechanisms for mutual problem definition, policy development, and program execution. Proponents see virtue in the model's ability to help reconcile the values, norms, and expectations of the professional bureaucracy with those held by the public. Coproduction, they suggest, seeks to accommodate the bureaucratic imperatives of professionalism, economy, and efficiency with the political imperatives of bureaucratic responsiveness and accountability.

It is unclear if TVA's — or any other regulatory target's — management or legislative sovereigns could ever feel comfortable with a full-scale coproduction program. Although not requiring the relinquishment of professional values, legal authority, or agency accountability, coproduction would entail some sharing of agency authority, responsibility, and perhaps even accountability with constituencies. Still, a case can be made for the inculcation of a coproduction ethic in public managers of the TVA ilk, one geared to the regulatory concerns of the 1980s and beyond. Faced anyway with de facto coproduction from those disgruntled with agency policies and having access to judicial and administrative remedies, regulatory targets institutionalizing the coproduction process would appear to be acting in their own self-interest. Efforts to structure timely, meaningful constituency involvement could avert costly, even mission-threatening legal battles with those excluded from policy deliberations.

But what would the development of a coproduction ethic entail, and how likely are regulatory targets like TVA to adopt such a philosophy in the 1980s? Operationalized by a proactive management style, a coproduction ethic would require public managers to: become catalysts for client participation in agency policy making; institutionalize consensual decision-making processes involving these clients; codevelop expertise-based solutions for mutually defined problems; and encourage a sense of shared client-agency responsibility for the policies adopted.[15] One cannot overestimate the difficulties of adopting and implementing such an administrative style; the problems associated with altering institutional cultures are widely heralded and well founded. What is more, since coproduction cannot eliminate the principled and legitimate policy differences of multiple clienteles, disillusionment with the process by those suffering policy disappointments might undermine its goals. Still, certain factors exist that are conducive to its adoption by regulatees. Most compelling are the need to obtain public cooperation with programs if they are to succeed (e.g., energy conservation) and the urgency to respond to persistent calls for involvement by constituencies flushed with judicial success when slighted in the past. Thus, the development of a coproduction service ethic might yet become a very attractive, cost-effective administrative strategy for targets of intragovernmental regulation in the 1980s.

What do the EPA/TVA cases indicate about the implications of the regulatory dilemma for the public interest? Two primary conclusions can be drawn. First, as a form of bureaucratic oversight such regulation is a promising supplement to traditional overhead democracy techniques. Second, challenges raised by public agencies to regulatory enforcement may not be as inappropriate, insurmountable, or dysfunctional as commonly assumed.

Toward Comprehensive Bureaucratic Oversight?   James Madison wrote that to thwart tyranny the components of government should be pitted against each other: "Ambition must be made to counteract ambition."[16] It was the tyranny of the congressional majority that most animated popular concerns in Madison's time — a tyranny thought principally diffused by the internal check of bicameralism.[17] It is the tyranny of the expert, unelected bureaucracy that most fires contemporary imaginations. But as Garry Wills has noted, Madison's scheme offers no comparable internal check for the executive branch. In enacting social regulatory policies that require federal agencies to hold others accountable to the law, however, Congress has "pitted the ambitions" of these bureaucracies against each other in true Madisonian fashion. In the process, as the EPA/TVA experience suggests, it has created a noteworthy supplement to legislative oversight.

According to Rourke, agencies that perform the regulatory role just described function as adversary bureaucracies overseeing particular aspects of federal family activities. That is, they seek to "bring the decisions and actions of other federal agencies under greater scrutiny and to deter them from malpractice" with regard to specific policy concerns.[18] As the EPA/TVA disputes illustrate, however, "bureaucratic oversight" can be fraught with frustration, demoralization, and embarrassment given the internecine conflict it can engender. Yet to focus exclusively on these problems is to risk overlooking the positive aspects of the process, aspects afforded even in a situation as trying as the SO_2 controversy.

As Schattschneider insightfully recognized, the breadth of the scope of conflict accompanying a policy issue profoundly defines the nature of the ultimate resolution of that issue: "The *audience* determines the outcome of the fight," with the public interest best served as the scope expands.[19] As the EPA/TVA controversies demonstrate, intragovernmental regulation can broaden substantially the scope of interagency conflict to accommodate the scrutiny and values of private citizens, state and local government officials, members of the agencies' respective subsystems, and even the president and his emissaries. From the lessons of these cases, one begins again to appreciate the logic, need, and workability of a system that does not rely exclusively upon internal checks as a control of governmental behavior. The history of the external effort to bring the TVA into compliance with the letter and the spirit of the CAA and the FWPCA — *as those outside the TVA envisioned that law* — provides an apt illustration of how agencies purposely set at odds with one another can generate the sort of contagious conflict from which some approximation of a public interest can emerge.

The disputes also suggest that the degree of bureaucratic oversight that intragovernmental regulation prompts is more comprehensive and reciprocal than previously appreciated. Most researchers addressing the topic imply that scrutiny is limited to compliance with the regulatory policy in question and to the activities of the regulated agency. But because policies involving social regulation typically affect a broad range of target agency operations, all facets of agency activities can become fair game for investigation. This scrutiny, in turn, can arouse the interests of elected sovereigns and become a tripwire for full-scale oversight proceedings. Indeed, TVA repeatedly had to joust publicly with critics in defense of nonenvironmental topics related to its rate structure, bonded indebtedness, and nuclear power program. Similarly, TVA's critiques of EPA's interpretation and application of environmental laws aroused the sustained attention of public and private sector actors alike.

Given its episodic nature and uneven application, legislative oversight is often criticized as inadequate. Because the congressional and political rewards for oversight are normally so fleeting, the maze of agency activities so impenetrable, and the resources of legislators so limited, some say oversight of the executive branch has a low priority on Capitol Hill. Conversely, it is also contended that when informal means of oversight — such as constituency case work

—are considered, the process is more continuous and pervasive than usually assumed.[20] Certainly, the EPA/TVA disputes do not resolve this issue. They do suggest, however, that the broadened scope of conflict that intragovernmental regulation can engender may bring a breadth of interest and value representation to the policy process that is seldom provided by traditional legislative oversight. Consequently, though it is no less episodic nor evenly applied, bureaucratic oversight might prove to be a valuable asset to overhead democracy.

Servant of the Public Interest?   The behavior displayed by TVA during the SO_2 dispute—protracted, uncompromising, and relentless noncompliance with the CAA—usually is depicted as contrary to the interests of the commonweal. Some analysts legitimately question how government can expect compliance from the private sector if members of the federal establishment flout regulations.[21] Others use examples of federal defiance by agencies such as TVA to warn us about the perils of an expanding public sector.[22] The EPA/TVA experiences, however, prompt one to ask if the public interest is not also served by regulatory challenges.

Whether principled or obstructionist in nature, challenges to intragovernmental regulation can do several things. First, the challenges of federal agencies—because they are so controversial and noteworthy—can bring the sustained attention of elected officials to bear on the unanticipated consequences of public policies. Secondly, challenges can provide elected, not just appointed, officials and an aroused public an opportunity to adjust, and perhaps even reconcile, conflicting policy goals in the light of implementation experience. Finally, since no one bureaucracy has a monopoly on virtue or wisdom, challenges can correct any technical, legal, or judgemental errors made by implementors in applying policies to target populations.

In summary, the travails spawned by intragovernmental regulation appear less insurmountable and dysfunctional than popularly assumed. Clearly, federal government activities and public regulation are not incompatible; adversary bureaucracies can hold other public agencies accountable to the law. What is more, doing this furnishes the advantages, noted by Schattschneider, of broadened scopes of conflict with multiple arenas for pursuit of the common good by interested parties and the public. Those who are disadvantaged or abused in one arena can shift to another where their influence may be heightened and their arguments sustained. Intragovernmental regulation, and the "preemptive creative redundance" it introduces to the policy process, provides opportunities to temper if not remedy the unintended and unwanted consequences that occur when disparate public policies interact.[23] In a political system prone to polycentric problems as complex, little understood, and costly to resolve as our own, agency challenges to the implementation of particular policies are probably unavoidable.[24] And given a legislative process ill suited to a priori consideration of policy interaction, they are sometimes essential.

Notes

PREFACE

1. Keith Hawkins, *Environment and Enforcement: Regulation and the Social Definition of Pollution* (Oxford: Clarendon Press, 1984).
2. Because a guarantee of anonymity was offered to all and was accepted by several of those interviewed, some of the quotations, comments, and insights in the text are not attributed to individuals. The bibliography lists those who waived anonymity.

NOTES FOR CHAPTER 1

1. Norton E. Long, "Bureaucracy and Constitutionalism," *American Political Science Review* 46 (Sept. 1952): 808.
2. Lawrence C. Dodd and Richard L. Schott, *Congress and the Administrative State* (New York: Wiley, 1979).
3. Francis E. Rourke, *Bureaucracy, Politics, and Public Policy*, 2d ed. (Boston: Little, Brown, 1976), 177.
4. James Q. Wilson, "The Bureaucracy Problem," *Public Interest* 6 (Winter 1967): 4.
5. E.E. Schattschneider, *The Semisovereign People* (Hinsdale, Ill.: Dryden Press, 1960), 69.
6. Charles Schultz, *The Public Use of Private Interest* (Washington, D.C.: Brookings Institute, 1977).
7. Charles Frankel, *The Democratic Prospect* (New York: Harper & Row, 1962), 8.
8. Anthony Downs, "Up and Down with Ecology—The Issue-Attention Cycle," *Public Interest* 28 (Summer 1972): 38-50; Samuel P. Huntington, "The Marasmus of the ICC: The Commission, the Railroads, and the Public Interest," *Yale Law Journal* 61 (Apr. 1952): 467-509; James Q. Wilson, "The Dead Hand of Regulation," *Public Interest* 25 (Fall 1971): 39-58; Gabriel Kolko, *Railroads and Regulation, 1877-1916* (Princeton: Princeton Univ. Press, 1965).

9. William Lilly and James C. Miller, "The New Social Regulation," *Public Interest* 47 (Spring 1977): 28–36.

10. Paul H. Weaver, "Regulation, Social Policy, and Class Conflict," *Public Interest* 50 (Winter 1978): 45–63.

11. Richard B. Stewart, "The Reformation of American Administrative Law," *Harvard Law Review* 88 (June 1975): 1811.

12. Francis E. Rourke, "Bureaucratic Autonomy and the Public Interest," *American Behavioral Scientist* 22 (May/June 1979): 543. It should be noted that Rourke is concerned about this development, fearing that the professional efficiency and responsiveness to the traditional clientele of a public agency may suffer.

13. Internal TVA memorandum, 10 Aug. 1973.

14. Certainly there is overlap in these three administrative eras. For example, TVA has always been a "yardstick" in the Rooseveltian sense of the term given its ability to produce power at rates considerably lower than its private utility cohorts in all three eras. Still, the distinctions offered allow appreciation of shifts in administrative and environmental emphases that occurred during TVA's history.

15. House Doc. 15, 73d Cong., 1st sess. (1933).

16. George E. Rawson, "The Process of Program Development: The Case of TVA's Power Program" (Ph.D. diss., Univ. of Tennessee, Knoxville, 1978), 53.

17. David E. Lilienthal, *TVA: Democracy on the March* (New York: Harper, 1944), 133–36. These allies have been helpful throughout TVA's history, especially during the extensive congressional hearings held from May to December of 1938 in the wake of the Morgan/Lilienthal feud.

18. Rawson, "TVA's Power Program," 50. Court cases include *Ashwander v. Tennessee Valley Authority*, 8 F. Supp. 893 (N.D. Ala. 1934), and *Tennessee Electric Power Co. v. Tennessee Valley Authority*, 21 F. Supp. 947 (E.D. Tenn. 1938).

19. A classic discussion of the Dixon-Yates controversy is presented in Aaron Wildavsky, "TVA and Power Politics," *American Political Science Review* 55 (Sept. 1961): 576–90.

20. The TVA Self-Financing Act of 1959, Pub. L. No. 86–137; "TVA Revenue Bonds," *Congressional Quarterly Almanac* (Washington, D.C.: Congressional Quarterly, 1959), 261.

21. Martha Derthick, "The Tennessee Valley Authority," in *Between State and Nation* (Washington, D.C.: Brookings Institute, 1974), 33. As the text suggests, the term "self-regulation" should not be interpreted as an absolute grant of autonomy to TVA. Avery Leiserson perhaps put it best when he wrote: "TVA's organizational history may be regarded as a shifting balance on a continuum between formal (legal) autonomy and informal (operating) accountability in an unstable environment of political forces and pressures." Avery Leiserson, "Administrative Management and Political Accountability," pp. 126–27 in Erwin C. Hargrove and Paul K. Conkin, eds., *TVA: Fifty Years of Grass-roots Bureaucracy* (Urbana: Univ. of Illinois Press, 1983).

22. Rawson, "TVA's Power Program," 71.

23. Dr. O.M. Derryberry and M.A. Churchill, paper presented at Public Hearing Concerning Proposed Water Quality Criteria for that Portion of the Tennessee River Basin in Alabama, Sheffield, Ala., 12 Dec. 1966, pp. 1–2.

24. Tennessee Valley Authority, *Tennessee Valley Authority Power Annual Report* (Knoxville: TVA, 1970–71).

25. Charles O. Jones, "Speculative Augmentation in Federal Air Pollution Policy-Making," in *Cases in Public Policy-Making*, ed. James E. Anderson (New York: Praeger, 1976); J. Gordon Arbuckle and Timothy A. Vanderver, Jr., "Water Pollution Control," in *Environmental Law Handbook*, ed. J. Gordon Arbuckle et al. (New York: Government Institutes, 1978), 95.

26. See Steven L. Del Sesto, *Science, Politics and Controversy: Civilian Nuclear Power in the United States* (Boulder, Colo.: Westview Press, 1979).

27. The National Environmental Policy Act, Pub. L. No. 91–190 (1970).

28. The Clean Air Act of 1970, Pub. L. No. 91-604 (1970), Section 304; The Federal Water Pollution Control Act of 1972, Pub. L. No. 92-500 (1972), Section 505; The Atomic Energy Act. This is not to say that TVA's regulatory predicament is any more threatening than challenges it has successfully met in the past, including the private power company assault on its very existence in the late 1930s or the Dixon-Yates controversy in the 1950s. As Avery Leiserson suggests, "controversiality has been endemic throughout the board's career" (Leiserson, "Administrative Management," p. 126). What is different, as Steven M. Neuse points out, is that the "costs to TVA of its newer battles . . . with environmental interests have been much dearer." Steven K. Neuse, "TVA at Age Fifty: Reflections and Retrospect," *Public Administration Review* 43 (Nov–Dec 1983): 497. Different as well is the breadth of value and interest representation that the agency must deal with on a regular basis.

29. John H. Shenefield, "Government Enterprises—a New Frontier for Regulatory Reforms," *Regulation* 3 (Nov./Dec. 1979): 18.

30. James Q. Wilson and Patricia Rachal, "Can the Government Regulate Itself?" *Public Interest* 46 (Winter 1977): 3–14.

31. 116 *Congressional Record* 19, 207 (1970).

NOTES FOR CHAPTER 2

1. James Harrington, "The Commonwealth of Oceana," in *Dictionary of Quotations*, ed. Bergen Evans (New York: Avenel, 1978), 378.

2. See Harold Seidman, *Politics, Position, and Power*, 2d ed. (New York: Oxford Univ. Press, 1975); Theodore J. Lowi, *The End of Liberalism* (New York: Norton, 1969); and Ronald Randall, "Presidential Power versus Bureaucratic Intransigence: The Influence of the Nixon Administration on Welfare Policy," *American Political Science Review* 73 (Sept. 1979): 795–810.

3. V.O. Key, Jr., *Public Opinion and American Democracy* (New York: Knopf, 1961), 14.

4. The most significant of these studies were John Esposito, *Vanishing Air* (New York: Grossman, 1970), and David Zwick and Marcy Benstock, *Water Wasteland* (New York: Grossman, 1971).

5. The Air Pollution Control Act of 1955, Pub. L. No. 84-159 (1955). Though originally titled the Air Pollution Control Act, the act is popularly known as the Clean Air Act.

6. The Clean Air Act of 1963, Pub. L. No. 88-206 (1963).

7. The Air Quality Act of 1967, Pub. L. No. 90-148 (1967). Despite its different title, this act actually constituted amendments to the Clean Air Act.

8. Clean Air Amendments of 1970, Pub. L. No. 91-604 (1970). Cited hereafter as CAA of 1970.

9. David P. Currie, "Federal Air Quality Standards and Their Implementation," *American Bar Foundation Research Journal* 2 (1976): 365.

10. Charles O. Jones, "Speculative Augmentation in Federal Air Pollution Policy-Making," in *Cases in Public Policy-Making*, ed. James E. Anderson (New York: Praeger, 1976), 62.

11. U.S. Congress, House, Subcommittee on Public Health and Welfare, Committee on Interstate and Foreign Commerce, *Hearings on Air Pollution Control and Solid Waste Recycling*, 91st Cong., 1st and 2d sess., 1969, 1970, p. 247.

12. Alfred A. Marcus, *Promise and Performance: Choosing and Implementing an Environmental Policy* (Westport, Conn.: Greenwood Press, 1980), 70.

13. Walter A. Rosenbaum, *The Politics of Environmental Concern* (New York: Praeger, 1977), 144.

14. CAA of 1970, sec. 108.

15. Ibid.

16. Ibid., sec. 110.

17. Ibid.

18. Ibid.

19. Ibid.

20. Ibid., sec. 113.

21. Ibid.

22. Ibid.

23. Lettie McSpadden Wenner, *One Environment Under Law* (Pacific Palisades, Cal.: Goodyear Publishing, 1976), 71.

24. The Federal Water Pollution Control Act of 1948, Pub. L. No. 80-845 (1948). Hereafter, this and related acts are cited after first, full reference as FWPCA and year.

25. J. Clarence Davies III and Barbara S. Davies, *The Politics of Pollution*, 2d ed. (Indianapolis: Bobbs-Merrill, 1975), 29.

26. The Federal Water Pollution Control Act Amendments of 1956, Pub. L. No. 84-660 (1956).

27. The Federal Water Pollution Control Act of 1961, Pub. L. No. 87-88 (1961).

28. The Water Quality Act of 1965, Pub. L. No. 89-234 (1965). Despite its different title, this act constituted amendments to the FWPCA.

29. Arbuckle and Vanderver, Jr., "Water Pollution Control," 95.

30. Wenner, *One Environment Under Law*, 85.

31. This provision was intended to prevent preemption of water quality

control by the federal government. It was also Sen. Muskie's intention to end a situation in which no agency had jurisdiction to prevent prospective thermal pollution. See Davies and Davies, *Politics of Pollution*, 36–39, for a more detailed discussion of Muskie's travails.

32. For example, Executive Order 11258, Prevention, Control and Abatement of Water Pollution by Federal Activities, 17 Nov. 1965, and Executive Order 11288, Prevention, Control and Abatement of Water Pollution by Federal Activities, 2 July 1966.

33. Environmental Protection Agency, *The First Two Years: A Review of EPA's Enforcement Program* (Washington, D.C.: Office of Enforcement and General Counsel, Feb. 1973), 8, 68–91.

34. Robert Zener, "The Federal Law of Water Pollution Control," in *Federal Environmental Law*, eds. Edmund Dolgin and Thomas Guilbert (New York: West, 1974), 1002.

35. The Rivers and Harbors Act of 1899, 33 U.S.C. Section 407, 2 *Environmental Law Review* 41142.

36. *United States v. Republic Steel Corp.*, 362 U.S. 482 (1960), and *United States v. Standard Oil Co.*, 384 U.S. 224 (1966).

37. *Kalur v. Resor*, 335 F. Supp. 1, 1 ELR 20637 (D.D.C., 1971).

38. The Federal Water Pollution Control Act of 1972, Pub. L. No. 92–5000 (1972); the quotation is from Davies and Davies, *Politics of Pollution*, 44.

39. FWPCA of 1972, sec. 402. The acronym "NPDES" refers to the National Pollutant Discharge Elimination System created by the act.

40. Ibid., sec. 309.

NOTES FOR CHAPTER 3

1. Key, *Public Opinion*, 14.

2. Murray Edelman, *The Symbolic Uses of Politics* (Urbana: Univ. of Illinois Press, 1964), 141.

3. Keith Casto, "Public Power and Public Interest: An Analysis of the TVA Air Pollution Litigation," *Tennessee Law Review* 49 (Summer 1982): 796.

4. Giandomenico Majone, "Process and Outcome in Regulatory Decision-Making," *American Behavioral Scientist* 22 (May/June 1979): 577.

5. In January and March of 1971 EPA issued proposed national SO_2 primary and secondary ambient air quality standards (36 *Fed. Reg.* 1502 et seq. [1971] and 36 *Fed. Reg.* 5867 [1971]); binding national ambient air quality standards for the pollutant were issued on 30 Apr. 1971 (36 *Fed. Reg.* 8186 et seq. [1971]).

6. 36 *Fed. Reg.* 8186.

7. Ibid.

8. Ibid.

9. Richard J. Tobin, *The Social Gamble* (Lexington: Lexington Books, 1979), 10.

10. CAA of 1970, sec. 110.

11. See Richard E. Ayres, "Enforcement of Air Pollution Controls on Stationary Sources Under the Clean Air Amendments of 1970," *Ecology Law Quarterly* 4 (1975): 453. Constant emission controls are defined as "either a manufacturing process that is inherently low polluting, or a system for continuously reducing the emissions before they reach the ambient air (such as flue gas desulfurization)." Christopher Davis et al., "The Clean Air Act Amendments of 1977: Away from Technology-Forcing?" *Harvard Environmental Law Review* 2 (1977): 35.

12. Intermittent control systems "require monitoring the air quality in an area and either shutting down or reducing emissions when meteorologic conditions adversely affect dispersion." They may also include the use of tall smokestacks to disperse "emissions over such a large area that they result in low ambient air concentrations at ground level near the source." Davis et al., "Clean Air Act Amendments of 1977," 35.

13. Ayres, "Enforcement of Air Pollution Controls," 454.

14. Davis et al., "The Clean Air Act Amendments of 1977," 35.

15. The proposed State Implementation Plan Guidelines were issued 7 Apr. 1971. See 36 *Fed. Reg.* 6680 et seq. (1971).

16. Tobin, *Social Gamble*, 95.

17. See 37 *Fed. Reg.* 10847 (1972); 37 *Fed. Reg.* 10894 (1972); and 37 *Fed. Reg.* 10868 (1972).

18. U.S. Environmental Protection Agency and the Tennessee Valley Authority, *Preliminary Assessment of Alternative Sulfur Oxide Control Strategies for TVA Steamplants* (Knoxville: TVA, June 1974; revised Jan. 1975), p. 4–4. Hereafter cited as the *EPA/TVA Task Force Report*.

19. *Buckeye Power, Inc. v. EPA*, 481 F 2d 162 (1973), citing letter from Jack E. Raven, U.S. Environmental Protection Agency, to Gov. Carter, 7 May 1972.

20. 37 *Fed. Reg.* 10842 et seq. (1972).

21. Ibid., 10842.

22. Ibid., 15095.

23. 38 *Fed. Reg.* 25697 et seq. (1973). Exactly how far this proposed regulation went in allowing tall-stack intermittent control systems is a matter of some dispute. TVA has contended that this regulation would only have allowed them on a temporary basis (Tennessee Valley Authority, "Chronology of TVA Sulphur Dioxide Control," provided by TVA Attorney Barry Walton [Knoxville: TVA June 1979], 2). Henceforth cited as "Walton Chronology." Critics of intermittent control systems saw this proposed regulation as a reversal of EPA's previously proposed disapproval of tall-stack systems (see Ayres, "Enforcement of Air Pollution Controls," 456–57). Apparently, this proposed regulation did not entirely satisfy either the proponents or opponents of tall-stack intermittent control systems.

24. See "Donald Cook vs. EPA," *New York Times*, 24 Nov. 1974, pp. F1, 14; and "Tall Stacks versus Scrubbers: $3.5 Million Publicity Campaign Fails to Discredit Emission Reduction Technology," *Environmental Law Reporter* 5 (1974): 10009–10.

25. See E.E. Kenworthy, "EPA Aides Say Commerce Department Amendments Would Weaken Clean Air Act," *New York Times*, 10 Dec. 1974, p. 31.

26. *EPA/TVA Task Force Report*, 4–4.

27. 38 *Fed. Reg.* 34476 (1973); 38 *Fed. Reg.* 34477 (1973).

28. 39 *Fed. Reg.* 10277 (1974).

29. Ibid., 38528; ibid., 38529.

30. Ibid., 28357.

31. Richard B. Stewart and James E. Krier, *Environmental Law and Policy* 2nd ed. (New York: Bobbs-Merrill, 1978), 553.

32. Bill M. Shaw, "Sovereign Immunity: Federal Compliance with State Permit Requirements Under the Clean Air Act and the Federal Water Pollution Control Act Amendments," *San Fernando Valley Law Review* 6 (Spring 1978): 120.

33. William R. Shaw, "The Procedures to Ensure Compliance by Federal Facilities with Environmental Quality Standards," *Environmental Law Reporter* 5 (1975): 50215.

34. Davis et al., "Clean Air Act Amendments of 1977," p. 77.

35. Ibid.

36. Louis C. Gawthrop, *Bureaucratic Behavior in the Executive Branch* (Toronto: Free Press, 1969), 63, 64.

37. *EPA/TVA Task Force Report*.

38. Interview with Paul Traina, EPA Region IV, Atlanta, 26 June 1980.

39. Interview with Harold Hodges, Tennessee Air Pollution Control Division, Nashville, 18 Sept. 1980.

40. Ibid.

41. Traina interview; interview with Arthur Linton, EPA Region IV, Atlanta, 27 June 1980.

42. Traina interview.

43. "Walton Chronology," 2.

44. Traina interview.

45. Interview with Aubrey J. Wagner, Former Chairman, TVA board of directors, Knoxville, 18 Feb. 1981.

46. Interview, Nashville, 17 Sept. 1980.

47. *Alabama v. TVA*, No. 72–939 (N.D. Alabama, 1972), and *Kentucky v. Ruckelshaus*, No. 74806 (N.D. Kentucky, 1972).

48. Chairman Wagner's speech was reproduced in U.S., Congress, House, Testimony of Aubrey J. Wagner before the Subcommittee of the Committee on Appropriations, *Hearings on Public Works for Water and Power Development and Research Appropriation Bill, 1976,* 94th Cong., 2d sess., 1976, pp. 13–16.

49. Environmental Protection Agency, Report of the Hearing Panel, *National Public Hearings on Power Plant Compliance with Sulfur Oxide Air Pollution Regulations*, Jan. 1974. TVA's presentation was likely, in part, a response to the EPA's call for "demonstration by each candidate source on a case-by-case basis that adequate constant emission reduction techniques [were] not available to attain and maintain the national standards, and that those techniques that [were] available would be applied to permanently reduce emissions to the maximum extent practicable prior to application of supplementary control systems." See 38 *Fed. Reg.* 25699 (1973).

50. 38 *Fed. Reg.* 25699 (1973).

51. *EPA/TVA Task Force Report*, p. 4–4.

52. Testimony of Nathaniel B. Hughes, Director of Power Resource Planning, TVA, before the Tennessee Air Pollution Control Board, 12 June 1976.

53. Testimony of M.L. Mullins, Manager of Environmental Protection and Utilities, Monsono Corporation, before the Tennessee Air Pollution Control Board, 12 June 1973.

54. Interview with Barry Walton, attorney, TVA Office of the General Counsel, Knoxville, 13 June 1979.

55. Interview with Keith Casto, attorney, EPA Region IV, Atlanta, 26 June 1980.

56. Letter from Russell E. Train, EPA administrator, to Aubrey J. Wagner, TVA board chairman, 24 May 1974, as presented in the *EPA/TVA Task Force Report*, p. 1–3.

57. *Kentucky v. Ruckelshaus*, 497 F 2d 1172 (6th Cir., 1974).

58. *Alabama v. Seeber*, 502 F 2d 1238 (5th Cir., 1974).

59. 39 *Fed. Reg.* 29357 (1974).

60. This suit was subsequently decided in *Big Rivers Electric Corp. v. EPA*, 523 F 2d 16 (1975).

61. William R. Shaw, "Procedures to Ensure Compliance by Federal Facilities with Environmental Quality Standards," 50216.

62. Confidential interview, EPA Region IV, Atlanta, 1979.

63. Wagner interview.

NOTES FOR CHAPTER 4

1. Memorandum to John Barron and F.E. Gartrell from Robert H. Marquis, TVA General Counsel, 10 Aug. 1973.

2. Ibid.

3. John Quarles, *Cleaning Up America* (Boston: Houghton Mifflin, 1976), 114.

4. FWPCA of 1972, sec. 303.

5. *Water Quality Standards-Setting Conference for the Interstate Waters of the State of Alabama* (Atlanta: Environmental Protection Agency, Water Quality Office, 1971), 18. Henceforth cited as *Standards-Setting Conference*.

6. Russell L. Johnson, "Thermal Pollution: The Electric Utility Industry and Section 21(b) of the Federal Water Pollution Control Act," *Hastings Law Journal* 22 (Feb. 1971): 688.

7. Robert S. Burd, "Water Quality Standards for Temperature," in *Engineering Aspects of Thermal Pollution*, eds. Frank L. Parker and Peter A. Krenkle (Nashville: Vanderbilt Univ. Press, 1969), 74–75.

8. *Standards-Setting Conference*, 22.

9. 33 *Fed. Reg.* 9877 (1968).

10. 37 *Fed. Reg.* 5260 (1972).

11. 33 *Fed. Reg.* 9879 (1968).

12. Bruce A. Brye, "TVA Activities to Control Heated Water Discharges," a paper presented to the Alabama Society of Professional Engineers State Convention, Huntsville, 2–3 June 1972, p. 8.

13. 33 *Fed. Reg.* 9877 (1968); Tennessee Valley Authority, *Final Environmental Statement—Sequoyah Nuclear Plant, Units 1 and 2* (Chattanooga: TVA, 13 Feb. 1974), p. 2.6–2.

14. Marcus, *Promise and Performance*, 149.

15. Ibid.

16. Ibid., 152.

17. 39 *Fed. Reg.* 8294 (1974).

18. FWPCA, sec. 316(a).

19. Tom Eblen, "TVA 50 Years Later, It's Still Trying to Develop Its Valley," *Albuquerque Journal*, 15 May 1983, pp. B1, B4. It should also be added that TVA recently announced that it would cancel four additional unfinished reactors and over the next eleven years write off the $2.7 billion it has spent on them. See "TVA to Cancel 4 N-Plants," *Atlanta Constitution*, 29 Aug. 1984, p. 9-B.

20. Paul R. Schulman, "The Reflexive Organization: On Decisions, Boundaries, and the Policy Process," *Journal of Politics* 38 (Nov. 1976): 1015–16.

21. S. David Freeman, "TVA and National Power Policy," *Tennessee Law Review* 49 (Summer 1982): 683.

22. Eblen, "TVA," B-4.

23. North Callahan, *TVA: Bridge Over Troubled Waters* (New York: Barnes, 1980), 312.

24. Ibid., 313.

25. Dr. O.M. Derryberry, TVA Director of Health, and M.A. Churchill, Chief, TVA Water Quality Branch, paper presented at Public Hearing Concerning Proposed Water Quality Criteria for that Portion of the Tennessee River Basin in Alabama (Sheffield, Ala., 12 Dec. 1966), 2.

26. Marquis to Barron and Gartrell Memorandum, 10 Aug. 1973, p. 1; interview with Howard Zeller, EPA Region IV, Atlanta, 14 May 1981; and memorandum from M.A. Churchill, Chief, TVA Water Quality Branch, to F.E. Gartrell, TVA Assistant Director of Health, 28 June 1967, p. 2.

27. Derryberry memo, 6.

28. Memorandum to the Files from M.A. Churchill, Chief, Water Quality Branch, TVA, May 1967.

29. Testimony of M.A. Churchill, Chief, Water Quality Branch, TVA, before the Alabama Water Quality Improvement Commission, 19 June 1967.

30. Churchill to Gartrell Memorandum, 28 June 1967, p. 2.

31. Ibid., 3.

32. Letter from Stewart Udall, Secretary of the Interior, to Alabama Governor George Wallace, 15 Feb. 1968, p. 1.

33. Memorandum from Howard Zeller, EPA Region IV Water Quality Standards Coordinator, to the Files, 27 June 1968.

34. Ibid.

35. Letter from M.A. Churchill, Chief, Water Quality Branch, TVA, to S.J. Trombetta, Director of Federal Activities, Coordination Program, Federal Water Pollution Control Administration, 4 Aug. 1967.

36. Zeller Memorandum to Files, 1968.

37. Ibid.

38. Memorandum from T.P. Gallagher, TVA, to the Files, 5 July 1968, p. 1.

39. "Heated Water Control Crux of Likely Federal Agencies Clash," *Electrical World*, 29 Sept. 1969, p. 20.

40. Wagner interview.

41. *New Hampshire v. AEC*, 406 F. 2d. 170 (1969).

42. Letter from C.F. Layton, Acting Deputy Assistant, Secretary of the Interior, to Mr. Price, Director of Regulations, U.S. Atomic Energy Commission, 25 Feb. 1969.

43. Del Sesto, *Science, Politics, and Controversy*, 49.

44. Letter from William Ruckelshaus, EPA Administrator, to Alabama Governor George Wallace, 5 Feb. 1971.

45. Memorandum from M.A. Churchill, Chief, TVA Water Quality Branch, to F.E. Gartrell, TVA Assistant Director of Health, 2 Mar. 1971.

46. Ibid.

47. Ibid.

48. Letter from Howard Zeller, EPA Region IV, to J.L. Crockett, Jr., Director of Technical Staff, Alabama Water Improvement Commission, 21 July 1971.

49. Memorandum from W.R. Nicholas, Assistant Chief, TVA Water Quality Branch, to M.A. Churchill, Chief, TVA Water Quality Branch, 2 Apr. 1971.

50. Memorandum from Larry Clark, TVA Special Project Staff, to R.A. Buckingham, Supervisor, TVA Special Project Staff, 4 Nov. 1971.

51. Ibid.

NOTES FOR CHAPTER 5

1. William H. Riker and Peter C. Ordeshook, *An Introduction to Positive Political Theory* (Englewood Cliffs: Prentice-Hall, 1973), 5.

2. David Lilienthal and Robert Marquis, "The Conduct of Business Enterprises by the Federal Government," *Harvard Law Review* 54 (1941): 545, 575. In 1941 Robert Marquis was a member of the TVA legal staff. He eventually served as TVA's general counsel from 1967 to 1975.

3. Dean Hill Rivkin, "The TVA Air Pollution Conflict: The Dynamics of Public Law Advocacy," *Tennessee Law Review* 49 (Summer 1982): 858.

4. See, for example, U.S., Congress, House, Testimony of Nathaniel B. Hughes, Jr., TVA Assistant Power Manager, before the Subcommittee on Health and the Environment, 94th Cong., 1st sess., 1975, pp. 773–74; U.S., Congress, Senate, Committee on Public Works, *TVA Oversight Hearings*, 94th Cong., 1st sess., 1975; U.S. Congress, Senate, Public Works Subcommittee on Environmental Pollution, *Hearings on the Implementation of the Clean Air Act of 1970: Proposed Amendments*, 94th Cong., 1st sess., 1975; and U.S., Congress, House, Committee on Appropriations, *Hearings on Public Works for Water and Power Development and Energy Research Appropriation Bill, 1976,* 94th Cong., 1st sess., 1975.

5. Letter from Aubrey J. Wagner, Chairman, TVA Board of Directors, to John S. Hoffman, Secretary, Department of Natural Resources and Environmental Protection, State of Kentucky, 14 Apr. 1975.

6. Written statement of Dr. Ruth Neff submitted to the Tennessee Air Pollution Control Board, 20 June 1975.

7. Testimony of Dr. Thomas L. Montgomery, Chief, Air Quality Branch, TVA, before the Tennessee Air Pollution Control Board, 20 June 1975.

8. Hearings before the Committee on Public Works, *Tennessee Valley Authority Oversight Hearings*, Pt. 2, 94th Cong., 1st sess., 1975. Hereafter cited as TVA *Oversight Hearings*.

9. Public Works Subcommittee on Environmental Pollution, *Hearings on the Implementation of the Clean Air Act of 1970: Proposed Amendments*, 94th Cong., 1st sess., 1975.

10. "Walton Chronology."

11. Letter from Russell E. Train, EPA Administrator, to Aubrey J. Wagner, Chairman, TVA Board of Directors, 30 May 1975.

12. *Big Rivers Electric Corp. v. EPA*, 523 F 2d 16 (1975).

13. 41 *Fed. Reg.* 7450 et seq. (1976).

14. *Big Rivers Electric Corp. v. EPA*, Crt. Denied, 425 U.S. 934 (1976).

15. *Hancock v. Train*, 426 U.S. 167 (1976).

16. Testimony of Dr. Thomas Montgomery, Chief, Air Quality Branch, TVA, before the Alabama Air Pollution Control Commission, 31 July 1975.

17. Letter from Lynn Seeber, General Manager, TVA, to Jack E. Raven, Region IV Administrator, EPA 12 Dec. 1976.

18. Ibid.

19. Traina interview.

20. Casto interview; interview with Dr. Ruth Neff, Tennessee Environmental Council, Nashville, 7 Nov. 1979; interview with attorney Dean Hill Rivkin, Univ. of Tennessee School of Law, Knoxville, 4 and 17 Dec. 1979.

21. Interview with Jack Raven, EPA Region IV Administrator, Atlanta, 28 June 1980.

22. Linton interview; Raven interview.

23. Linton interview.

24. Letter from John Van Mol, Director of Information, TVA, to Dr. Ruth Neff, Executive Director, Tennessee Environmental Council, 24 Mar. 1975.

25. Neff interview; interview with Mary Wade, Tennessee League of Women Voters, Nashville, 7 Nov. 1979.

26. Van Mol to Neff, 24 Mar. 1975.

27. Letter from Jonathan Gibson, Coordinator, Tennessee Environmental Council (TEC), to Citizens Attending TVA Symposia, 16 July 1976.

28. Letter from John Gibbons, Director, Univ. of Tennessee Environmental Center, to Jonathan Gibson, Coordinator, TEC, TVA Symposia, 19 Jan. 1976.

29. Letter from Jonathan Gibson, Coordinator, TEC,TVA Symposia, to S. David Freeman, 23 Dec. 1975.

30. Letter from John Van Mol, Director of Information, TVA, to Jonathan Gibson, Coordinator, TEC, TVA Symposia, 16 Jan. 1976.

31. Letter from John Van Mol, Dir. of Information, TVA, to Dr. Ruth Neff, TEC, 1 Dec. 1975.

32. Letter from Neil McBride, Board of Directors, TVA, to Mary Wade, President, TEC, 29 Mar. 1976.

33. 38 *Fed. Reg.* 25701 (1973).

34. Memorandum from John Walton, Tennessee Air Pollution Control Division, to Harold Hodges, Director, Tennessee Air Pollution Control Division, 12 Apr. 1977.

35. *TVA News*, 10 Jan. 1977, p. 1.

36. "Officials Tour TVA Steam Plant," *Roane County News*, 11 July 1977, pp. 1, 2.

37. "Constituents Answer Poll for Atchley," *Knoxville Journal*, 9 May 1977, p. 1.

38. Tennessee House Joint Resolution 44, 90th General Assembly, 1977, Tennessee Public Acts 1575.

39. Interview with S. David Freeman, Chairman, TVA Board of Directors, Knoxville, 30 Dec. 1980.

40. Confidential interview, EPA Region IV, Atlanta.

41. Freeman interview.

42. Casto interview; interview with William Chandler, Environmental Policy Center, Washington, D.C., 28 Jan. 1980.

43. Casto interview.

44. "TVA to Burn Low-Sulfur Coal to Meet Emissions Standards," TVA News Release, 21 Mar. 1977, pp. 2, 3.

45. Letter from Larry Hammond, Deputy Assistant Attorney General, Office of Legal Counsel, U.S. Department of Justice, to Douglas Costle, Administrator, EPA, 22 Aug. 1977, p. 3.

46. Sen. Rep. No. 1196, 91st Cong., 2d sess., 36–37 (1970).

47. Durning interview; Traina interview.

48. "TVA to Burn Low-Sulfur Coal."

49. Chandler interview.

50. Rivkin interview.

51. Rivkin interview; Neff interview. The citizen groups serving as plaintiff intervenors in the Alabama suit were: Alabama Lung Association, Sierra Club, and Natural Resources Defense Council. The citizen groups serving as plaintiffs in the Tennessee suits were: Tennessee Thoracic Society, East Tennessee Energy Group, League of Women Voters in Tennessee, Natural Resources Defense Council, Save Our Cumberland Mountains, Sierra Club, Tennessee Citizens for Wilderness Planning, Tennessee Environmental Council, and Vanderbilt Environmental Group.

52. Casto interview; Traina interview.

53. Traina interview.

54. Ibid.

55. Rivkin interview.

56. Chandler interview.

57. Letter from Lynn Seeber, General Manager, TVA, to Dean Hill Rivkin, Attorney, Citizen Coalition, 8 Apr. 1977, p. 4.

58. Memorandum to files from Barry Stevens, Tennessee Air Pollution Control Division, 11 May 1979.

59. Confidential interview, TAPCD, Nashville.

60. Ibid.

61. Hodges interview.

62. Barry Stevens Memorandum.

63. The Clean Air Act Amendments of 1977, Pub. L. No. 95-95 (1977), secs. 111 and 123. Henceforth cited as the CAA of 1977.

64. Ibid., sec. 118.

65. Ibid., secs. 113 and 129.

66. 123 *Congressional Record*, S9443, 10 June 1977.

67. Rivkin interview.

68. Rivkin, "The TVA Air Pollution Conflict," p. 870, n. 88.

69. *New York Times*, 26 May 1977, p. 14, 1.

70. Rivkin interview.

71. Jim Ballock, "Frustrated Bill Jenkins Quits TVA," *Knoxville News-Sentinel*, 6 May 1978, pp. 1, 3.

72. Carson Brewer, "Wagner Refuses to Sign EPA Settlement," *Knoxville News-Sentinel*, 18 May 1978, pp. 1, 2.

73. Executive Order 12088, Federal Compliance with Pollution Control Standards, 13 Oct. 1978; 43 *Fed. Reg.* 47707 et seq. (1978).

74. Interview with Charles Hungerford, EPA Attorney, Washington, D.C., 28 Jan. 1980.

75. Casto interview.

76. Freeman interview. Also see U.S., Congress, Senate, Committee on Environment and Public Works, *Hearings on the Nomination of S. David Freeman*, 95th Cong., 1st sess., 1977, pp. 60–70.

77. Traina interview; interview with James Bycott, EPA Region IV Attorney, Atlanta, 29 June 1980; and interview with Charles Hungerford, EPA Staff Attorney, Washington, D.C., 28 Jan. 1980.

78. U.S., Congress, Senate, Committee on Environment and Public Works, Hearings on the Nomination of Marvin B. Durning, 95th Cong., 1st sess., 1977, p. 14.

79. Interview with Marvin B. Durning, EPA Deputy Administrator for Enforcement, Washington, D.C., 30 Jan. 1980.

80. Ibid.

81. Freeman interview; Durning interview.

82. Freeman interview.

83. Ibid.

84. Ibid. It should be noted that we contacted Mr. Seeber for an interview, but he did not wish to discuss the SO_2 or thermal dispute with us.

85. Ibid.

86. Wagner interview.

87. Freeman interview.

88. Hungerford interview.

89. Specifically, what the plaintiffs took advantage of was the "credit against the penalty" provision of the act. As explained by Marvin Durning, "The 'credit against the penalty' feature provides that a violating source may offset against the penalty the economic value of pollution control or other

acceptable environmentally beneficial expenditures above (or sooner than) those required by law. Frequently, the credit completely offsets the penalty and the public obtains environmental benefits in lieu of money. Usually, moreover, expenditures for such credits also have advantages for the source . . . and may facilitate settlement by providing a psychologically more acceptable alternative than the paying of penalties."

90. Hungerford interview.

91. Consent Decree, entered in the U.S. District Court for the Middle District of Tennessee, Nashville Division, for the case of *Tennessee Thoracic Society et al. v. Wagner*; and Consent Decree, entered in the U.S. District Court for the Northern District of Alabama, in the case of *Alabama v. TVA*. The original five suits filed in the Tennessee litigation were transferred to the Northern District Court in Nashville to be handled by a single judge. Hereafter, unless otherwise specified, both documents will be referred to simply as the Consent Decree. Specific page citations will be taken from the decree entered before the U.S. District Court of Middle Tennessee, 102. The quotation is from the Freeman interview.

92. Consent Decree, 102.

93. In this way plaintiffs ended, at least for the period covered in the agreement, concern over the economic impact of TVA's relying on low-sulfur western coal as an element of its compliance program. This provision, in addition to providing some security for the companies and miners working in the Cumberland region, also alleviated the plaintiffs' concern over the environmental hazards inherent in burning the western coal with its reduced btu content (from Rivkin interview).

94. Consent Decree, 45. This provision was "dear to the hearts" of the citizen group plaintiffs and was especially objected to by TVA board chairman Wagner before he resigned (Chandler interview).

95. These cost estimates are the official ones made by the parties to the settlement. They were produced in response to an order from the Middle Tennessee District judge to whom the Consent Decree was submitted. *Statement of Economic Impacts of Consent Agreement*, for the case of *Tennessee Thoracic Society et al. v. Wagner*, tables 1 and 2. As will be discussed later, these figures became the subject of great controversy, with many interested parties contending that they actually were too low. Certainly, they represent a baseline figure and probably represent the lowest estimate available at present. This document is hereafter cited as *Statement of Economic Impacts*.

96. Rivkin and Hungerford interviews.

97. Wagner interview.

98. Ibid. In Wagner's own words, "Once we were brought into compliance, we were going to be thrown in everybody's face as a standard. We had a responsibility to do everything we could to see that the standards made sense."

99. Ballock, "Frustrated Bill Jenkins Quits TVA."

100. Freeman interview.

101. Ibid.

102. Freeman interview; Traina interview.

103. The letter is included in Senate Committee on Environment and Public Works, Subcommittee on Environmental Pollution, *Hearings on Executive Branch Review of Environmental Regulations*, 96th Cong., 1st sess., 1979, p. 173. Hereafter cited as the *Executive Branch Review Hearings*.

104. Apparently the letter was made public by the aluminum company. The immediate effect of its release was to create the impression that the Carter administration opposed the settlement as inflationary. See, for example, "What Price Regulation?" *Newsweek*, 19 Mar. 1979, p. 80. The timing of the release, and the nature of the contents of the Bosworth letter, led some to allege that it caused the district judge in Tennessee to hold up the settlement. Judge Wiseman denied, however, that he had been influenced by receipt of a copy of the letter from Sen. Jim Sasser (D-Tenn.). Philip Shabecoff, "White House is Cool to Charges of Interference in Role of EPA," *New York Times*, 23 Feb. 1979, p. A23. Later, supporters of the agreement would argue during Senate hearings that the Bosworth incident was evidence of administration (outside EPA) and industry attempts to sabotage the agreement. See the testimony of Richard E. Ayres during the *Executive Branch Review Hearings*, 29–33.

105. On 9 Mar. 1979, Michael J. Egan, Associate Attorney General of the United States, sent a letter to Sanford Sagalkin, also of the Department of Justice and in charge of handling the sec. 304 litigation against TVA, stating (on behalf of Assistant to the President Stuart Eizenstat) that "the President has reviewed this matter carefully and believes that entry of the consent decrees is in the public interest and consistent with the President's policies. The Executive Branch is firmly of one mind in its support of the TVA agreement." The Egan letter authorized his Department of Justice colleague, Sagalkin, to submit the letter for the consideration of the courts in the pending case. Letter included in the *Executive Branch Review Hearings*, 477.

106. As quoted in Shabecoff, "White House is Cool," A23.

107. *Executive Branch Review Hearings*, 355. Sen. Edmund Muskie took Bosworth severely to task for his involvement in the settlement and in particular criticized the director of COWPS for allowing his letter to get to the federal judge and create the impression that the administration was critical of the consent agreement. *Executive Branch Review Hearings*, 358–59.

108. S. David Freeman was, eventually, to defend his settlement with EPA in the national press and severely criticize Bosworth's intervention: "It was an act that was not appropriate, not justified and not in the public interest." See "What Price Regulation," 19 Mar. 1979, p. 80. The TVA/EPA consent agreement was discussed in the *Executive Branch Review Hearings*; the *TVA Bond Ceiling Hearings*; and the Senate Committee on Environment and Public Works, Subcommittee on Environmental Pollution, *Hearings on the Enforcement of Environmental Regulations*, 96th Cong., 1st sess., 1979.

109. "UCEMC Joining Co-Ops in Lawsuit Against TVA," *Carthage Courier,* 3 May 1979.

110. Ray Campbell, "U.S. Seeks to Keep Co-Ops Off EPA-TVA Pact," *Nashville Banner*, 9 May 1979, p. 28. Eventually 37 co-ops were to join the suit.

111. "Electric Cooperatives Admitted to Pollution Suit," *Nashville Banner*, 29 May 1979, p. 10.

112. The objections to the consent decree raised by distributors who intervened were as follows: (1) The proposed consent decree did not give appropriate recognition to the Baker Amendment for the Kingston Steam Plant. (2) The emission limit at Paradise was overly stringent. (3) The proposed consent decree failed to specify in detail the method of disposal of the waste material generated by the pollution control equipment at TVA's coal-fired power plants. (4) The proposed consent decree failed to absolve TVA from payment of administrative noncompliance penalties under section 120 of the act. (5) Creation of the Implementation Committee was not in the public interest because the presence of representatives of the plaintiff environmental organizations would usurp the power of TVA to regulate its internal affairs and because the plaintiffs were not publicly accountable. Keith Casto, "Public Power and Public Interest: An Analysis of the TVA Air Pollution Litigation," *Tennessee Law Review* 49 (Summer 1982): 819.

113. *Statement of Economic Impacts*, 6.

114. "EPA Chief's TVA Visit Called Symbolic," *Knoxville News-Sentinel*, 5 June 1979, p. 8.

115. "TVA Defends Buying of Pollution Equipment," *Knoxville News-Sentinel*, 1 Feb. 1980, p. 13.

116. Ibid.

117. Ibid.

118. "TVA Distributors Criticize Freeman," *Knoxville Journal*, 2 Feb. 1980, p. 1.

119. As quoted in "TVA's 'Overcompliance' on Clean Air is Challenged," *Knoxville News-Sentinel*, 17 Mar. 1979, pp. 1, 7.

NOTES FOR CHAPTER 6

1. Austin Sarat and Joel B. Grossman, "Courts and Conflict Resolution: Problems in the Mobilization of Adjudication," *American Political Science Review* 69 (Dec. 1975): 1200–1217.

2. Rawson, "The Process of Program Development."

3. Wagner interview.

4. "TVA Power Plant Said Environmentally Okay," *Mobile Register*, 4 Nov. 1972, p. 1.

5. Tarlock, A. Dan, Roger Tippy, and Frances E. Francis, "Environmental Regulation of Power Plant Siting," *Southern California Law Review* 45 (1972): 529–33.

6. Memorandum from M.A. Churchill, Chief, Water Quality Branch, TVA, to Dr. F.E. Gartrell, Asst. Director of Health, TVA 10 Feb. 1972.

7. GAO, *Sequoyah Nuclear Plant: Tennessee Valley Authority* (Washington, D.C.: GAO, Jan. 1975), 37, 39.

8. Letter from Jack E. Raven, EPA Region IV Administrator, to F.E. Gartrell, TVA, 17 Dec. 1971.

9. Zeller interview; interview with Charles Kaplan, EPA Region IV, At-

lanta, 14 May 1981; and interview with Bruce Brye, TVA, Chattanooga, 16 May 1981.

10. Del Sesto, *Science, Politics, and Controversy*, 159.

11. TVA *News*, 2 Feb. 1972, p. 1.

12. Memorandum from Charles Kaplan, EPA Region IV, to Sanitary Engineer, EPA Federal Facilities Branch, 28 Jan. 1972.

13. Interview with Howard Zeller, EPA Region IV, Atlanta, 15 May 1981.

14. Letter from G.F. Stone and W.R. Nicholas to J.A. Oppold, 23 Jan. 1974.

15. Linton interview.

16. *TVA Annual Report: 1973*, 43–44.

17. *TVA News*, 2 Feb. 1972, p. 1.

18. Letter from Charles D. Kelly, Director, Alabama Game and Fish Division, to the Editor of the *Environmental Control News for Southern Industry*, 7 Aug. 1973, p. 1.

19. "The Economics of Clean Water," *Environment Reporter*, 12 May 1972.

20. Frank Sikora, "N-Plant Will Open Without Cooling Unit," *Birmingham News*, 23 Aug. 1972, p. 1.

21. Zeller interview; Linton interview; Brye interview; interview with James Morris, TVA, in Chattanooga, 16 May 1981.

22. Jack E. Raven, EPA, to Dr. F.E. Gartrell, TVA, 22 May 1972, TVA Office of Health and Environmental Science, *Final Environmental Statement — Browns Ferry Nuclear Plant — Units 1, 2, and 3*, vol. 1 (Chattanooga: TVA, 1972), pp. 3.12-1 to 3.12-2.

23. Ibid.

24. Sikora, "N-Plant," p. 1.

25. Bob Dunnavant, "State May Try to Delay Plant's Start, Cooling Towers Termed a Must at Browns Ferry," *Huntsville Times*, 26 Sept. 1972.

26. Ibid.

27. Letter from Aubrey J. Wagner, Chairman, TVA Board of Directors, to Sen. James B. Allen (D-Ala.), 17 Nov. 1973.

28. Brye interview. In Brye's own words, AEC "passed the buck" to EPA.

29. "Stipulation of Petitioner, State of Alabama, and Applicant, Tennessee Valley Authority Browns Ferry Nuclear Plants, Units One, Two, and Three," 26 Mar. 1973.

30. Frank L. Parker and Marcus Jernigan, "To Cool or Not to Cool?: Benefit Cost Analyses with Specific Application to Browns Ferry Power Plant Cooling Towers" (unpublished paper, 1973).

31. David G. Powell, TVA Division of Law, to Frank L. Parker, Professor, Vanderbilt Univ., 2 Jan. 1973.

32. Memorandum from N.B. Hughes, Jr., TVA Director of Power Resource Planning, to F.E. Gartrell, TVA Director of Environmental Planning, and T.H. Ripley, TVA Director of Forestry, Fisheries and Wildlife Development, 9 Mar. 1973.

33. Ibid.

34. Memorandum from M.B. Hughes, Jr., Director of Power Resource

Planning, TVA, to F.E. Gartrell, Director of Environmental Planning, TVA, and T.H. Ripley, Director of Forestry, Fisheries and Wildlife Development, TVA, 9 Nov. 1972.

35. "Utility Water Act Group (UWAG) Report No. 10," presented by Hunton, Williams, Gay, and Gibson, Richmond, Va., 19 Dec. 1973. The following description of the three alternatives relies on 39 *Fed. Reg.* 36181 (1974).

36. Memorandum from E.D. Dougherty, Environmental Engineer, TVA Power Research Staff, to the Manager's Files, 8 June 1973.

37. Internal TVA memorandum from the Environmental Biology Branch to Billy Isom, 20 Dec. 1973.

38. Ibid.

39. *Final Environmental Impact Statement Comments, Browns Ferry Nuclear Plant, Units 1, 2, and 3* (Washington, D.C.: EPA, 19 Dec. 1972), 2.

40. Ibid.

41. Memorandum to the Manager's Files from E.O. Dougherty, Environmental Engineer, TVA Power Research Staff, 8 June 1973.

42. Ibid.

43. Letter from Lynn Seeber, General Manager, TVA, to John Quarles, Acting Administrator, EPA, 30 Aug. 1973.

44. Letter from Herbert Sanger, TVA General Counsel, to Allan Cywin, Director, EPA Effluent Guidelines Division, 11 Feb. 1976.

45. Letter from David G. Powell, TVA Division of Law, to Charles Kaplan, EPA Region IV, 13 Sept. 1973.

NOTES FOR CHAPTER 7

1. James E. Anderson, *Public Policy-Making*, 2d ed. (New York: Holt, Rinehart and Winston, 1979), 136.

2. Erwin C. Hargrove, *The Missing Link* (Washington, D.C.: Urban Institute, 1975).

3. Examples of recent efforts to study regulatory policy implementation include: Paul A. Sabatier,"Regulatory Policy-Making: Toward a Framework for Analysis," *Natural Resources Journal* 17 (July 1977): 415–60; Randall B. Ripley and Grace A. Franklin, *Bureaucracy and Policy Implementation* (Homewood, Ill.: Dorsey, 1982); Alfred A. Marcus, *Promise and Performance: Choosing and Implementing an Environmental Policy* (Westport, Conn.: Glenwood Press, 1980); James Q. Wilson, ed., *The Politics of Regulation* (New York: Basic Books, 1980); James Q. Wilson and Patricia Rachal, "Can the Government Regulate Itself?" *Public Interest* 46 (Winter 1977): 3–14; John Mendelott, *Regulating Safety: An Economic and Political Analysis of Occupational Safety and Health Policy* (Cambridge: MIT Univ. Press, 1979); Lawrence S. Bacow, *Bargaining for Job Safety and Health* (Cambridge: MIT Univ. Press, 1980); Eugene Bardach and Robert A. Kagan, *Going by the Book: The Problem of Regulatory Unreasonableness* (Philadelphia: Temple Univ. Press, 1982); Eugene Bardach and Robert A. Kagan, eds., *Social Regulation: Strategies for Reform* (San Francisco: Institute for Contemporary Studies, 1982); Michael S. Lewis-Beck and John R. Alford,

"Can Government Regulate Safety? The Coal Mine Example," *American Political Science Review* 74 (Sept. 1980): 745–55; Paul D. Downing and Kenneth Hane, eds., "Cross-National Comparisons in Environmental Protection: A Symposium," *Policy Studies Journal* 11 (Sept. 1982): 38–187; and Beryl A. Radin, *Implementation, Change, and the Federal Bureaucracy: School Desegregation Policy in HEW, 1964–1968* (New York: Teachers College Press, 1977).

4. See, e.g.: Paul H. Culhane, *Public Lands Politics* (Baltimore: Johns Hopkins Univ. Press, 1981); Paul Sabatier and Daniel Mazmanian, "Regulating Coastal Land Use in California, 1973–1975," *Policy Studies Journal* 11 (Sept. 1982): 88–102; and Jochen Hucke, "Implementing Environmental Regulations in the Federal Republic of Germany," *Policy Studies Journal* 11 (Sept. 1982): 130–40.

5. See, e.g.: Harold Luft, "Benefit-Cost Analysis and Public Policy Implementation," *Public Policy* 24 (Fall 1976): 437–62, and Charles S. Bullock III and Harell R. Rodgers, Jr., *Coercion to Compliance* (Lexington: Lexington Books, 1976).

6. For excellent summaries of the conceptual frameworks associated with these factors, as well as the propositions associated with each, see: Robert T. Nakamura and Frank Smallwood, *The Politics of Policy Implementation* (New York: St. Martin's Press, 1980); George C. Edwards III, *Implementing Public Policy* (Washington, D.C.: Congressional Quarterly, 1980); and Daniel A. Mazmanian and Paul A. Sabatier, *Implementation and Public Policy* (Glenview: Scott, Foresman, 1983).

7. Marcus, *Promise and Performance*.

8. Mazmanian and Sabatier, *Implementation and Public Policy*.

9. Bardach and Kagan, *Going by the Book*.

10. Bullock and Rodgers, *Coercion to Compliance*.

11. Traina interview.

12. Wagner's contention was recently supported in a staff study done by J.C. Noggle, TVA biologist in Muscle Shoals, Ala. Noggle maintained that soil sulfur deficiencies would result from clean-up efforts. Ironically, this study was funded by EPA.

13. Walton interview; Neff interview; and Casto interview.

14. Linton interview; Rivkin interview; and Durning interview.

15. Morris interview.

16. Traina interview; Linton interview.

17. Raven interview.

18. Traina interview; Durning interview; and Bycott interview.

19. Traina interview.

20. Brye interview; Morris interview. These men were highly laudatory of EPA's attitudes and behavior during the thermal dispute.

21. Memorandum from G.F. Stone, TVA, and W.R. Nicholas, Asst. Chief, TVA Water Quality Branch, to J.A. Oppold, TVA, 23 Jan. 1974.

22. Traina interview.

23. Ibid.

24. Robert S. Montjoy and Lawrence J. O'Toole, "Toward a Theory of

Policy Implementation: An Organizational Perspective," *Public Administration Review* 39 (Sept./Oct. 1979): 465–75.

25. See, for example: Bardach and Kagan, *Going by the Book*; Jeremy Rabkin, "Office for Civil Rights," 304–53 in James Q. Wilson, ed., *The Politics of Regulation*; and Lawrence J. White, "U.S. Mobile Source Emissions Regulation: The Problems of Implementation," *Policy Studies Journal* 11 (Sept. 1982): 77–87.

26. One excellent comparative treatment is Mazmanian and Sabatier, *Implementation and Public Policy*.

27. Some have attempted to convey the perspectives of regulatory targets, but most have done so either in passing, without in-depth analyses of particular application efforts, or with a focus at the aggregate level. See, for example, Bardach and Kagan, *Going by the Book*; Wilson and Rachal, "Can Government Regulate Itself?"; and Arieh A. Ullmann, "The Implementation of Air Pollution Control in German Industry," *Policy Studies Journal* 11 (Sept. 1982): 141–52.

28. See, for example, Jeffrey L. Pressman and Aaron B. Wildavsky, *Implementation* (Berkeley: Univ. of California Press, 1973).

29. Philip Selznick, *Leadership in Administration* (New York: Harper & Row, 1957); Gary L. Wamsley and Meyer N. Zald, *The Political Economy of Public Organizations: A Critique and Approach to the Study of Public Administration* (Lexington: Lexington Books, 1973); and James D. Thompson, *Organizations in Action* (New York: McGraw-Hill, 1967). The concepts of institutional mission and organizational goals are admittedly controversial ones. Some suggest that organizational missions and goals are multiple not unified, evolving not static, and symbolic not real. See, for example, Amitai Etzioni, "Two Approaches to Organizational Analysis: A Critique and a Suggestion," *Administrative Science Quarterly* 5 (Sept. 1960), and Charles Perrow, *Complex Organizations*, 2d ed. (Glenview: Scott, Foresman, 1979). Still, many argue that most organizations have functions that are clearly secondary given the allocation of "fewer resources and less time to those functions which they perceive as marginal" (Edwards, *Implementing Public Policy*, 95).

30. Mazmanian and Sabatier, *Implementation and Public Policy*; Montjoy and O'Toole, *Toward a Theory of Policy Implementation*; Edwards, *Implementing Public Policy*.

31. Pressman and Wildavsky, *Implementation*.

32. Ibid., 116–20.

33. Robert L. Lineberry, *American Public Policy* (New York: Harper & Row, 1977), 78.

34. Paul D. Downing, "Cross-National Comparisons in Environmental Protection: Introduction to the Issues," *Policy Studies Journal* 11 (Sept. 1982): 40.

35. See, for example, Donald S. Van Meter and Carl E. Van Horn, "The Policy Implementation Process: A Conceptual Framework," *Administration and Society* 6 (Feb. 1975): 445–88; Paul Sabatier, "Social Movements and Regulatory Agencies," *Policy Science* 6 (Fall 1975): 301–342; and Mazmanian and Sabatier, *Implementation and Public Policy*, 31–34.

36. For an excellent discussion of ally mobilization in the intragovernmental arena, see Wilson and Rachal, "Can Government Regulate Itself?"

NOTES FOR CHAPTER 8

1. Official Transcript of Proceedings, *Tennessee Thoracic Society v. Freeman*, No. 77–3286 and Consolidated Cases (M.D. Tenn., 31 July 1979).

2. Memorandum from Robert H. Marquis, TVA General Counsel, to John Barron and F.E. Gartrell, 10 Aug. 1973.

3. E.E. Schattschneider, *The Semisovereign People*, 15.

4. Another outstanding example of this kind of behavior was the unsuccessful attempt by environmentalists and the Department of Interior to prevent the TVA from building the Tellico Dam. In a dispute that produced the famous Supreme Court "Snail Darter" decision, TVA lost every battle but the last — in Congress — when it won a last-minute exemption from the Endangered Species Act. For a detailed account of the dispute, see Stephen Rechichar and Michael R. Fitzgerald, *The Contagiousness of Conflict: TVA's Tellico Dam Project* (Knoxville: Bureau of Public Administration, 1983).

5. Traina interview; Casto interview.

6. Matthew Holden, Jr., "'Imperialism' in Bureaucracy," *American Political Science Review* 60 (Dec. 1966): 944.

7. George E. Rawson, "The Implementation of Public Policy by Third-Sector Organizations," paper presented at the 1978 Annual Meeting of the American Political Science Association, New York, N.Y., 31 Aug.–3 Sept. 1978, p. 14; *TVA Oversight Hearings*.

8. Derthick, "The Tennessee Valley Authority," 39.

9. Between 1972 and 1979, TVA's industrial rates have quadrupled and its residential rates tripled. James Branscome, "TVA Chairman David Freeman Talks About TVA and Power," *Mountain Eagle*, Whitesburg, K.Y., 25 Jan. 1979.

10. Interview with Frank Perkins, Nashville, 18 Sept. 1980.

11. See Rourke, "Bureaucratic Autonomy," for an excellent treatment of the case for protecting bureaucratic independence.

12. This discussion of Wagner and Freeman's attitudes toward regulation and citizen participation is based on interviews conducted by the author and Michael R. Fitzgerald of the Univ. of Tennessee.

13. Jeffrey L. Brudney and Robert E. England, "Urban Policy Making and Subjective Service Evaluations: Are They Compatible?" *Public Administration Review* 42 (Mar./Apr. 1982): 133.

14. This discussion of the coproduction model of service delivery is based on two excellent treatments of the subject: Gordon P. Whitaker, "Coproduction: Citizen Participation in Service Delivery," *Public Administration Review* 40 (May/June 1980): 240–46; and Brudney and England, "Urban Policy Making."

15. It should be noted that even though Freeman agreed to establish the citizen implementation committee, he proceeded to implement the consent decree prior to the committee's creation and without soliciting outside input. (Note: the committee could not be convened prior to court approval

of the decree.) It is likely that Freeman felt it important to implement the pollution control terms of the agreement and thus render court approval or disapproval of the decree a moot point. For an excellent treatment of the proactive versus the professional-technocratic administrative styles, see Michael M. Harmon, *Action Theory for Public Administration* (New York: Longman, 1981). Also, while TVA has created a citizen action office, initiated issue-based, ad hoc citizen participation programs, and held more than 300 public meetings throughout the region, its efforts to involve the public have been criticized. President Reagan's transition team termed its efforts "more form than substance" and "flawed in execution and concept" (Rivkin, *The TVA Air Pollution Conflict*, p. 853, fn 37). Similarly, a report issued by a regional task force of Common Cause in April 1983 stated that "no meaningful avenues for public participation by the residential ratepayers [existed] in TVA's decision making" (Louis M. Gwin, "Mechanisms for Public Participation at the Tennessee Valley Authority," *Public Relations Quarterly* 29 (Spring 1984): 30.

16. James Madison, "Federalist 51," in *The Federalist Papers*, Alexander Hamilton, James Madison, and John Jay (New York: New American Library of World Literature, 1961), 322.

17. Garry Wills, *Explaining America: The Federalist* (New York: Penguin, 1981), xx, xxi.

18. Francis E. Rourke, *Bureaucracy, Politics, and Public Policy*, 2d ed. (Boston: Little, Brown, 1976), 177.

19. Schattschneider, *The Semisovereign People*, 2.

20. See, for example, Michael W. Kirst, *Government Without Passing Laws* (Chapel Hill: Univ. of North Carolina Press, 1969).

21. See, e.g., Dean Hill Rivkin, "The TVA Air Pollution Conflict"; Zygmunt J. B. Plater, "Reflected in a River: Agency Accountability and the TVA Tellico Dam Case," *Tennessee Law Review* 49 (Summer 1982): 747–87.

22. For example, Wilson and Rachal, "Can Government Regulate Itself?"

23. Thanks to an anonymous reviewer for suggesting the term "preemptive creative redundance."

24. The concept "polycentric problem" refers to the tendency of issues to be interrelated and consequently for the policy solutions of one problem to have implications for the others. For the frustrations involved in dealing with these problems as seen through the eyes of policy makers, see David S. Broder, *Changing of the Guard: Power and Leadership in America* (New York: Penguin, 1981).

Bibliography

BOOKS AND ARTICLES

Anderson, Frederick R. *NEPA in the Courts*. Baltimore: Resources for the Future, distributed by the Johns Hopkins Univ. Press, 1973.

Anderson, James E. *Emergence of the Modern Regulatory State*. Washington, D.C.: Public Affairs Press, 1962.

———. *Public Policy-Making*. 2d ed. New York: Holt, Rinehart and Winston, 1979.

Anderson, Paul. "Implementing Air Pollution Control Policy: The Sulfur Dioxide Emission Limitations Program in Ohio." In *Energy and Environmental Issues: The Making and Implementation of Public Policy*, ed. Michael Steinman. Lexington: Lexington Books, 1979. Pp. 117–36.

Arbuckle, J. Gordon, and Timothy A. Vanderver, Jr. "Water Pollution Control." In *Environmental Law Handbook*, ed. J. Gordon Arbuckle et al. New York: Government Institutes, 1978. Pp. 95–164.

Ayres, Richard E. "Enforcement of Air Pollution Controls on Stationary Sources under the Clean Air Amendments of 1970." *Ecology Law Quarterly* 4 (1975): 441–78.

Bacow, Lawrence S. *Bargaining for Job Safety and Health*. Cambridge: MIT Univ. Press, 1980.

Ball, Bruce P. "Water Pollution and Compliance Decision Making." In *Public Policy Making in a Federal System*, ed. Charles O. Jones and Robert D. Thomas. Beverly Hills: Sage Publications, 1976. Pp. 169–87.

Baram, Michael S. "The Legal and Regulatory Framework for Thermal Discharge from Nuclear Power Plants." *Environmental Affairs* 2 (Winter 1972): 505–529.

Bardach, Eugene. *The Implementation Game*. Cambridge: MIT Univ. Press, 1977.

———, and Robert A. Kagan. *Going by the Book: The Problem of Regulatory Unreasonableness*. Philadelphia: Temple Univ. Press, 1982.

———. *Social Regulation: Strategies for Reform*. San Francisco: Institute for Contemporary Studies, 1982.

Bockrath, Joseph T. *Environmental Law for Engineers, Scientists, and Managers*. New York: McGraw-Hill, 1977.

Broder, David S. *Changing of the Guard: Power and Leadership in America*. New York: Penguin, 1981.

Browning, Rufus P., and Dale Rogers Marshall. "Implementation of Model Cities and Revenue Sharing in Ten Bay Area Cities: Design and First Findings." In *Public Policy Making in a Federal System*, ed. Charles O. Jones and Robert D. Thomas. Beverly Hills: Sage Publications, 1976. Pp. 191–216.

————, and David H. Tabb. "Implementation and Political Change: Sources of Local Variations in Federal Social Programs." *Policy Studies Journal* 8 (1980): 616–32.

Brudney, Jeffrey L., and Robert E. England. "Urban Policy Making and Subjective Service Evaluations: Are They Compatible?" *Public Administration Review* 42 (Mar./Apr. 1982): 127–35.

Bullock, Charles, and Harell R. Rodgers. *Coercion to Compliance*. Lexington: Lexington Books, 1976.

Burd, Robert S. "Water Quality Standards for Temperature." In *Engineering Aspects of Thermal Pollution*, eds. Frank L. Parker and Peter A. Krenkle. Nashville: Vanderbilt Univ. Press, 1969. Pp. 72–78.

Callahan, North. *The TVA: Bridge Over Troubled Waters*. New York: Barnes, 1980.

Casto, Keith. "Public Power and Public Interest: An Analysis of the TVA Air Pollution Litigation." *Tennessee Law Review* 49 (Summer 1982): 789–841.

Cater, Douglas. *Power in Washington*. New York: Random, 1964.

Culhane, Paul H. *Public Lands Politics*. Baltimore: Johns Hopkins Univ. Press, 1981.

Currie, David P. "Federal Air Quality Standards and Their Implementation." *American Bar Foundation Research Journal* 2 (1976): 365–409.

Cushman, Robert E. *The Independent Regulatory Commissions*. New York: Oxford Univ. Press, 1941.

Dahl, Robert A., and Charles E. Lindblom. *Politics, Economics and Welfare*. New York: Harper & Row, 1953.

Davies, J. Clarence III, and Barbara S. Davies. *The Politics of Pollution*. 2d ed. Indianapolis: Bobbs-Merrill, 1975.

Davis, Christopher, et al. "The Clean Air Act Amendments of 1977: Away from Technology-Forcing?" *Harvard Environmental Law Review* 2 (1977): 1–102.

Davis, David Howard. *Energy Politics*. 2d ed. New York: St. Martin's Press, 1978.

Del Sesto, Steven L. *Science, Politics and Controversy: Civilian Nuclear Power in the United States, 1946–1974*. Boulder, Colo.: Westview Press, 1979.

Derthick, Martha. *New Towns In-Town*. Washington, D.C.: Urban Institute, 1972.

――――. "The Tennessee Valley Authority." In *Between State and Nation*. Washington, D.C.: Brookings Institute, 1974. Pp. 18–45.

Dodd, Lawrence C., and Richard L. Schott. *Congress and the Administrative State*. New York: Wiley, 1979.

Dolbeare, Kenneth M., and Philip E. Hammond. *The School Prayer Decisions: From Court Policy to Local Practice*. Chicago: Univ. of Chicago Press, 1971.

Downing, Paul D. "Cross-National Comparisons in Environmental Protection: Introduction to the Issues." *Policy Studies Journal* 11 (Sept. 1982): 38–43.

――――, and Kenneth Hanf, eds. "Cross-National Comparisons in Environmental Protection: A Symposium." *Policy Studies Journal* 11 (Sept. 1982): 38–187.

Downs, Anthony. *Inside Bureaucracy*. Boston: Little, Brown, 1967.

――――. "Up and Down with Ecology—The Issue-Attention Cycle." *Public Interest* 28 (Summer 1972): 38–50.

Durisch, Lawrence, L., and Robert E. Lowry. "The Scope and Content of Administrative Decision—the TVA Illustration." *Public Administration Review* 4 (Autumn 1953): 219–26.

Ebbin, Steven and Raphael Kasper. *Citizen Groups and the Nuclear Power Controversy: Uses of Scientific and Technological Information*. Cambridge: MIT Univ. Press, 1974.

"The Economics of Clean Water." *Environment Reporter*. 12 May 1972, pp. 1110–14.

Edelman, Murray. *The Symbolic Uses of Politics*. Urbana: Univ. of Illinois Press, 1964.

Edwards, George C., III. *Implementing Public Policy*. Washington, D.C.: Congressional Quarterly, 1980.

Edwards, George C., III, and Ira Sharkansky. *The Policy Predicament: Making and Implementing Public Policy*. San Francisco: W.H. Freeman, 1978.

Eichholz, Geoffrey G. *Environmental Aspects of Nuclear Power*. Ann Arbor: Ann Arbor Science, 1976.

Esposito, John. *Vanishing Air*. New York: Grossman, 1970.

Etzioni, Amitai. "Two Approaches to Organizational Analysis: A Critique and a Suggestion." *Administrative Science Quarterly* 5 (Sept. 1960): 257–78.

Frankel, Charles. *The Democratic Prospect*. New York: Harper & Row, 1962.

Freeman, J. Leiper. *The Political Process*. 2d ed. New York: Random, 1965.

Freeman, S. David. "TVA and National Power Policy." *Tennessee Law Review* 49 (Summer 1982): 679–85.

Friedrich, Carl J. *Constitutional Government and Politics*. New York: Harper & Row, 1937.

Friendly, Henry J. *The Federal Administrative Agencies*. Cambridge: Harvard Univ. Press, 1962.

Gawthrop, Louis C. *Bureaucratic Behavior in the Executive Branch*. Toronto: Free Press, 1969.

Gerth, H.H., and C. Wright Mills. From *Max Weber: Essays in Sociology*. New York: Oxford Univ. Press, 1946.

Goodwin, Leonard, and Phyllis Moen. "The Evolution and Implementation of Family Welfare Policy." *Policy Studies Journal* 8 (1980): 633–51.

Gwin, Louis M. "Mechanisms for Public Participation at the Tennessee Valley Authority." *Public Relations Quarterly* 29 (Spring 1984): 27–30.

Halperin, Morton H. *Bureaucratic Politics and Foreign Policy*. Washington, D.C.: The Brookings Institute, 1974.

———. "Implementing Presidential Foreign Policy Decisions: Limitations and Resistance." In *Cases in Public Policy-Making*, ed. James E. Anderson. New York: Praeger, 1976. Pp. 208–236.

Hargrove, Erwin C. *The Missing Link*. Washington, D.C.: Urban Institute, 1975.

Harmon, Michael M. *Action Theory for Public Administration*. New York: Longman, 1981.

Harrington, James. "The Commonwealth of Oceana." In *Dictionary of Quotations*, ed. Bergen Evans. New York: Avenel, 1978. P. 378.

Hawkins, Keith. *Environment and Enforcement: Regulation and the Social Definition of Pollution*. Oxford: Clarendon Press, 1984.

Hayes, Lynton R. *Energy, Economic Growth, and Regionalism in the West*. Albuquerque: Univ. of New Mexico Press, 1980.

"Heated Water Control Crux of Likely Agencies Clash." *Electrical World*, Sept. 29, 1969, p. 20.

Heclo, Hugh H. "Review Article: Policy Analysis." *British Journal of Political Science* 2 (Jan. 1972): 83–108.

Hobday, Victor C. *Sparks at the Grass Roots*. Knoxville: Univ. of Tennessee Press, 1969.

Holden, Matthew. "'Imperialism' in Bureaucracy." *American Political Science Review* 60 (Dec. 1966): 943–51.

———. "Political Bargaining and Pollution Control." In *Politics and Economic Policy-Making*, ed. James E. Anderson. Reading: Addison-Wesley, 1970. Pp. 433–52.

Hucke, Jochen. "Implementing Environmental Regulations in the Federal Republic of Germany."*Policy Studies Journal* 11 (Sept. 1982): 130–40.

Huntington, Samuel P. "The Marasmus of the ICC: The Commission, the Railroads, and the Public Interest." *Yale Law Journal* 61 (Apr. 1952): 467–509.

Ingram, Helen. "Policy Implementation through Bargaining: The Case of Federal Grants-in-Aid." *Public Policy* 25 (Fall 1977): 499–526.

Johnson, Russell L. "Thermal Pollution: The Electric Utility Industry and Section 21(b) of the Federal Water Pollution Control Act." *The Hastings Law Journal* 22 (Feb. 1971): 685–704.

Jones, Charles O. *Clean Air*. Pittsburgh: Univ. of Pittsburgh Press, 1975.

———. *An Introduction to the Study of Public Policy*. 2d ed. North Scituate: Duxbury Press, 1977.

———. "Speculative Augmentation in Federal Air Pollution Policy-Making." In *Cases in Public Policy-Making*, ed. James E. Anderson. New York: Praeger, 1976. Pp. 54–79.

Key, V.O., Jr. *Public Opinion and American Democracy*. New York: Knopf, 1961.

Kirst, Michael W. *Government Without Passing Laws*. Chapel Hill: Univ. of North Carolina Press, 1969.

Kohlmeier, Louis M., Jr. *The Regulators: Watchdog Agencies and the Public Interest*. New York: Harper & Row, 1969.

Kolko, Gabriel. *Railroads and Regulation, 1877–1916*. Princeton: Princeton Univ. Press, 1965.

Lambright, W. Henry. *Governing Science and Technology*. New York: Oxford Univ. Press, 1976.

Leiserson, Avery. "Administrative Management and Political Accountability." *TVA: Fifty Years of Grass-roots Bureaucracy*, ed. Erwin C. Hargrove and Paul K. Conkin. Urbana: Univ. of Illinois Press, 1983. Pp. 122–49.

Lewis-Beck, Michael, and John R. Alford. "Can Government Regulate Safety? The Coal Mine Example." *American Political Science Review* 74 (Sept. 1980): 745–56.

Lijphart, Arend. "Comparative Politics and the Comparative Method." *American Political Science Review* 65 (Dec. 1971): 682–93.

Lilienthal, David E. *TVA: Democracy on the March*. New York: Harper, 1944.

———, and Robert Marquis. "The Conduct of Business Enterprises by the Federal Government." *Harvard Law Review* 54 (Feb. 1941): 545–601.

Lilly, William, and James C. Miller. "The New Social Regulation." *The Public Interest* No. 47 (Spring 1977): 28–36.

Lineberry, Robert L. *American Public Policy*. New York: Harper & Row, 1977.

Liroff, Richard A. *A National Policy for the Environment: NEPA and Its Aftermath*. Bloomington: Indiana Univ. Press, 1976.

Long, Norton E. "Bureaucracy and Constitutionalism." *American Political Science Review* 46 (Sept. 1952): 808–18.

Lowi, Theodore J. *The End of Liberalism*. New York: Norton, 1969.

Luft, Harold. "Benefit-Cost Analysis and Public Policy Implementation." *Public Policy* 24 (Fall 1976): 437–62.

MacAvoy, Paul. *The Crisis of the Regulatory Commissions*. New York: Norton, 1970.

———. *The Regulated Industries and the Economy*. New York: Norton, 1979.

Madison, James. "Federalist 51." In *The Federalist Papers*, by Alexander Hamilton, James Madison, and John Jay. New York: New American Library of World Literature, 1961. Pp. 320-25.

Majone, Giandomenico. "Process and Outcome in Regulatory Decision-Making." *American Behavioral Scientist* 22 (May/June 1979): 561-83.

Marcus, Alfred A. *Promise and Performance: Choosing and Implementing an Enviromental Policy*. Westport, Conn.: Greenwood Press, 1980.

Martin, Roscoe C. "Retrospect and Prospect." In *TVA: The First Twenty Years*, ed. Roscoe C. Martin. Kingsport: Univ. of Tennessee Press and Univ. of Alabama Press, 1956. Pp. 266-67.

———. *TVA: The First Twenty Years*. Kingsport: Univ. of Tennessee Press and Univ. of Alabama Press, 1956.

Mazmanian, Daniel, and Paul Sabatier. *Implementation and Public Policy*. Glenview: Scott, Foresman, 1983.

———. "Symposium on Successful Policy Implementation." *Policy Studies Journal* 8 (1980): 531.

McCraw, Thomas K. *Morgan vs. Lilienthal: The Feud Within TVA*. Chicago: Loyola Univ. Press, 1970.

———. *TVA and the Power Fight: 1933-1939*. Philadelphia: J.B. Lippincott, 1971.

McLaughlin, Milbrey. *Evaluation and Reform: ESEA, Title I*. Cambridge: Ballinger, 1975.

Meier, Kenneth J. *Politics and the Bureaucracy: Policymaking in the Fourth Branch of Government*. North Scituate: Duxbury Press, 1979.

Mendelott, John. *Regulating Safety: An Economic and Political Analysis of Occupational Safety and Health Policy*. Cambridge: MIT Univ. Press, 1979.

Milner, Neal A. *The Court and Local Law Enforcement: The Impact of Miranda*. Beverly Hills: Sage Publications, 1971.

Montjoy, Robert S., and Lawrence J. O'Toole. "Toward a Theory of Policy Implementation: An Organizational Perspective." *Public Administration Review* 39 (Sept./Oct. 1979): 465-75.

Moore, Mark H., and Graham T. Allison. "Introduction." *Public Policy* 3 (Spring 1978): 152-56.

Murphy, Jerome. *State Education Agencies and Discretionary Funds*. Lexington: Lexington Books, 1974.

Nakamura, Robert T., and Frank Smallwood. *The Policies of Policy Implementation*. New York: St. Martin's Press, 1980.

Neuse, Steven M. "TVA at Age Fifty: Reflections and Retrospect." *Public Administration Review* 43 (Nov.-Dec. 1983): 491-99.

Parker, Frank L., and Peter A. Krenkle. *Engineering Aspects of Thermal Pollution*. Nashville: Vanderbilt Univ. Press, 1969.

Perrow, Charles. *Complex Organizations*. 2d ed. Glenview: Scott, Foresman, 1979.

Plater, Zygmunt J.B. "Reflected in a River: Agency Accountability and the TVA Tellico Dam Case." *Tennessee Law Review* 49 (Summer 1982): 747–87.

Pressman, Jeffrey L., and Aaron B. Wildavsky. *Implementation*. Berkeley: Univ. of California Press, 1973.

Quarles, John. *Cleaning Up America*. Boston: Houghton Mifflin, 1976.

Rabkin, Jeremy. "Office for Civil Rights." In *The Politics of Regulation*, ed. James Q. Wilson. New York: Basic Books, 1980. Pp. 304–353.

Radin, Beryl A. *Implementation, Change, and the Federal Bureaucracy: School Desegregation Policy in HEW, 1964–1968*. New York: Teachers College Press, 1977.

Randall, Ronald. "Presidential Power versus Bureaucratic Intransigence: The Influence of the Nixon Administration on Welfare Policy." *American Political Science Review* 73 (Sept. 1979): 795–810.

Rechichar, Stephen, and Michael R. Fitzgerald. *The Contagiousness of Conflict: TVA's Tellico Dam Project*. Knoxville: Bureau of Public Administration, 1983.

Redford, Emmette S. *Democracy in the Administrative State*. New York: Oxford Univ. Press, 1969.

Regens, James L., Thomas M. Dietz, and Robert W. Rycroft. "Risk Assessment in the Policy-Making Process: Environmental Health and Safety Protection." *Public Administration Review* 43 (Mar./Apr. 1983): 137–45.

Reich, Charles A. "The New Property." *Public Interest* 3 (Spring 1966): 57–89.

Rein, Martin, and Francine Rabinovitz. "Implementation: A Theoretical Perspective." In *American Politics and Public Policy*, ed. Walter D. Burnham and Martha W. Weinberg. Cambridge: MIT Univ. Press, 1978. Pp. 205–11.

Riker, William H., and Peter C. Ordeshook. *An Introduction to Positive Political Theory*. Englewood Cliffs: Prentice-Hall, 1973.

Ripley, Randall B., and Grace A. Franklin. *Bureaucracy and Policy Implementation*. Homewood, Ill.: Dorsey, 1982.

Rivkin, Dean Hill. "The TVA Air Pollution Conflict: The Dynamics of Public Law Advocacy." *Tennessee Law Review* 49 (Summer 1982): 843–83.

Rosenbaum, Nelson. "Statutory Structure and Policy Implementation: The Case of Wetlands Regulation." *Policy Studies Journal* 8 (1980): 575–96.

Rosenbaum, Walter A. *The Politics of Environmental Concern*. New York: Praeger, 1977.

Rourke, Francis E. *Bureaucracy, Politics, and Public Policy*. 2d ed. Boston: Little, Brown, 1976.

———. "Bureaucratic Autonomy and the Public Interest." *American Behavioral Scientist* 22 (May/June 1979): 537–46.

Sabatier, Paul A. "Regulatory Policy-Making: Toward A Framework for Analysis." *Natural Resources Journal* 17 (July 1977): 415–60.

———. "Social Movements and Regulatory Agencies." *Policy Science* 6 (Fall 1975): 301–342.

———, and Daniel Mazmanian. "The Implementation of Public Policy: A Framework of Analysis." *Policy Studies Journal* 8 (1980): 538–60.

———. "Regulating Coastal Land Use in California, 1973–1975." *Policy Studies Journal* 11 (Sept. 1982): 88–102.

Saloma, John S. *Congress and the New Politics*. Boston: Little, Brown, 1969.

Sarat, Austin, and Joel B. Grossman. "Courts and Conflict Resolution: Problems in the Mobilization of Adjudication." *American Political Science Review* 69 (Dec. 1975): 1200–1217.

Schattschneider, E.E. *The Semisovereign People*. Hinsdale, Ill.: Dryden Press, 1960.

Scher, Seymour. "Conditions for Legislative Control." *Journal of Politics* 25 (Aug. 1963): 526–51.

Schuck, Peter H. "Litigation, Bargaining, and Regulation." *Regulation* 3 (July/Aug. 1979): 26–39.

Schulman, Paul R. "The Reflexive Organization: On Decisions, Boundaries, and the Policy Process." *Journal of Politics* 38 (Nov. 1976): 1014–23.

Schultz, Charles. *The Public Use of Private Interest*. Washington, D.C.: Brookings Institute, 1977.

Seidman, Harold. *Politics, Position, and Power*. 2d ed. New York; Oxford Univ. Press, 1975.

Selznick, Philip. *Leadership in Administration*. New York: Harper & Row, 1957.

"Senate Discussion of Baker Amendments." *Congressional Quarterly Weekly Report,* 13 Aug. 1977, p. 1715.

Settle, John E., Jr. "Guarding the Guardian: The 'Citizen Suit' for Clean Air." *Environmental Law* 3 (Spring 1973): 1–21.

Shaw, Bill M. "Sovereign Immunity: Federal Compliance with State Permit Requirements under the Clean Air Act and the Federal Water Pollution Control Act Amendments." *San Fernando Valley Law Review* 6 (Spring 1978): 117–25.

Shaw, William R. "The Procedures to Ensure Compliance by Federal Facilities with Environmental Quality Standards." *Environmental Law Reporter* 5 (1975): 50211–28.

Shenefield, John H. "Government Enterprises — A New Frontier for Regulatory Reforms." *Regulation* 3 (Nov./Dec. 1979): 16–18.

Stewart, Richard B. "The Reformation of American Administrative Law." *Harvard Law Review* 88 (June 1975): 1769–1813.

Stewart, Richard B., and James E. Krier. *Environmental Law and Policy.* 2d ed. New York: Bobbs-Merrill, 1978.

Tabb, David H. "Implementation and Political Change: Sources of Local Variations in Federal Social Programs." *Policy Studies Journal* 8 (1980): 616–32.

"Tall Stacks versus Scrubbers: $3.5 Million Publicity Campaign Fails to Discredit Emission Reduction Technology." *Environmental Law Reporter* 5 (1974): 10009–10.

Tarlock, A. Dan, Roger Tippy, and Frances E. Francis, "Environmental Regulation of Power Plant Siting." *Southern California Law Review* 45 (1972): 502–69.

Thompson, Frank J. "Bureaucratic Discretion and the National Health Service Corps." *Political Science Quarterly* 97 (Fall 1982): 427–45.

Thompson, James D. *Organizations in Action.* New York: McGraw-Hill, 1967.

Tobin, Richard J. *The Social Gamble.* Lexington: Lexington Books, 1979.

"TVA Revenue Bonds." *Congressional Quarterly Almanac.* Washington, D.C.: Congressional Quarterly, 1959. P. 261.

Ullman, Arich. "The Implementation of Air Pollution Control in German Industry." *Policy Studies Journal* 11 (Sept. 1982): 141–52.

Van Meter, Donald, and Carl Van Horn. "The Policy Implementation Process: A Conceptual Framework." *Administration and Society* 6 (Feb. 1975): 445–88.

Wamsley, Gary L., and Mayer N. Zald. *The Political Economy of Public Organizations: A Critique and Approach to the Study of Public Administration.* Lexington: Lexington Books, 1973.

Weatherly, Richard, and Michael Lipsky. "Street Level Bureaucrats and Institutional Innovation: Implementing Special Education Reform." *Harvard Education Review* 47 (May 1977): 171–97.

Weaver, Paul H. "Regulation, Social Policy, and Class Conflict." *Public Interest* 50 (Winter 1978): 45–63.

Welborn, David M. *Governance of Federal Regulatory Agencies.* Knoxville: Univ. of Tennessee Press, 1977.

Wenner, Lettie McSpadden. *One Environment Under Law.* Pacific Palisades: Goodyear Publishing, 1976.

Whitaker, Gordon P. "Coproduction: Citizen Participation in Service Delivery." *Public Administration Review* 40 (May/June 1980): 240–46.

Whitaker, John. *Striking a Balance.* Washington, D.C.: American Enterprise Institute, 1976.

White, Lawrence J. "U.S. Mobile Source Emissions Regulation: The Problems of Implementation." *Policy Studies Journal* 11 (Sept. 1982): 77–87.

Wildavsky, Aaron. "TVA and Power Politics." *American Political Science Review* 55 (Sept. 1961): 576–90.

Williams, Walter. "Special Issue on Implementation: Editor's Comments." *Policy Analysis* 1 (Summer 1975): 451.

Wills, Garry. *Explaining America: The Federalist*. New York: Penguin, 1981.

Wilson, James Q. "The Bureaucracy Problem." *Public Interest* 6 (Winter 1967): 3–22.

———. "The Dead Hand of Regulation." *Public Interest* 25 (Fall 1971): 39–58.

———. *The Politics of Regulation*. New York: Basic Books, 1980.

———, and Patricia Rachal. "Can the Government Regulate Itself?" *Public Interest* 46 (Winter 1977): 3–14.

Zener, Robert. "The Federal Law of Water Pollution Control." In *Federal Environmental Law*, eds. Edmund Dolgin and Thomas Guilbert. New York: West, 1974. Pp. 682–792.

Zwerling, Stephen. *Mass Transit and the Politics of Technology: A Study of BART and the San Francisco Bay Area*. New York: Praeger, 1974.

Zwick, David, and Marcy Benstock. *Water Wasteland*. New York: Grossman, 1971.

UNPUBLISHED MATERIALS

Brye, Bruce A. "TVA Activities to Control Heated Water Discharges." Paper presented to the Alabama Society of Professional Engineers State Convention, Huntsville, Ala., 2–3 June 1972.

Churchill, M.A., Chief, Water Quality Branch, TVA. Testimony before the Alabama Water Quality Improvement Commission, 19 June 1967.

Derryberry, O.M., TVA Director of Health, and Churchill, M.A., Chief, TVA Water Quality Branch. Paper presented at Public Hearing Concerning Proposed Water Quality Criteria for that Portion of the Tennessee River Basin in Alabama, Sheffield, Ala., 12 Dec. 1966.

Hughes, Nathaniel B., TVA Director of Power Resource Planning. Testimony before the Tennessee Air Pollution Control Board, 12 June 1976.

Montgomery, Thomas L., Chief, Air Quality Branch, TVA. Testimony before the Tennessee Air Pollution Control Board, 20 June 1975.

Mullins, M.L., Manager of Environmental Protection and Utilities, Monsono Corporation. Testimony before the Tennessee Air Pollution Control Board, 12 June 1973.

———. Testimony before the Tennessee Air Pollution Control Board, 31 July 1975.

Neff, Dr. Ruth. Written statement to the Tennessee Air Pollution Control Board, 20 June 1975.

Parker, Frank L., and Marcus Jernigan. "To Cool or Not to Cool?: Benefit-

Cost Analyses with Specific Application to Browns Ferry Power Plant Cooling Towers." 1973.

Rawson, George E. "The Implementation of Public Policy by Third-Sector Organizations." Paper presented at the Annual Meeting of the American Political Science Association, New York, N.Y., 1978.

————. "The Process of Program Development: The Case of TVA's Power Program." Ph.D. diss., Univ. of Tennessee, Knoxville, 1978.

Stephenson, Charles M. "Administrative Decision Revisited: TVA Experience Since 1953." Unpublished paper, TVA, Knoxville, 1975.

"Utility Water Act Group (UWAG) Report No. 10." Unpublished report presented to TVA by Hunton, Williams, Gay, and Gibson, Richmond, Va., 19 Dec. 1973.

Waldo, Dwight. "Reflections on Technoscience Policy and Administration in a Turbulent Milieu." Paper presented at the Conference on Public Science and Administration at the Univ. of New Mexico, Albuquerque, Sept. 1969.

PUBLIC DOCUMENTS

The Air Pollution Control Act of 1955. Pub. L. No. 84–159 (1955).

The Air Quality Act of 1967. Pub. L. No. 90-148 (1967).

The Clean Air Act Amendments of 1977. Pub. L. No. 95-95 (1977).

The Clean Air Act of 1963. Pub. L. No. 88-206 (1963).

The Clean Air Act of 1970. Pub. L. No. 91-604 (1970).

116 *Congressional Record* 19, 207 (1970).

123 *Congressional Record* S9443, 10 June 1977.

Department of the Interior. *Water Quality Criteria, Report of the National Technical Advisory Committee to the Secretary of the Interior*. Washington, D.C.: Department of the Interior, 14 April 1968.

Executive Order 11258. Prevention, Control and Abatement of Water Pollution by Federal Activities. 17 Nov. 1965.

Executive Order 11288. Prevention, Control and Abatement of Water Pollution by Federal Activities. 2 July 1966.

Executive Order 12088. Federal Compliance with Pollution Control Standards. 13 Oct. 1978, 43 *Fed. Reg.* 47707 et seq. (1978).

33 *Fed. Reg.* 9877 (1968).

33 *Fed. Reg.* 9879 (1968).

36 *Fed. Reg.* 1502 et seq. (1971).

36 *Fed. Reg.* 3085 (1971).

36 *Fed. Reg.* 5867 (1971).

36 *Fed. Reg.* 6680 et seq. (1971).

36 *Fed. Reg.* 8186 et seq. (1971).

37 *Fed. Reg.* 5260 (1972).

37 *Fed. Reg.* 10842 et seq. (1972).
37 *Fed. Reg.* 10842 (1972).
37 *Fed. Reg.* 10845 (1972).
37 *Fed. Reg.* 10846 (1972).
37 *Fed. Reg.* 10847 (1972).
37 *Fed. Reg.* 10868 (1972).
37 *Fed. Reg.* 10894 (1972).
37 *Fed. Reg.* 15095 (1972).
38 *Fed. Reg.* 25697 et seq. (1973).
38 *Fed. Reg.* 25699 (1973).
38 *Fed. Reg.* 25701 (1973).
38 *Fed. Reg.* 34476 (1973).
38 *Fed. Reg.* 34477 (1973).
39 *Fed. Reg.* 10277 (1974).
39 *Fed. Reg.* 11434 (1974).
39 *Fed. Reg.* 28357 (1974).
39 *Fed. Reg.* 29357 (1974).
39 *Fed. Reg.* 36176 (1974).
39 *Fed. Reg.* 36181 (1974).
39 *Fed. Reg.* 36187 (1974).
39 *Fed. Reg.* 38528 (1974).
39 *Fed. Reg.* 38529 (1974).
39 *Fed. Reg.* 8294 (1974).
41 *Fed. Reg.* 7450 et seq. (1976).
The Federal Water Pollution Control Act of 1948. Pub. L. No. 80-845
    (1948).
The Federal Water Pollution Control Act Amendments of 1956. Pub. L. No.
    84-660 (1956).
The Federal Water Pollution Control Act of 1961. Pub. L. No. 87-88 (1961).
The Federal Water Pollution Control Act of 1972. Pub. L. No. 92-500 (1972).
General Accounting Office. *Sequoyah Nuclear Plant: Tennessee Valley Au-
    thority*. Washington, D.C.: GAO, Jan. 1975.
House Doc. 15, 73rd Cong., 1st sess. (1933).
The National Environmental Policy Act. Pub. L. No. 91-190 (1969).
The National Environmental Policy Act of 1969. Pub. L. No. 91-190, 1970,
    83 Stat. 852, U.S.C. sec. 4321–47.
The Rivers and Harbors Act of 1899. 33 U.S.C. Section 407, 2. *Environmen-
    tal Law Review* 41142.
Senate Report No. 1196, 91st Congress, 2d sess. (1970). "Stipulation of Peti-
    tioner, State of Alabama, and Applicant, Tennessee Valley Authority
    Browns Ferry Nuclear Plants, Units One, Two, and Three," 26 March 1973.
Tennessee House Joint Resolution 44, 90th General Assembly, 1977, Tennes-
    see Public Acts 1575.
The TVA Self-Financing Act of 1959, Pub. L. No. 86-137 (1959).
Tennessee Valley Authority. *Draft Environmental Statement, Hartsville Nu-
    clear Plants*. Chattanooga: TVA, 1974.

————. *Final Environmental Statement — Browns Ferry Nuclear Plant, Units 1, 2, and 3*. Vol. 1. Chattanooga: TVA, 1972.

————. *Final Environmental Statement — Sequoyah Nuclear Plant, Units 1 and 2*. Chattanooga: TVA, 13 February 1974.

U.S. Congress. Hearings before the Joint Committee on Atomic Energy. *Environmental Effects of Producing Electric Power*. Pt. 2 (vol. I). 91st Cong., 2d sess., 1970.

————. Hearings before the Joint Committee on Atomic Energy. *Environmental Effects of Producing Electric Power*. Pt. 2 (vol. II). 91st Cong., 2d sess., 1970.

U.S. Congress. House. Committee on Appropriations. *Hearings on Public Works for Water and Power Development and Energy Research Appropriation Bill, 1976*. 94th Cong., 1st sess., 1975.

————. Public Works Subcommittee on Investigations and Review. *Hearings on the Steam Electric Power Generating Point Source Category*. 93d Cong., 2d sess., 1974.

————. Subcommittee on Public Health and Welfare, Committee on Interstate and Foreign Commerce. *Hearings on Air Pollution Control and Solid Water Recycling*. 91st Cong., 1st and 2d sess., 1969, 1970.

————. Testimony of Gordon Clapp before the Subcommittee of the Committee on Appropriations. *Government Corporations. Appropriations for 1949*. 80th Cong., 2d sess., 1948.

————. Testimony of Nathaniel B. Hughes, Jr., TVA Assistant Power Manager, before the Subcommittee on Health and the Environment. *Hearings on Public Works for Water and Power Development and Research Appropriation Bill*. 94th Cong., 1st sess., 1975.

————. Testimony of Aubrey J. Wagner before the House Subcommittee of the Committee on Appropriations. *Hearings on Public Works for Water and Power Development and Research Appropriation Bill*. 94th Cong., 2d sess., 1976.

U.S. Congress. Senate. Committee on Environment and Public Works. *Hearings on the Nomination of Marvin B. Durning*. 95th Cong., 1st sess., 1977.

————. Committee on Environment and Public Works. *Hearings on the Nomination of S. David Freeman*. 95th Cong., 1st sess., 1977.

————. *Hearings on Executive Branch Review of Environmental Regulations*. 96th Cong., 1st sess., 1979.

————. Hearings before the Committee on Public Works. *Tennessee Valley Authority Oversight Hearings*. Pt. 2. 94th Cong., 1st sess., 1975.

————. Public Works Subcommittee on Environmental Pollution. *Hearings on the Enforcement of Environmental Regulations*. 96th Cong., 1st sess., 1979.

————. Public Works Subcommittee on Environmental Pollution. *Hearings on the Implementation of the Clean Air Act of 1970: Proposed Amendments.* 94th Cong., 1st sess., 1975.

————. Subcommittee on Flood Control — Rivers and Harbors of the Committee on Public Works. *Increase in Statutory Limitation of TVA to Issue Bonds.* 89th Cong., 2d sess., 1966.

————. Testimony of Richard E. Ayres before the Subcommittee on Air and Water Pollution of the Committee on Public Works. *Hearings on the Implementation of the Clean Air Act Amendments of 1970.* Pt. 1. 92d Cong., 2d sess., 1972.

U.S. Statutes at Large, 48 Stat. 58.

The Water Quality Act of 1965. Pub. L. No. 89-234 (1965).

The Water Quality Improvement Act of 1970. Pub. L. No. 91-224 (1970).

ENVIRONMENTAL PROTECTION AGENCY AND
TENNESSEE VALLEY AUTHORITY REPORTS

Environmental Protection Agency. *The First Two Years: A Review of EPA's Enforcement Program.* Washington, D.C.: Office of Enforcement and General Counsel, Feb. 1973.

Environmental Protection Agency. Report of the Hearing Panel. *National Public Hearings on Power Plant Compliance with Sulfur Oxide Air Pollution Regulations.* Washington, D.C.: Government Printing Office, Jan. 1974.

Environmental Protection Agency. Tennessee Valley Authority Task Force Report. *Preliminary Assessment of Alternative Sulfur Oxide Control Strategies for TVA Steamplants.* June 1974; revised Jan. 1975.

Environmental Protection Agency, *Water Quality Standards-Setting Conference for the Inter-State Waters of the State of Alabama.* Atlanta: EPA, Water Quality Office, 5–7 Apr. 1971.

Tennessee Valley Authority. *Annual Report of the Tennessee Valley Authority: 1973.* Knoxville: TVA, 1973.

————. *Annual Report of the Tennessee Valley Authority: 1975.* Knoxville: TVA, 1975.

————. *Tennessee Valley Authority Power Annual Report.* Knoxville: TVA, 1970–1971.

————. "Chronology of TVA Sulfur Dioxide Control" (provided by TVA attorney Barry Walton). Knoxville: TVA, June 1979.

COURT CASES

Alabama v. Seeber, 502 F 2d 1238 (5th Cir., 1974).

Alabama v. TVA, No. 72-939 (N.D. Alabama, 1972).

Ashwander v. Tennessee Valley Authority, 8 F. Supp. 893 (N.D. Ala. 1934).

Big Rivers Electric Corp. v. EPA, 523 F 2d 16 (1975).

Big Rivers Electric Corp. v. EPA, Crt. Denied, 425 U.S. 934 (1976).

Buckeye Power, Inc. v. EPA, 481 F 2d 162 (5th Cir., 1973), citing letter from Jack E. Raven, U.S. Environmental Protection Agency, to Governor Carter, 7 May 1972.

Calvert Cliffs Coordinating Committee v. Atomic Energy Commission, 499 F 2d 1109 (1971).

Hancock v. Train, 426 U.S. 167 (1976).

Kalur v. Resor, 335 F. Supp. 1, 1 ELR 20637 (D.D.C., 1971).

Kentucky v. Ruckelshaus, No. 74806 (N.D. Kentucky, 1972).

Kentucky v. Ruckelshaus, 497 F 2d 1172 (6th Cir., 1974).

New Hampshire v. AEC, 406 F. 2d 170 (1969).

Official Transcript of Proceedings. *Tennessee Thoracic Society v. Freeman.* No. 77-3286 and Consolidated Cases (M.D. Tenn., July 31, 1979).

Tennessee Electric Power Co. v. Tennessee Valley Authority, 21 F. Supp. 947 (E.D. Tenn. 1938).

Tennessee Thoracic Society et al. v. Wagner, Civil Action No. 77-3286-NA-CU (U.S. Court for the Middle District of Tennessee, Nashville Division, 1978). Consent Decree.

United States v. Republic Steel Corp., 362 U.S. 482 (1960).

United States v. Standard Oil Co., 384 U.S. 224 (1966).

NEWSPAPERS

Ballock, Jim. "Frustrated Bill Jenkins Quits TVA." *Knoxville News-Sentinel.* 6 May 1978, pp. 1, 3.

Beazley, Ernie. "TVA-EPA Settlement Approved." *Knoxville Journal.* 23 Dec. 1980, pp. 1, 11.

Branscomb, James. "TVA Chairman David Freeman Talks About TVA Power." *Mountain Eagle.* 25 Jan. 1979, p. 1.

Brewer, Carson. "Wagner Refuses to Sign EPA Settlement." *Knoxville News-Sentinel.* 18 May 1978, pp. 1, 2.

Campbell, Ray. "U.S. Seeks to Keep Co-ops off EPA–TVA Pact." *Nashville Banner.* 9 May 1979, p. 28.

"Constituents Answer Poll for Atchley." *Knoxville Journal.* 9 May 1977, p. 1.

"Donald Cook vs. EPA." *New York Times.* 24 Nov. 1974, pp. F1, 14.

Dunnavent, Bob. "State May Try to Delay Plant's Start, Cooling Towers Termed a Must at Browns Ferry." *Huntsville Times.* 26 Sept. 1972.

Eblen, Tom. "TVA: 50 Years Later, It's Still Trying to Develop Its Valley." *Albuquerque Journal.* 15 May 1983, pp. B1, B4.

"Electric Cooperatives Admitted to Pollution Suit." *Nashville Banner.* 29 May 1979, p. 10.

"EPA Chief's TVA Visit Called Symbolic." *Knoxville News-Sentinel*. 5 June 1979, p. 8.

Kenworthy, E.E. "EPA Aides Say Commerce Department Amendments Would Weaken Clean Air Act." *New York Times*. 10 Dec. 1974, p. 31.

Moulton, John. "TVA Steam Plant Pollution Plan Approved." *Knoxville News-Sentinel*. 23 Dec. 1980, p. 12.

New York Times. 26 May 1977, p. 14, 1.

"Officials Tour TVA Steam Plant." *Roane County News*. 11 July 1977, pp. 1, 2.

Shabecoff, Philip. "White House is Cool to Charges of Interference in Role of EPA." *New York Times*. 23 Feb. 1979, p. A23.

Sikora, Frank. "N-Plant Will Open Without Cooling Unit." *Birmingham News*. 23 Aug. 1972, p. 1.

"TVA Defends Buying of Pollution Equipment." *Knoxville News-Sentinel*. 1 Feb. 1980, p. 13.

"TVA Distributors Criticize Freeman." *Knoxville Journal*. 2 Feb. 1980, p. 1.

TVA News. 10 Jan. 1977, p. 1.

"TVA to Cancel 4 N-plants." *The Atlanta Constitution*. 29 Aug. 1984, p. 9-B.

"TVA Power Plant Said Environmentally Okay." *Mobile Register*. 4 Nov. 1972, p. 1.

"TVA to Burn Low-Sulfur Coal to Meet Emissions Standards." TVA News Release. 21 Mar. 1977, pp. 2, 3.

"TVA's 'Overcompliance' on Clean Air is Challenged." *Knoxville News-Sentinel*. 17 Mar. 1979, pp. 1, 7.

"UCEMC Joining Co-ops in Lawsuit Against TVA." *Carthage Courier*. 3 May 1979.

"What Price Regulation?" *Newsweek*. 19 Mar. 1979, p. 80.

"Will Comply, TVA Pledges." *Birmingham News*. 6 Nov. 1972, p. 1.

LETTERS AND MEMORANDA

Atomic Energy Commission. Memorandum to the Files. Sept. 1973.

Churchill, M.A., Chief, TVA Water Quality Branch. Memorandum to F.E. Gartrell, TVA Assistant Director of Health. 28 June 1967.

———. Memorandum to F.E. Gartrell, TVA Assistant Director of Health. 2 Mar. 1971.

———. Memorandum to Dr. F.E. Gartrell, TVA Assistant Director of Health. 10 Feb. 1972.

———. Memorandum to the Files. May 1967.

———. Letter to S.J. Trombetta, Director of Federal Activities, Federal Water Pollution Control Administration. 4 Aug. 1967.

Clark, Larry, TVA Special Project Staff. Memorandum to R.A. Buckington, Supervisor, TVA Special Project Staff. 4 Nov. 1971.

Derryberry, O.M., TVA Manager of Environmental Science. Letter to John Bolton, Chief Administrative Officer, Alabama Water Improvement Commission. 12 June 1972.

Dougherty, E.D., Environmental Engineer, TVA Power Research Staff. Memorandum to the Manager's Files. 8 June 1973.

Gallagher, T.P., TVA. Memorandum to the Files. 5 July 1968.

Gibbons, John, Director, University of Tennessee Environmental Center. Letter to Jonathon Gibson, Coordinator, Tennessee Environmental Council. 19 Jan. 1976.

Gibson, Jonathon, Coordinator, Tennessee Environmental Council. Letter to Citizens Attending TVA Symposium. 16 July 1976.

———. Letter to S. David Freeman. 23 Dec. 1975.

Hammond, Larry, Deputy Assistant Attorney General, Office of Legal Counsel, U.S. Dept. of Justice. Letter to Douglas Costle, Administrator, EPA. 22 Aug. 1977.

Hughes, N.B., Jr., TVA Director of Power Resource Planning. Memorandum to F.E. Gartrell, TVA Director of Environmental Planning, and T.H. Ripley, TVA Director of Forestry, Fisheries and Wildlife Development. 9 Mar. 1973.

———. Nov. 9, 1972.

Internal TVA Memorandum. Aug. 10, 1973.

Internal TVA Memorandum from the Environmental Biology Branch to Billy Isom. 20 Dec. 1973.

Kaplan, Charles, EPA Region IV. Memorandum to Sanitary Engineer, EPA Federal Facilities Branch. 28 Jan. 1972.

Kelly, Charles D., Director, Alabama Game and Fish Division. Letter to the Editor, *Environmental Control News for Southern Industry*. 7 Aug. 1973, p. 1.

Layton, C.F., Acting Deputy Assistant, Secretary of the Interior. Letter to Mr. Price, Director of Regulations, U.S. Atomic Energy Commission. 25 Feb. 1969.

Marquis, Robert H., TVA General Counsel. Memorandum to John Barron and F.E. Gartrell. 10 Aug. 1973.

McBride, Neil, Board of Directors, TVA. Letter to Mary Wade, President, Tennessee Environmental Council. 29 Mar. 1976.

Nicholas, W.R., Assistant Chief, TVA Water Quality Branch. Memorandum to M.A. Churchill, Chief, TVA Water Quality Branch. 2 Apr. 1971.

Powell, David G., TVA Division of Law. Letter to Frank L. Parker, Professor, Vanderbilt University. 2 Jan. 1973.

———. Letter to Charles Kaplan, EPA Region IV. 13 Sept. 1973.

Raven, Jack E., EPA Region IV Administrator. Letter to F.E. Gartrell, TVA Assistant Director of Health. 22 May 1972.

———. 17 Dec. 1971.

————. Letter to David G. Powell, TVA Division of Law. 16 Oct. 1973.

Ruckelshaus, William, EPA Administrator. Letter to Alabama Governor George Wallace. 5 Feb. 1971.

Sanger, Herbert, TVA General Counsel. Letter to Allan Cywin, Director, EPA Effluent Guidelines Division. 11 Feb. 1976.

Seeber, Lynn, General Manager, TVA. Letter to John Quarles, Acting Administrator, EPA. 30 Aug. 1973.

————. Letter to Jack E. Raven, Region IV Administrator. 12 Dec. 1976.

————. Letter to Dean Hill Rivkin, Attorney, Citizen Coalition, 8 Apr. 1977.

Stevens, Barry, Tennessee Air Pollution Control Division. Memorandum to the Files. 11 May 1979.

Stone, G.F., TVA, and Nicholas, W.R., Assistant Chief, TVA Water Quality Branch. Memorandum to J.A. Oppold, TVA. 23 Jan. 1974.

Train, Russell E., EPA Administrator. Letter to Aubrey J. Wagner, Chairman, TVA Board of Directors. 24 May 1975.

————. Letter to Aubrey J. Wagner, Chairman, TVA Board of Directors. 30 May 1975.

Udall, Stewart, Secretary of the Interior. Letter to Alabama Governor George Wallace. 15 Feb. 1968.

Van Mol, John, Director of Information, TVA. Letter to Jonathon Gibson, Coordinator, Tennessee Environmental Council, TVA Symposia. 16 Jan. 1976.

————. Letter to Dr. Ruth Neff, Executive Director, TEC. 24 Mar. 1975.

————. 1 Dec. 1975.

Wagner, Aubrey J., Chairman, TVA Board of Directors. Letter to Senator James B. Allen (D-Ala.). 17 Nov. 1973.

————. Letter to John S. Hoffman, Secretary, Department of Natural Resources and Environmental Protection, State of Kentucky. 14 Apr. 1975.

Walton, John, Tennessee Air Pollution Control Division. Memorandum to Harold Hodges, Director, Tennessee Air Pollution Control Division. 12 Apr. 1977.

Zeller, Howard, EPA Region IV Water Quality Standards Coordinator. Letter to J.L. Crockett, Jr., Director of Technical Staff, Alabama Water Improvement Commission. 21 July 1971.

————. Memorandum to the Files. 27 June 1968.

INTERVIEWS

Brye, Bruce. TVA. Interview in Chattanooga, Tenn. 16 May 1981.

Bycott, James. Attorney, EPA Region IV. Interview in Atlanta, Ga. 29 June 1980.

Casto, Keith. Attorney, EPA Region IV. Interview in Atlanta, Ga. 26 June 1980.

Chandler, William. Environmental Policy Center. Interview in Washington, D.C. 28 Jan. 1980.

Durning, Marvin B. EPA Deputy Administrator for Enforcement. Interview in Washington, D.C. 30 Jan. 1980.

Freeman, S. David. Chairman, TVA Board of Directors. Interview in Knoxville, Tenn. 30 Dec. 1980.

Hodges, Harold. Tennessee Air Pollution Control Division. Interview in Nashville, Tenn. 18 Sept. 1980.

Hungerford, Charles. Attorney, EPA Staff. Interview in Washington, D.C. 28 Jan. 1980.

Kaplan, Charles. EPA Region IV. Interview in Atlanta, Ga. 14 May 1981.

Linton, Arthur. EPA Region IV. Interview in Atlanta, Ga. 27 June 1980.

Morris, James. TVA. Interview in Chattanooga, Tenn. 16 May 1981.

Neff, Ruth. Tennessee Environmental Council. Interview in Nashville, Tenn. 7 Nov. 1979.

Perkins, Frank. Executive Director, Tennessee Rural Electrical Cooperative Association. Interview in Nashville, Tenn. 18 Sept. 1980.

Raven, Jack. EPA Region IV Administrator. Interview in Atlanta, Ga. 28 June 1980.

Richardson, Michael. Former EPA Staff Attorney. Interview in Washington, D.C. 30 Jan. 1980.

Rivkin, Dean Hill. Attorney, University of Tennessee Law School. Interviews in Knoxville, Tenn. 4 and 17 Dec. 1979.

Traina, Paul. EPA Region IV. Interview in Atlanta, Ga. 26 June 1980.

Wade, Mary. Tennessee League of Women Voters. Interview in Nashville, Tenn. 7 Nov. 1979.

Wagner, Aubrey J. Former Chairman, TVA Board of Directors. Interview in Knoxville, Tenn. 18 Feb. 1981.

Walton, Barry. Attorney, TVA Office of the General Counsel, Interview in Knoxville, Tenn. 13 June 1979.

Wilder, John. Lieutenant Governor, State of Tennessee. Interview in Nashville, Tenn. 17 Sept. 1980.

Zeller, Howard. EPA Region IV. Interview in Atlanta, Ga. 15 May 1981.

Index

About the Book and Author

Robert Francis Durant was born in Northampton, Massachusetts in 1949. He graduated from Northampton High School in 1966 and received his B.A. in Political Science from Maryville College, Maryville, Tennessee in 1970. He holds an MPA degree (1979) and a Ph.D. in Political Science (1981) from the University of Tennessee, Knoxville. From 1977 to 1981 he served as a research associate at the Bureau of Public Administration, University of Tennessee. He then joined the faculty at New Mexico State University (1981–1984). He is presently an assistant professor of Political Science at the University of Georgia. This book was conceived while the author was employed by the Bureau of Public Administration, and much of the research funding and support services needed to complete it were provided by the bureau. All errors of fact or interpretation, however, are the sole responsibility of the author.

This book has been set into type on a Compugraphic digital phototypesetter in ten point Times Roman with two points of spacing between the lines. Times Roman was also used as display. The book was designed by Jim Billingsley, composed by Metricomp, Inc., printed offset by Thomson-Shore, Inc., and bound by John H. Dekker & Sons. The acid-free paper on which the book is printed is designed for an effective life of at least three hundred years.

THE UNIVERSITY OF TENNESSEE PRESS : KNOXVILLE

DATE DUE